28936
ED

United Mind Workers

Charles Taylor Kerchner

Julia E. Koppich

Joseph G. Weeres

United Mind Workers

Unions and Teaching in the Knowledge Society

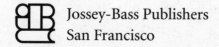

Jossey-Bass Publishers
San Francisco

Substantial discounts on bulk quantities of Jossey-Bass books are available to corporations, professional associations, and other organizations. For details and discount information, contact the special sales department at Jossey-Bass Inc., Publishers (415) 433–1740; Fax (800) 605–2665.

For sales outside the United States, please contact your local Simon & Schuster International Office.

Jossey-Bass Web address: http://www.josseybass.com

 Manufactured in the United States of America on Lyons Falls Turin Book. This paper is acid-free and 100 percent totally chlorine-free.

Library of Congress Cataloging-in-Publication Data

Kerchner, Charles T.
    United mind workers : unions and teaching in the knowledge society
    / Charles Taylor Kerchner, Julia E. Koppich, Joseph G. Weeres. —
1st ed.
        p.   cm — (The Jossey-Bass education series)
    Includes bibliographical references and index.
    ISBN 0-7879-0829-0 (cloth : acid-free)
    1. Teachers' unions—United States.   2. Collective bargaining—
Teachers—United States.   3. School personnel management—United
States.   4. Educational change—United States.   I. Koppich, Julia.
II. Weeres, Joseph G., date.   III. Title.   IV. Series.
LB2844.53.U6K48   1997
331.88'113711'0973—dc21   97-4636

FIRST EDITION
HB Printing   10 9 8 7 6 5 4 3 2 1

The Jossey-Bass Education Series

Contents

⟨⟩— Preface

Dear Reader,

This is a book about teacher unions, not as they are, but as they might be. It is a book about an institution of public education not as it is but as it may become if we respond intelligently to changes in the postindustrial economy, the increasing diversity of our society, and changes in the nature of knowledge and learning. It is a book about social forecasting, thinking about a reality that isn't here yet. It is a book about the place of knowledge workers in the American democracy of the twenty-first century, and how teachers can help define how these workers are organized. Most of all it is a book about *organizing,* organizing all of teaching work—not just the economic part— organizing both education and labor in ways that look forward rather than back.

When institutions change, all their parts face both unprecedented vulnerability and unprecedented opportunity. This world of change, we believe, is what teacher unions face over the next twenty-five years.

Because education faces a world alive with threat and opportunity, we believe forward-thinking unionists should find this book compelling reading. Indeed, we hope it becomes required reading in the bastions of the National Education Association and the American Federation of Teachers, but not only there. Unions have been in the blind spot on the radar scope of educational reform. In the hundreds of commissions and thousands of reports written about changing public education in the United States since 1983, unions are mostly invisible. And when they have been mentioned, they are almost universally pictured as part of the problem rather than as a critical element of the solution. The failure to consider what unions do and what they potentially add to the institution of public education in the United States leaves a gaping hole in educational reform policy. This book is aimed squarely at those who make public policy and those who wish to influence it: governors, state school officers, federal and state legislators and their staffs, and that small, happy band of academics interested in educational politics and policy.

Practitioners who think about the future should also read this book. There are no checklists of helpful hints or magic solutions; there is nothing that one can take back and use next Tuesday. What this book offers teachers and practicing school administrators is a way of thinking: a way to connect the day-to-day activities they are undertaking now with the big changes in institutional life that are swirling around them. It presents ways in which school people can see themselves as actors in the social drama being played out rather than victims. It offers the promise of empowerment and the challenge of leadership.

Prefaces are often the most revealing parts of books. The authors drop their academic personas and speak directly to readers, revealing themselves in conversations frequently missing in the rest of the text. But prefaces also present problems to authors. Because not all readers linger on their way to the body of the book, books sometimes have to begin twice: once informally in the preface, and once in the first chapter. For that reason, we decided to delay our rather personalized introduction to the book, building it into the first chapter. Readers interested in how we came to write this book or why the book is structured the way it is can find their answers there. Readers who want a preview of each chapter so that they can pick and choose what they read can also find descriptions in the opening chapter.

We also want to take this opportunity to acknowledge that the preparation of this book has been conspicuously helped by a number of individuals and organizations. The Carnegie Corporation of New York, the U.S. Department of Labor, and the Stuart Foundation of San Francisco provided research and project funds, the results of which greatly influenced our thinking about the frontiers of labor relations. Susan Moore Johnson, Miles Myers, and Adam Urbanski read the entire draft text and made helpful suggestions for its revision. Our editors at Jossey-Bass have proved to be both diligent and patient as we worked our way through several drafts. To Leslie Iura, Christie Hakim, Pamela Berkman, and Hilary Powers go our appreciation and thanks.

We bid you good reading.

Claremont, California   CHARLES TAYLOR KERCHNER
February 1997   JULIA E. KOPPICH
                                                 JOSEPH G. WEERES

~~~ The Authors

Charles Taylor Kerchner is the Hollis P. Allen professor of education at the Claremont Graduate School. He is the author of two previous books on teacher unions: *The Changing Idea of a Teachers' Union* (with Douglas Mitchell) and *A Union of Professionals* (with Julia Koppich). He is currently studying the connections between education and the development of postindustrial cities. Kerchner earned his Ph.D. at Northwestern University and his M.B.A. and B.A. at the University of Illinois.

Julia E. Koppich is managing partner of Management Analysis & Planning Associates, an educational consulting firm based in San Francisco, California, and holds an appointment as associate professor of education at the Claremont Graduate School. She was previously a member of the faculty of the Graduate School of Education at the University of California at Berkeley and served as director of Policy Analysis for California Education (PACE). Koppich has written widely on matters of educational reform and school politics and policy and is the author, with Charles Kerchner, of *A Union of Professionals*. She earned her M.A. and Ph.D. at the University of California, Berkeley, and her B.A. at the University of California, Davis.

Joseph G. Weeres earned his Ph.D. at the University of Chicago, where he specialized in the study of the politics of education. He earned the B.A. and M.A. in philosophy at St. Mary's College. Since coming to Claremont in 1971, Weeres has taught courses that examine how the political and economic environments of education shape the structure and decisions of schools and other educational organizations. He chaired the Education Faculty from 1986 to 1993 and was director of the Center for Educational Studies from 1991 to 1993.

Weeres is in the second year of a study of the impact of work technologies on educational expectations for employees, in an effort to understand how the instructional core of education needs to be designed to prepare students to participate in the new economy. He and

Kerchner recently published "This Time It's Serious: Postindustrialism and the Coming Institutional Change in Education" in the *Politics of Education Association Yearbook,* and his chapter "Public Choice Perspective on Urban School Politics" appeared in Cibulka, Reed, and Wong's *Politics of Urban Schools* (1992) and in the *Journal of Education Policy* (winter 1991).

United Mind Workers

PART ONE

A Postindustrial Unionism

CHAPTER ONE

Organizing the Other Half of Teaching

Book ideas are born in odd places. After a gestation period that would frustrate an elephant, this one revealed its true form in an elevator. A National Education Association organizer approached Charles Kerchner, saying, "These changes you're talking about—it's not just reforming the union. We have to organize teachers all over again. The first time we organized their economic rights; now we have to organize them as educators. We have to organize the other half of their jobs."

Yes—that was the point.

Transforming labor relations so as to get away from industrial-style collective bargaining was not simply a matter of attitude or bargaining style. And it certainly was not a matter of being cooperative versus confrontational. We had understood that deep organizational change was necessary. *The Changing Idea of a Teachers' Union* (Kerchner and Mitchell, 1988), written nearly a decade ago, recognized different "generations" of labor relations, each separated by organizational struggles. But we had missed the scope of institutional change facing public education.

THE DIFFICULTY OF
INSTITUTIONAL CHANGE

Our failure to see the institutional change dimensions of labor relations caused us frustration with the pace and scale of labor-management reforms. No one involved—not even ourselves—recognized the enormous difficulty of changing fundamental employee-employer relationships within the existing institution. We witnessed gradual attempts at decentralizing decision making in schools, giving teachers and principals more say in the decisions that affected them, only to see those efforts dissipate. Process paralysis replaced the instinct to create distinctive schools. We saw bold ideas such as peer review start with a flurry of interest, and then not spread. Most unions, and most managements, were too mired in conventional wisdom to see the importance of teachers' taking responsibility for their own work and the performance of their colleagues. Even large-scale and seemingly permanent reforms bogged down when economic times turned tough or a key leader departed. School boards seemed to have an unerring instinct for replacing reformist superintendents with enforcers of the conventional wisdom—as if school reform were an exercise in small-scale equilibrium.

We were also frustrated with labor's critics. Organized labor is often ossified, and it deserves criticism. But the journalistic critics of teacher unions have missed by a mile. They have often been wrong on the facts, and almost always appear to write from ignorance about the history of working people in the United States and the social necessity that employees be able to represent their interests and aspirations for their work and their lives. In an age in which many American workers lead perilous economic lives, the social value of income security and decent wages receives a blind eye. Unions have surely talked too much and done too little about educational reform. Yet to criticize unions for opposing a particular reform assumes that reforms themselves don't deserve vigorous debate.

Politicians and educational reformers likewise show a blind side. In a decade of educational reform, including hundreds of commissions and reports, unions were largely ignored except for a general backhanded criticism that they were a block on reform. For a while, we thought the problem was Republicans. The carping critics of the right were determined to impose vouchers or other alleged marketforce solutions without a shred of evidence that school markets would prosper in inner cities, from which every other market—even the supermarket—had fled. But teacher-bashing and education-thumping became a bipartisan sport. No serious attempt to shape a reform teacher union policy has been undertaken by either political party.

Even our dearest friends, the teachers who carried most of the burden of change, proved baffling. Why did it seem impossible for teachers to focus hard on student learning? Why was it that our rule of thumb said it took *three years* for a school faculty to move from discussions about who got access to the Xerox machine to substantive conversations about how children learned, how it could be documented, and how learning could be increased? It often seemed that the psychological comfort of the participants was the main criterion for moving forward. There was no urgency to it, no clarion call.

MISSING SOMETHING BIG

We had missed something big. While teachers and school managers were grappling with the problems of interest-based bargaining and school site management, the tectonic plates of institutional change were rumbling underneath public education. Belief in the capacity of government declined and with it the belief that schools could solve their own problems. As the rocks of the old institution shook, noninstitutional magma bubbled to the surface, white hot and beautiful. One flow suggested that education's problems would be solved by more equitable representation of vigorous interest groups. Another flow glowed with the allure of the market.

As we investigated a noteworthy set of educational reforms born in the 1980s, we thought we were witnessing a rebuilding of the grand coalition that had supported public education earlier in this century. The developments, reported in *A Union of Professionals* (Kerchner and Koppich, 1993) illustrated the possibility of reform, but also the difficulty of sustaining it. Originally, we thought that a union-management coalition based on rebuilding the schools would be sufficiently powerful to stabilize urban politics and give schools the time they needed to change within the existing institution. We were wrong.

Incremental change in public education proved difficult when the rest of society was unstable. When the big tectonic plates of the society and the economy move, everything else changes, too. The educational implications of what has been called the "third industrial revolution" of the 1970s and 1980s were not confined to rethinking vocational education or introducing computer literacy. The changes that depopulated Buffalo and Detroit and nearly made a ghost town of Flint—the ones that gave rise to Japan, Inc.—were sign and signal that the social and economic world was changing rapidly. Other institutions—including the most conservative, such as medicine and banking—heaved from their bedrock. Why would we think of schools and of teacher unionism with the slightest expectation that they would continue within the same institutional shell? The answer is that we are not used to thinking in terms of institutional change.

The last time education changed in a massive way coincided with the movement from an agricultural society to an industrial society, a change that gained speed rapidly in the late nineteenth century and fostered the social imbalances of the Gilded Age and the subsequent rise of the Progressive Movement. With the exception of collective bargaining and desegregation, almost all the contemporary structures of schooling, and of school governance, flow from this era. We work in organizations designed in 1916.

KNOWLEDGE AS SOCIETY'S MASTER CONCEPT

Institutional change is as pervasive when it occurs as it is rare in the life of a society. When schools last underwent institutional change, they reorganized around new ideas of social life. Urbanism and industrialism became the *master concepts* of society, replacing the nineteenth-century ideals of agriculturalism and small-town life. It wasn't that the schools were factories; anyone who ever worked in a real factory knows that. But industrial assumptions came to rule educational decisions. The idea that bigger was better drove the consolidation of school districts in rural areas and the unification of districts in cities. The number of school districts in the country fell from three hundred thousand to fewer than fifteen thousand today. The idea that specialized was efficient gave rise to high school departmentalization and to separate career paths for school administrators and teachers. The idea of scientific management gave school administrators the mantle of technical expertise, some freedom from school board domination, and a clearly established organizational superiority over teachers. This arrangement was most clearly visible in the pre–collective bargaining National Education Association, where for fifty years teachers were members, but superintendents ran the place.

As we examined the attempts at educational reform over the last decade, we gradually recognized that the master concept of society was changing from industrialism to something new, and that schools were in the midst of the change. The new master concept doesn't yet have a name. *Postindustrial* tells us what's past, not what's coming. Urban economists such as Manuel Castells use the term *informational society*, signaling the importance of information and data flows. We prefer the term *knowledge society* because it suggests not only the flow of information, but its manipulation and use. Knowledge joins the traditional trio of labor, land, and capital as a source of wealth and power.

In Chapter Two, we examine the implications of changing from an industrial society to a knowledge society. We look at the uncanny parallels between the last half of the nineteenth century and the last half of the twentieth, and the implications for education as an institution.

Surprisingly, the largest implication is not for how schools are governed or run, but for how people teach and learn and what they should know. Industrial-era curriculum and pedagogy was different from that transmitted by *McGuffey's Reader*. Why would we not expect knowledge-era learning and teaching to be different from Dick and Jane?

Teachers care about changes in teaching and learning. They know more about how children think and learn—and the conditions that promote thinking and learning—than do governors, business leaders, and most college professors. Why, we thought, is this voice of expertise not well articulated? And the answer kept coming back, "But teaching isn't organized that way." Collective bargaining legitimated teachers' economic interests, but it never recognized them as experts about learning. The idea of *knowledge workers* who create, synthesize, and interpret information dominates the literature on modern workplaces, but teaching is still organized around the industrial-era assumption that teachers are essentially manual workers, pouring curriculum into passive minds. Thus in this book, we ask: If workers could organize around industrial life, why not organize around mental work? For us, the idea of *united mind workers* is more than a play on words.

IMAGINING A NEW INSTITUTION OF PUBLIC EDUCATION

To write a book about an educational institution in which teacher unions organize around teachers' knowledge of learning, we had to imagine an educational institution built around what some call a *professional community*. That is, to think about unions differently, we had to imagine schools organized differently. Even as the rumbling beneath us gathers strength, we had to imagine at least the elements of a new institution of education. To write about teacher unionism in the 1990s requires that we think of education in the United States as having entered a new age of institutional stability, even though we recognize that the immediate future is almost certain to be tumultuous.

Thus throughout writing this book, we struggled with the logical divide between designing a new institution of education and describing what we knew about unions and their organization. We took many long diversions into the speculative unknown: What would a school district look like? Would there be school boards? But these trails took us too far away from the heart of teacher unionism, and ultimately we decided to pick only a few structural elements of the new institution and build our idea of unionism around them.

All institutions have a means of defining quality and of enforcing it. They all have some idea about the size and shape of the organization that gets work done. And they all have some way of dividing up work and assigning it to different workers. These are the three elements that we use to describe how knowledge workers might be organized.

Ways of Defining and Creating Quality

The first structural elements of the emerging educational institution are the mechanisms for defining and measuring educational quality. We argue that quality is particularly important because the mechanisms for quality assurance are changing from those that assure quality by category, such as assignment of teachers with the right credentials, to those that assure quality by individual outcomes, such as student assessment and teacher performance review.

Knowledge-era quality is different from industrial-era quality. Thus we should not be surprised that a furious debate about standards, tradition, individual rights, and community values is being played out.

A similar history was unfolded as a precursor to the reforms of the Progressive Era. We argue that defining and measuring quality—for students, for teachers, for schools—is central to what unions need to do. We cover this topic in Part Two, examining the union's role in setting standards, educating new teachers, evaluating performance, and promoting teacher discipline.

Organizing Around Individual Schools

The second structural element in the emerging institution of labor relations is scale of union organization. We argue that unions should be organized around individual schools rather than school districts. This would be a drastic change, and a counterintuitive one. We take this position for two reasons: one strategic, the other pedagogical.

Our strategic reason for arguing that unions ought to organize around individual schools derives from the inherent instability of school districts themselves. The shape, scope, and function of school districts appears increasingly problematic. Every reform experiment—from school site management to charter schools—threatens the social order of the existing school system. And every experiment that structurally alters a district threatens one of the elements by which unions now gain influence and stability. While it is true that not all these reforms are good ones, it makes no strategic sense for unions to make their organization dependent on propping up what are often dysfunctional school districts. To do so positions teacher unions to be left behind, trapped on the wrong side of the gulf opened by historic change.

Education stands at the beginning of a reform cycle, not at the end, and there is every reason to expect it to undergo the kinds of large structural changes that have rippled through health care and financial services in the last decade. A better strategy is to organize around the smallest feasible unit of organized learning, the school. Schools may look different than they do now, but we think that they will be stable organizational entities for the foreseeable future.

Our pedagogical reason for arguing that unions should be organized around schools derives from the need for diversity and efficiency during unsettled times. It won't solve the educational design problem to recreate massive systems, searching for what David Tyack calls the *one best system*. Change will require much experimentation and a lot of adaptation. This is also a time of great social diversity and substantial contention. The racialization of politics and the prolifer-ation of voices paralyzes many urban school decision processes. One way for social diversity to work is to attach it to educational decisions at schools.

In Part Three, we describe a labor relations system built around rel-atively autonomous schools. These could be charter schools, schools within a district having substantive site management and governance provisions, or schools in a governance arrangement not yet practiced. We describe what a contract would look like at a school-site level and how it could be negotiated and administered without an undue bur-den on either teachers or administrators.

An Expansive Labor Market for Teacher Talent

The third structural element is the labor market. Industrial organiza-tions were built around the idea of careers within organizations, what economists call *internal* labor markets. Organizing in this way distin-guished industrial employment from the prior system of craft-based work, where workers frequently moved among employers and where they identified more heavily with their occupation than with their employer. Although we see the imprint of industrial-era labor mar-kets most clearly in the promotion pattern for school administrators in large school districts, teaching was also organized as an internal market. Under both civil service and collective bargaining, job pro-tection rights attached to the individual school district, and there were often substantial disincentives for moving among school districts, and sometimes from moving among subdivisions of a school district. When teachers gained collective bargaining, they organized around protections for the jobs they had—the only ones they were likely to get unless they became administrators. Job protection became a nat-ural and understandable goal of teacher unions. Although far from absolute, due process and seniority protections were very important elements of personal security for teachers.

However, job protection unionism has serious drawbacks. It pro-tects teachers, but it also constrains them. To sort out what workers are entitled to what protections, jobs and the protections associated with them must be tightly specified. Almost any substantive change in teaching work requires altering the web of protections. New com-binations of work and energy become difficult.

Moreover, job protection unionism is predicated on the continuing of an internal versus an external labor market for teachers, and that, in turn, is predicated on public schools maintaining a virtual monopoly on schooling and direct instruction. Almost any change in the structure of schooling becomes a threat to these protections. Home schooling, contracting out, charter schools, vouchers, private schools—all threaten existing teachers because teachers' economic security is almost exclusively tied to continued employment in the same school district. Even radical demographic shifts—through changes in birth rates, suburbanization, or deindustrialization—threaten teachers' economic security. A number of pressures limit the effects of job protection unionism built around internal labor markets.

In Chapters Eight and Nine, we describe how a labor market for teachers might work if it were designed around an *external* labor market. If individual schools, rather than school districts, were the central organizing feature of teacher unions and of schooling, then teachers would need a way to enter and leave employment and to move from school to school.

Our primary mechanism is a modern and professionalized version of the historic craft union hiring hall. Unions, we argue, should take on many of the job finding and job placement functions that were undertaken by school districts in the era of bureaucratic organization.

Three core ideas become the structures of our notions about school organization and thus about union organization:

- *Organize around quality:* Advocate, implement, and enforce standards for student learning and standards for teaching. Back these up with adequate professional development and strong peer review systems.

- *Organize around schools:* Slim the district contract and create individual school compacts covering resource allocation, hiring, quality assurance, and how teachers take joint responsibility for reforms.

- *Organize around an external labor market:* Create modern hiring halls that allow teachers to switch jobs more easily. Make pensions and benefits portable, and shape a career ladder that allows people to enter education as classroom aides and advance through education and experience to teaching.

ORGANIZING AN AMERICAN INSTITUTION

In the last two chapters, we return to the question of institutional change. Education will surely get better by organizing from the classroom up, but organizing an institution requires thinking about how a system of schools can be put together that looks and acts differently from an industrial hierarchy. This is a daunting task because it cuts against everything we know or have experienced in our lifetimes. Our instincts about such vital organizational functions as control may well be wrong. We make no pretense at all of tackling vital institution-building questions such as the conduct of school governance in this book; rather, we concentrate on the two elements we feel are necessary to institutionalizing teacher unions for the knowledge society.

The first institutional element is a new labor statute, one that recognizes requirements of knowledge work and then builds legal structures to support it. Chapter Ten argues that statutes become powerful patterning and institution-building devices and that the current labor relations framework does not create the necessary balance between worker protections and inducements for a productive workforce in the knowledge society. It then suggests the changes that need to be made in the National Labor Relations Act structure, which is the basis for most state teacher statutes.

Chapter Eleven returns to the theme of organizing. Teacher unions face two organizing tasks. One is to organize a new institution of education. The other is to serve as a prototype or vanguard for knowledge workers in general. The questions that teachers face in their work find strong parallels among highly educated, skilled workers in health care, finance, communications, and other industries undergoing massive restructuring. Organized labor has traditionally not been attractive to these workers, precisely because it was focused around industrial work patterns rather than professional ones. We believe organized teachers can demonstrate how it is possible to pursue quality and productivity simultaneously with dignity and "simple justice."

These are not short-run tasks, yet time is of the essence. In the postindustrial age, the future often arrives ahead of schedule.

CHAPTER TWO

From Siege Mentality to Transformational Vision

—⁓—

America's teacher unions face a period of simultaneous strength and vulnerability. Unions appear strong because they are the most stable and well-organized constituents of the existing institution of education. The massive 2.2-million-member National Education Association (NEA) and the articulate, urban-centered 900,000-member American Federation of Teachers (AFT) have arguably been the strongest forces in American public education over the last half-century.

Over the past decades, the two national unions have been active and visible symbols of the existing institution and the struggles to change it. The growth of strong teacher unions, along with desegregation and the advent of categorical programs, represents the largest policy intervention in public education since World War II. Union influence dwarfed that of school administrators and deans of university education schools, the other two legs of the historic "iron triangle" of education. Union political power is respected in statehouses and on Capitol Hill. Unions are a bulwark of the Democratic Party, and, more important, are among the few national organizations with a powerful presence in nearly every congressional district. Union presidents have attained unquestioned leadership status within the loosely formed institution of education. Each organization has a new and impressive national headquarters close to the seats of power in Washington.

Still, teacher unionism remains highly vulnerable. Unions are utterly dependent on the existing structure and power alignments within public education: a massive, rule-bound, hierarchical public bureaucracy that is increasingly seen as anachronistic and ill-fitted to the requirements of postindustrial society. All the labor relations reforms of the 1980s and early 1990s took place within the existing institution. No major labor relations statutes were changed, and changes in school operation and governance were handled largely as exceptions to more general rules. The underlying *institution* of public schooling hardly changed. Teacher unions have committed themselves to its defense, and have become vulnerable both because they are seen as self-serving apologists and because they spend enormous energy defending the old institution and relatively little designing and bringing about a new one.

An amazingly muddled *Forbes* article about the NEA underscores this ideological point and the associated strategic logic. "NEA's strategic problem is acute: It must resist threats to the government school cartel everywhere; it can afford to lose nowhere. Give the parents choice almost anywhere, and the dam breaks. The union panjandrums know this. The strain is starting to show" (Brimelow and Spencer, 1995, p. 122).While erroneous in the particulars, the statement illustrates the dilemma unions face as defenders of the existing institution. With only a modest expenditure of resources, attackers can trigger a large and expensive union response, one that ultimately the NEA and AFT cannot afford. The California Teachers Association spent $12 million and almost a year of its staff and elected leadership's time defeating a poorly drawn voucher initiative presented in a hapless and fractionated campaign (Doyle, 1994). Meanwhile, substantive educational reforms such as the state's assessment system were left unattended. Voucher proponents in California, as well as those supporting structural changes in schools nationwide, now see that they can fight the unions in a war of attrition.

The *Forbes* article language is instructive in another way, too. The words "government school cartel" strike at the legitimacy of the entire institution of public education, even the PTA, not just unionism. The capacity of existing institutions is being questioned (Block, 1990;

Chubb and Moe, 1990). Reforms on both the political left and right originate from a critique that holds that existing institutions are incapable of performing as they should. Ironically, having achieved power after organizing around its abuses, unions find themselves the chief defenders of an educational establishment that was among the proudest accomplishments of the Progressive Era.

THE ARGUMENT OF THIS BOOK

We argue here that the task of unionism lies not simply in sustaining the existing institution through political protection or confidence-building public relations, but in constructing a successor to industrial-era education. By this we do not mean to proclaim or advocate the end of public education. Ours is not an autopsy of public education (Lieberman, 1993), but rather the herald's call to alert unions and others that the institution faces basic questions about its direction and composition.

However, institutional reinvention—building an institution from the classroom up—is a fundamentally different organizing task from the one unions faced in the 1960s, different from "expanding the rights of one of the participants" in the existing institution of public education with known organizational structures and employment relationships (Grant and Murray, 1996). Where industrial-era labor relations successfully organized the economic rights of teachers, connecting them to the power of collective bargaining and the shield of procedural due process, the "other half" of teaching remains unorganized. Involving teachers' voice in the substance of education is still controversial, and it should be. Such a huge expansion of teacher rights needs to be firmly coupled with collective responsibility to align schooling in America with the requirements of the knowledge society.

Over the past decade, teacher unions have taken tentative steps toward reform within the existing institution of public education, and these steps have almost always proved frustrating. Change has been harder and more contentious than expected. And change did not spread from the few seedbeds of reform to unions and school districts nationally. Fundamental professional and teacher-empowerment reforms have taken place in no more than a few hundred of the nation's thousands of public school districts. These changes are therefore a tribute to the courage and dedication of union leaders throughout the country who have taken risks, departed from the conventional wisdom, and risked the criticism of their colleagues—and sometimes the wrath of their members. But it's far too little and almost too late.

The problem, we believe, is that marginal changes in school operations, exemplified by school site management reforms, are buffeted by much larger societal events, and thus the institution lacks the stability necessary for incremental change to grow and prosper (March and Olsen, 1989). School districts (particularly in big cities), the federal education establishment, and the icons of the existing institution such as the Educational Testing Service are themselves under siege.

In making the case for a teacher unionism fitted to a new institution of education we argue four points:

- Fundamental changes are taking place in the organization of society and the economy, changes that parallel those that occurred during the transition from an agricultural to an industrial society.

- These changes will cause fundamental reorganization of education as an institution similar to that which occurred in the Progressive Era early in this century.

- At their core, these changes are about reorganization of learning: What is learning, who is capable of learning, and what is the responsibility of teachers in creating learning?

- Institutional change will cause major dislocations to the way schools are organized and governed. These changes will alter the power and influence relationships of teacher unions, vastly diminishing conventional sources of power and influence, and opening new terrain for union organization.

Thus, we conclude, the primary task of unions is to reorganize around the emerging aspects of what we call the knowledge society.

FUNDAMENTAL CHANGES IN THE ECONOMY AND SOCIETY

In each historical era, society organizes itself around a *master concept*. For the last century, industrialism defined social reality in the United States. Industrial notions of organization told us that hierarchies were efficient. Industrial ideas about work design told us that specialization was the way to handle complex tasks. Industrial ideas about learning coincided with the growth of behavioral psychology and a one-best-system approach to learning. Most important, industrial notions of progress told us that a market economy and the opportunity to go to school could provide solutions to the problems of industrialism—class conflict, economic crisis, and exploitation (Block, 1990).

Master concepts change rarely, but we believe that the modern world is on the verge of such a change. We believe that we live in an age of parenthesis, a historical interlude between an industrial society and the coming knowledge society (Block, 1990; Drucker, 1993; Kerchner, 1986; Marshall and Tucker, 1992; Reich, 1991). We believe the conditions that existed at the end of the nineteenth century, when the structural and political basis of contemporary schools took shape, are recurring. Just as at the turn of the century, the economy is in the midst of reorganization. Now, as at the end of the last century, people are redefining work, creating new jobs, and redefining the necessary skills. Now, as at the turn of the century, migration proceeds on a large scale. Now, as at the turn of the last century, society is redefining the skills and knowledge one needs to participate in economic and civil life.

From Agriculture to Industry

A comparison of the trends and social forces illustrates our point. Schumpeter (1942) described capitalism as a process of creative destruction. Destruction is an apt term for what took place in America's rural communities during the latter half of the nineteenth century. As the application of machines to farming vastly increased the economic efficiency of agriculture, millions of small subsistence farmers were pushed into debt and eventual bankruptcy. In 1880, it took more than twenty man-hours to harvest an acre of wheat. By 1936, it took only a fraction over six man-hours. One leading agriculturist of the day noted, "We no longer raise wheat here, we manufacture it. . . . We are not husbandrymen, we are not farmers. We are producing a product to sell" (Rifkin, 1995, p. 109).

Today, new information-based technologies are imposing similar destructive efficiencies on both the industrial and service sectors of our economy. Millions of workers are already losing jobs due to corporate downsizing, outsource contracting of personnel, and offshore

manufacturing. Figure 2.1 shows these parallel patterns in employment: between 1870 and 1910, the percentage of the labor force
employed in farming declined from 53 percent to 35 percent, and
between 1950 and 1990, employment in the goods-producing sector
fell from 40 percent to 20 percent of nonagricultural payrolls. Similar
patterns present themselves when one compares the sectors' relative
contribution to GNP during these time periods. The industrial sector
will experience even greater declines if future trends parallel what hap-
pened in agriculture. In less than a century, the proportion of the labor
force working on farms declined from approximately 40 percent in
1900 to less than 5 percent today.

From Industry to Knowledge

Ironically, union organization around mass manufacturing occurred
just as manufacturing employment began to decline relative to the rest
of the workforce. As early as 1940, the number of workers in service-
producing industries became greater than those in goods-producing
industries, and the trend toward service employment continues. But
this shift in the labor market was masked by the tremendous boom in
the manufacturing economy in the post–World War II years. Increasing manufacturing productivity allowed the rapid expansion in the
service sector. The standard of living doubled in just twenty-seven
years, productivity increased rapidly, and unemployment was low
because the service sector, including government and education, was
growing (Peterson, 1994).

The post–World War II labor market had three supposedly endur-
ing features. One was employment stability. The second was a career
ladder within corporations, the internal labor market (Doeringer and
Piore, 1971). The third was middle-class rewards for nominal skills.
These three elements created an implicit bargain between the country's corporations and workers: security and good pay in return for
loyalty to the company, refusal to advocate European-style socialism
(which would otherwise have threatened basic industries with public
ownership), and dedication to consumer goods (which made the economic wheel go around). American society accepted big business with
relatively few regulations; big business accepted big labor. However,
beginning in the 1970s—with the decline in well-paid manufacturing
jobs that Harrison and Bluestone (1990) call "the great U-turn"—the

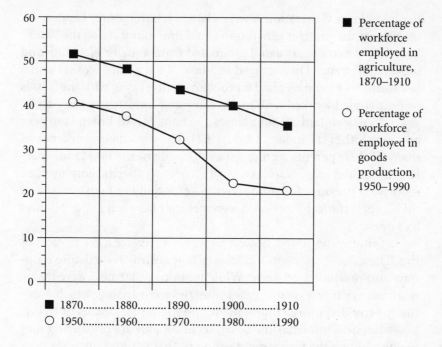

**Figure 2.1.   Percentage of Employment in Sector,
1870–1910 and 1950–1990.**

Sources: U.S. Bureau of the Census, 1972, 1992.

old economy stalled, the shape of the labor market changed radically, and with it the employment stability bargain was broken. Some 900,000 manufacturing jobs disappeared *each year* between 1978 and 1982 (Bluestone and Bluestone, 1992).

Ever since, we have been faced with contradictory images of our economic future. There is a vision of techno-paradise in which increasingly versatile robots, ever-advancing computers and software, and accelerating information exchange will set off a continued upward spiral of production and profit. Armed with smart technologies, workers will break down some of the isolation and mindlessness of industrial-era jobs and reinject craft and artisanship characteristics into their work (Piore and Sabel, 1984).

However, this image of progress is illusory to many and a bitter irony to a generation of workers who find good jobs hard to get and harder to keep. Generation X writes letters rebuffing Ann Landers for saying that the younger generation could find jobs if it had the "stuff" hers did. "Twelve years ago, I graduated from a major New England university," writes Discouraged in Mass. "I am a hard worker and a fast learner. I have never had a problem getting along with my bosses or the people I worked with in the computer industry. In the past 12 years, I've been laid off four times . . . I am 34. All I own is my car and my clothes" (Landers, 1995, p. E2). These younger workers and many of their parents see the dark underside of the new labor market: more fluid jobs with less security from any specific employer, an increasing pressure for productivity—especially in managerial and mid-level technical jobs—and a greater gulf between good jobs and bad ones.

As Schumpeter noted, however, there is a creative force in capitalism. The gains in economic efficiency that destroy the existing economy also produce a new one. While millions of farmers were losing work in agriculture, whole new industries were arising, which eventually provided more employment and higher standards of living. Likewise, new information-based technologies are producing new wealth, though the future distribution of that wealth remains a matter of uncertainty and debate (Berryman and Bailey, 1992; Reich, 1991). For unions, a change in the nature of work threatens the bedrock of their organization, just as did the shift from craft to industrial production.

Migration and Immigration

The social dislocations created by the economic shifts of the late nineteenth and late twentieth centuries both prompted large segments of the population to migrate. People followed jobs, moving from locations where the old economy languished to those being occupied by the emerging growth sectors. For example, from 1870 to 1910 the percentage of the population living in urban areas increased from 25 percent to 47 percent. By the 1940s, nearly 70 percent of the manufacturing jobs in the country were located in cities with populations greater than one million people. Now we see a parallel trend accompanying the shift from the industrial to the knowledge society (Figure 2.2). The flight from central cities to the suburbs was the beginning of this process. But as availability of telecommunications increases and

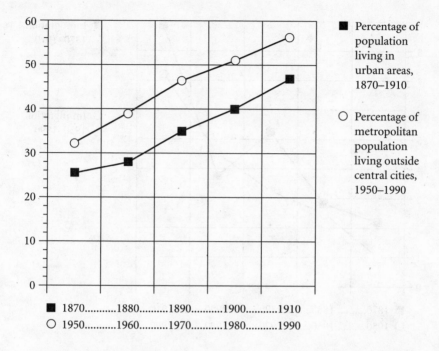

Figure 2.2.　Distribution of Population, 1870–1910 and 1950–1990.
Sources: U.S. Bureau of the Census, 1972, 1992.

costs of usage diminish we may see population declines even in sub-urban communities as people follow jobs to exurban locations.

Migration also has occurred in the form of immigration into the country (Figure 2.3). Approximately twenty-three million new immigrants were admitted during the 1870–1910 period, and eighteen million (*not* counting those who arrived illegally) during the 1950–1990 period. Controversy surrounded each of these periods of immigration, as public education sought to define its nation-building function.

Social and economic changes of this magnitude are inevitably reflected in changes in underlying institutions. The late nineteenth

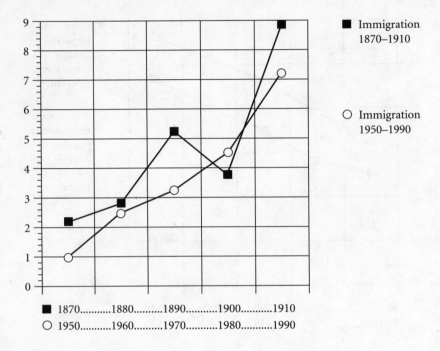

**Figure 2.3.   Immigration to the United States,
1870–1910 and 1950–1990 (in millions).**
Sources: U.S. Bureau of the Census, 1972, 1992.

century was a time of intense social conflict, a Gilded Age for some, a period of hardship and deprivation for many. Fortunes were made and lost, farms and businesses went bankrupt, and it was widely believed that class warfare was brewing in America as well as Europe.

It was this age that gave rise to a remarkable realignment of civic life in the United States: the Progressive Movement, which initiated most of the features of contemporary public life, including virtually all the structures of public education. Progressivism helped to reform the country from an agricultural nation owned by an omnipotent oligarchy and governed by corrupt party machines into an industrial urban society. It brought system and organization to the life of the republic, most particularly to its school systems.

PARALLELS WITH THE PROGRESSIVE ERA: REDESIGNING THE INSTITUTION

The common criticism that nothing changes very much very fast in education misstates reality on two counts. First, the long-wave changes are extraordinary. When education takes on a different identity and purpose, as public schooling did in the first two decades in this century, things change rapidly around new structures and functions (Cremin, 1962; Iannoccone and Lutz, 1970). Also, the period *before* the shift to a new identity is one of great uncertainty, public debate, and apparent confusion, with competing proposals for reform and simultaneous consternation that not much is happening very fast (DiMaggio and Powell, 1991).

The rural school problem, as Cubberly (1916) labeled it, became the focus of numerous reform efforts during the latter half of the nineteenth century. He called the system of small rural schools "expensive, inefficient, inconsistent, short-sighted, unprogressive and penurious." In a telling statement about the coming clash between education professionals and the localists he notes, "Most of the progress that has been made in rural education in the past two decades has been made without the support and often against the opposition of the district-school trustees and the people they represent" (p. 52).

Industrialization demanded essential changes in the purposes of schools, the pedagogy, and the organization of teaching. The revolution in technology, the rise of urbanization, and the emergence of the large-scale, bureaucratic corporation required that public education serve functions not envisioned when the common school was created early in the nineteenth century. The separation of work from family life, the intensification of labor specialization, the shift in the locus of work from natural groups to formal organizations, and the rise of a nation-state interconnected by rail, roads, and waterways all necessitated a fundamental change in what children learned in school. And this change was associated with urbanization. As Cubberly noted then, "It is not too much to say that the great educational advance which we, as a nation, have made during the past half-century has been, to a very large degree, the advance which our cities have made in the organization, administration, equipment, instruction, and the extension of educational advantages" (p. 61).

Whereas rural schools had sought to impart basic literacy, industrialization called for a much broader and more specialized range of curricular content. "The grading of schools, the development of high schools, the introduction of instruction in special subjects, night and continuation schools, vacation schools, playgrounds, evening lectures, schools for adults, the kindergarten, schools for dependents and delinquents, compulsory education, health supervision, vocational guidance and vocational instruction, free textbooks and supplies, the establishment of the value of good supervision and business organization, and the working-out and establishment of sound principles in educational organization and administration—these have been distinctive contributions which the city school district has made to our educational theory and practice" (p. 61).

In addition to reading, writing, and arithmetic, urban reformers expanded the curriculum to include formal training in such subjects as spelling, geography, literature, history, physiology, natural science, and mathematics. They also called upon schools to prepare students for an occupation, something that was not necessary in agrarian society when virtually all jobs involved simple manual labor. Given the occupational differentiation accompanying industrialization, this prescription invariably meant some form of curricular tracking: vocational education for those who would be going into the trades and more advanced training in the academic disciplines for those moving into the professions and management. Schools also needed to socialize students for entry into the workplace, so they placed great emphasis upon inculcating habits of punctuality, discipline, obedience, regularity, attention, and silence. This new socialization function set aside the kind of voluntary school attendance that had been associated with rural education and resulted in the establishment and enforcement of strict compulsory attendance laws. Schools also sought to transcend the allegiances of particular groups and communities and to instill in students common, national values of citizenship, loyalty, and submission to the rule of law. Liberal immigration policies and the mass migration of population from the farm to the city made nation building an essential purpose of schools in an industrialized society.

The imposition of this agenda on public education necessitated profound changes in pedagogy and the organization of teaching. The ungraded classroom of the one-room schoolhouse and the jack-of-all-trades teacher were no longer appropriate for a curriculum with the scope and specialization associated with industrialization. Effective transmittal of each curriculum subject matter required a specialized pedagogical approach, and the knowledge base teachers needed to master demanded a much greater degree of formal, specialized education.

CHANGES IN THE INSTRUCTIONAL CORE

Changes in society's master concept are most visible when school governance or organizational structures change, but they are most significant when they affect the instructional core of schools:

- Who should go to school?
- What should they learn?
- What are the respective roles of students, teachers, and families?

The remarkably resilient instructional core put into place around 1916 by the educational progressives sent everyone to school—but for differing lengths of time and with differing expectations. Changing this pattern requires an enormous change in beliefs and practices. As Grant and Murray (1996) argue, "It involves nothing less than a shift from the system of sorting and selecting and tracking to one of inclusion that aims to raise the average achievement of all children and to assure that none fall below an acceptable minimum" (p. 94).

The institutional discontinuity facing America is not so much a matter of totally new values as of reordered expectations. For the past century, we valued most the individual opportunity to persist in school. We created a system of increasingly inclusive enrollment, one that over the years extended the expectation of secondary schooling to all racial and ethnic groups and all levels of health or disability. It created a system of upward opportunity that both selected and sorted students and opened more chances for social mobility than had ever before existed.

This system of individual opportunity won out over the more elite, single-standard system favored by the 1893 Committee of Ten, a group commissioned by the National Education Association and chaired by Harvard president Charles W. Eliot. That group had advocated a modernized curriculum, including choices, but "every subject which is taught at all in a secondary school should be taught in the same way and to the same extent to every pupil so long as he pursues it, no matter what the probable destination of the pupil may be or at what point his education is to cease" (quoted in Toch, 1991, p. 42).

Instead, the system developed multiple destination points fitting education to the needs of industrial society. Cubberly's 1916 textbook on school administration graphically illustrates how the change in school structure in Newton, Massachusetts, paralleled the needs of industrial society. In earlier times, students persisted or failed to persist in school with little consideration to vocational preparation. In Newton's modern (circa 1908) schools, there were specific pathways with evening schools, industrial schools, and special schools for "backward" children, each connected to the new occupational order and designed "to meet the needs of every child in the community" (p. 315).

Expanding access to school, it was thought, required tailoring school to what were termed the endowments and the social condition of children. In a phrase made famous by psychologist Stanley Hall, the school should be fitted to the child and not the other way around.

The invention of intelligence tests armed urban reformers with a powerful means for responding to the challenge of individual student differences. By testing for the child's *aptitude* for learning, schools could sort and channel students into curricular tracks where they would find the educational experiences most meaningful, because these experiences would be congruent with their capacity to learn. Tracking also would allow schools to develop curricular packages that would facilitate the child's eventual transition into the workplace, thereby forging more differentiated linkages between school and community. In the process, educators built the bell curve into schooling.

The tracking, sorting system worked because it produced workers for the large numbers of jobs urban industrialism was creating. There were relatively low social opportunity costs for not completing a rigorous course of study in high school. Although the number of craft and professional jobs increased because the population and the economy were growing, the employment boom took place in basic manufacturing and assembly work. The transference from farm labor to factory labor was less a matter of cognitive achievement than of acculturation and work discipline. As Table 2.1 illustrates, as late as World War II, an eighth-grade education fully qualified one for more than 95 percent of jobs in the automobile industry.

Educational Requirement	Number of Jobs Requiring It	Percent of Total	Cumulative Percent
Ability to speak, read, and write English	194	67.7	67.7
Grammar school graduation	81	28.5	96.2
High school graduation	9	3.1	99.3
Some high school education	1	.35	99.65
College graduation	1	.35	100.0
Total	286	100.0	

Table 2.1. Educational Requirements for Auto Jobs.

Source: Johnston, 1939, p. 62. Data compiled from job specifications of the U.S. Employment Service.

The new economy of the late twentieth century is more demanding and less forgiving than its predecessor. It is not creating good jobs for the unskilled—indeed, there is a hearty debate about whether it is creating enough jobs for the skilled and educated—but it is clear that the premium placed on educational attainment is increasing. Moreover, the dependence of the economy on educated human resources is also increasing.

Between 1949 and 1992, as Table 2.2 shows, the income premium received by high school graduates compared with dropouts increased from 21 percent to 31 percent. The income premium attached to college graduation reached 130 percent. The 1992 data give a somewhat exaggerated picture of the increase because of changing demographics—for both 1949 and 1961, the general population included a large number of men who dropped out before entering high school, and whose low earnings were thus excluded from the base being compared with the earnings of the educated contingent. In 1992, there were relatively few in that category, and the entire distribution was thus pushed upward relative to the distributions reported for 1949 and 1961. The overall trend, however, is still relevant for our discussion.

	1949	1961	1992
High school graduation	21.9	16.2	31.7
Some college	42.0	41.4	64.2
Bachelor's degree or higher	98.0	86.8	130.0

Table 2.2.   Lifetime Income Advantage of Educated Males Aged 25–64.
Note: Figures indicate percent increase over income of men who dropped out of
high school.
Sources: Data for 1949 and 1961 calculated from U.S. Bureau of the Census, 1962;
data for 1992 calculated from U.S. Bureau of the Census, 1994.

The contribution of education to economic well-being is not
strictly private. Private earnings appear to accrue because of the educated worker's greater economic productivity. A recent study by the
U.S. Bureau of the Census (1994) indicates that a 10 percent increase
in educational attainment produced an 8.6 percent increase in economic productivity. For each additional year of schooling in the workforce, employers gained in productivity roughly what employees
gained in income. Over the past fifty years, increases in educational
attainment appear to have produced almost twice the gain in workplace efficiency as comparable increases in the value of tools and
machinery (Schultz, 1981).

Given these advantages, it is little wonder that there are strong pressures on public education to retain and graduate students from high
school and to qualify as many as possible for college entrance. Yet the
question of staying in school in virtually inseparable from what is
learned there.

The question of social and ethnic identity, the question of preparation for participation in a democratic society, and the question of
student attributes for participation in the knowledge society are all
ones that occupy educational reformers. They are questions teachers
care deeply about and in which they should be able to represent themselves through their unions and through discipline or subject-matter
organizations. They are the essence of identifying educational quality, and the next part of this book is dedicated to that issue. Here, we
want to address the ways in which the educational quality issue is
destabilizing the old instructional core: reaching new conclusions
about who should go to school, what they should study, and how
teachers should teach and students should learn. The answers to these
questions change teaching work and create a crisis for unionism.

DESTABILIZING THE OLD INSTITUTION

In the early 1980s, the National Commission on Educational Excellence report *A Nation at Risk* changed the focus of educational politics from discussions about achieving equity to discussions about achieving excellence. While we argue, as others have, that the two goals are mutually interdependent, the shift changed educational politics in Washington and state capitols.

The quality debate destabilizes the existing institution of education because it asserts that education as an institution has failed. Educational analyst Paul Cooperman started the debate by proclaiming, "Each generation of Americans has outstripped its parents in education, in literacy, and in economic attainment. For the first time in the history of the country, the educational skills of one generation will not surpass, will not equal, will not even approach, those of their parents" (National Commission on Excellence in Education, 1983, p. 9).

As it turned out, Cooperman's statement, and much of *A Nation at Risk,* exaggerated the academic performance problems of public education. The longer one looked, the more difficult it became to find the great decline in American education. Although the widely watched SAT scores had fallen in the early 1970s, much of their decline has been attributed to changes in the pool of test takers. Moreover, the reading and mathematics achievement of virtually all of the groups monitored by the National Center for Education Statistics have not shown net declines over the past two decades. Scores for African American and Latino students have actually improved, though they still remain substantially below those of white students.

In fact, in 1993, the National Assessment of Educational Progress (NAEP) announced that three-fourths of twelfth graders had reached a basic level at which they can "develop interpretations from a variety of texts," "understand overall arguments," "recognize explicit aspects of plot and characters," "support global generalizations," "respond personally to texts," and "use major documents to solve real-world problems" (Myers, 1996, p. 1).Thus the vast majority of American students had met the lofty standards set out in the early part of the century.

Is the crisis over student achievement and standards a fraud, a manufactured crisis, as asserted by Berliner and Biddle (1995)? We believe not. We believe that although public officials, journalists, and even union officers have been reckless in their statements about declining student achievement, the nation does face a deep crisis over creating and meeting standards that match the society of 2016 rather than that of 1916. Miles Myers, executive director of the National Council of Teachers of English and former president of the California Federation of Teachers, believes that the country is rapidly defining a new standard of literacy in which students are expected to make inferences, draw conclusions, analyze the use of literary devices, and make connections between literature and their own lives. (See Myers, 1996, for an excellent treatment of how the definition of literacy has evolved through our country's history.)

The bad news from the NAEP evaluation was that only one-third of twelfth graders met this higher standard.

Reform efforts, such as the New Standards Project, the Coalition of Essential Schools, the National Board for Professional Teaching Standards, and the standards projects of the different educational disciplines will profoundly destabilize the existing institution of public education. As Myers puts it: "Reading these reports it is possible to forget that changing the nation's standard of literacy will require changes in schools beyond those in curriculum content. . . . Changing our standard of literacy and our curriculum will require many changes in many parts of the school system, not just changes in the curriculum guides or in the assessments. In my opinion, the whole idea of the publicly funded common school in the United States may be now at stake in these discussions" (p. 2).

Implicitly or explicitly, reformers say that the existing institution of education cannot perform, and that it is the civic duty of those outside the institution to reform it—in the words of Finn's *We Must Take Charge* (1991). "We," in this case, does not mean school superintendents and certainly not unionized teachers. "We" almost certainly means anyone else: mayors, governors, business executives, community activists.

The destabilizing tendencies have been repeated in school district after school district across the country, but particularly in the big cities, creating a not-quite-hostile takeover of many school districts. In each of these instances, the traditional governance and organization of schools has been undermined and hybrid forms of governance have been put into place as part of experiments in school site management, flattening the hierarchy, intensifying the curriculum, clustering groups of schools together. These reforms have been most intense in the central cities, and both AFT (in Chicago, New York, Miami, Rochester, Pittsburgh, Cincinnati) and NEA locals (in Seattle,

Denver, Louisville) have been involved. Regardless of whether the teacher union opposed or supported the reform agenda, the stronger the reform and the closer to the classroom, the more profound the destabilization.

The reason that small changes in teaching yield big changes in the institution derives from the institutional nature of schooling. Education is difficult to change because it is a system in fact, not just in name. The pieces fit together, and it has worked remarkably well to produce the kind of education that reformers envisioned at the turn of the twentieth century.

To create the reforms needed at the turn of the twenty-first century, teachers' work will change significantly (a topic we address in the next chapter). To shift from presenting lessons to diagnosing learning, teachers need much more information about student learning and about ways to frame useful responses. As schools that have attempted to change their teaching know, conventional resource allocation practices rapidly fall short of the new requirements. Teachers need time. They need flexibility to teach some students for a longer period of time and others hardly at all. The logic of six- or seven-period days, with fifty-minute classes and thirty students in a class, flies out the window. So does the logic of existing authority and responsibility structures. When the basic structures of school cannot yield the standards we need, everything else is up for grabs, including union rules.

Like all industrial-era unions, teachers organized around what former labor secretary John Dunlop ([1958] 1993) called "a web of rules." The tactics and strategies of unionization created political and legal strength in the enforcement of those rules. The social function of labor relations, Dunlop held, is to create rules of the workplace that contribute to social stability and economic efficiency. Strikes, grievance adjudication procedures, unfair labor practices charges, demonstrations, and lawsuits all enforced the web of rules with the collective bargaining contract as the centerpiece.

There are two types of rules. The first rules establish and maintain the institution surrounding the workplace. In any era, an institution such as public education holds together because of common shared and enforced understandings. These both constrain and liberate. They constrain by creating political and social limits on what is expected and what is discussable. They liberate by freeing the institution to organize around its chosen goals without having to redebate them.

The second set of rules concerns the workplace itself. These include the conventional topics of labor relations—wages, hours, and conditions of employment—as well as expectations about commitment, caring, and expertise, sometimes called the psychological contract.

The irony in the current educational debates is that teacher unions themselves first forcefully questioned the three underlying institutional rules of industrial-era education. Union activity made it obvious that the old institution was not performing as it should.

First, unions organized against the bureaucratic control system installed by the business-dominated progressive reformers. Collective bargaining limited managerial discretion and authority, and its presence made it clear that the "neutral professional competence" ascribed to school administrators was not necessarily either neutral or competent. Teacher unionism flourished in the 1960s, the decade that spawned the bumper sticker: "Question Authority."

Second, union organization broke the back of elite governance of school districts. The educational progressives sought to remove education from local politics by vesting it in the hands of community elites. Through electoral activity and lobbying, unions became a part of an already pronounced tendency toward making school boards themselves a political arena: a focus for community discontent, a stepping-stone for higher elective political office.

Third, unions weighed into public education the side of social equity and thus helped question the primary pedagogical structure around which schools were organized, the social sorting function in which kids were associated with futures according to their racial and social backgrounds. Although imperfectly and unevenly, unions and their members campaigned against the bell curve of education.

The breakdown of bureaucratic control, elite governance, and bell-curve education leads us to the point of profound questioning of the current institution of public education. Unions feel this most acutely when labor relations disputes raise questions about the schools' capacity to solve educational problems. The questions raised by *Detroit Free Press* writer Joe Stroud could be found in almost any recent big city labor dispute. In the midst of the 1992 strike he wrote: "The city is losing its long twilight struggle against ignorance and failure. And the tragedy is that nobody—not the [Detroit Federation of Teachers] that Mr. [John] Elliott heads, not the board that [former superintendent Deborah] McGriff serves, nobody—seems to know how to break the pattern. . . . I'm not ready to give up on public education, but it surely tries my patience and tests my faith" (1992, p. 2F).

The most fundamental institutional rule is the grant of legitimacy that society gives to those who work in education. When society has confidence in an institution, it grants freedom and self-governance to those who work in it. No matter how powerful an interest group may seem, when it loses confidence, its actions are questioned. When, as Dunlop writes ([1958] 1993), the basic grants of legitimacy are withdrawn, none of the rest of the rules have much power.

Thus institutional rules form an important part of thinking about education and unions, and these are discussed in the final chapters of this book. In particular, we discuss the requirements for new labor relations statutes fitted to the needs of knowledge-era workplaces, and we connect the discussion of statutes to an acute need for union organizing, the only mechanism that will recreate unions as a vital influence in American life.

Most of this book, however, concerns the second set of rules, those about the content and process of work. This set of rules was carefully fitted to the structures of industrial-era workplaces, and produced what is called "job control unionism," a form of worker organization built around the assumption that the organizations carrying out work are largely permanent and stable, that jobs build into careers, and that large, hierarchical organizations are efficient and thus likely to persist. Collective action—or its threat—has enforced the rules.

Transforming unionism requires working on both sets of rules more or less at once. The Progressive Era reformers were successful because they were able to connect the work of teachers and schools to larger social purposes, everyday things like what students studied in school to very large concerns such as the national economy and what was called the "democratic experiment." The next transformation will have to do the same.

A VISION OF KNOWLEDGE WORKERS

Organizing teachers as knowledge workers assumes political and social importance beyond educational reform. Just as industrial work and workers were the fulcrum across which American society was organized in this century, knowledge work and workers will be the fulcrum in the next century. Teachers are by far the largest group of knowledge workers currently associated with organized labor. How teaching organizes around knowledge work creates the model for organizational life and distributive justice in the twenty-first century. Teachers become its vanguard.

The question is whether knowledge workers can be organized successfully, and whether occupations such as teaching that are already unionized can be organized around knowledge work. One of industrialism's signal accomplishments was the advent of large-scale permanent worker organization. Never before in history had the bulk of workers organized to such an extent. Urban and craft workers joined guilds, but the vast majority of the population had no comparable structure. Peasants revolted occasionally, but they did not stay organized. Craft union organization and then industrial organization proved to be powerful mechanisms raising working people from poverty to solid middle class. It is this status that changes in master concept from industrialism to knowledge society threaten. As Drucker (1994) notes, "No class in history has ever risen faster than the blue-collar worker. And no class has ever fallen faster" (p. 56).

Past attempts by the AFL-CIO to organize white-collar workers have largely been unsuccessful. The open question is whether workers will organize around their interests in autonomy, self-discipline, and self-direction. Knowledge workers appear highly individualistic, lacking the essential solidarity industrial workers possess (or possessed). But it must be remembered that up until the 1930s it was thought that industrial workers were too indifferent to support unions. "These same workers, only a few years later, gathered into the most powerful labor organizations the country has ever seen" (Heckscher, 1995, p. 65). Like other knowledge workers, teachers' insecurities come not from a decline in their industry but from the rapid restructuring of their work lives. Teaching is being restructured now just as it was during the Progressive Era (Murphy, 1990).

A number of writers in education think that teachers are already in the midst of organizing around these elements in their work. Grant and Murray (1996) see the outline of a "second academic revolution" not unlike the one through which college professors gained independence of university oligarchies in the 1950s. They write, "The conviction is growing among teachers that the kinds of reforms that are being demanded for children—namely that all of them become competent problem solvers and critical thinkers—cannot be fulfilled if the teachers themselves are not similarly empowered with respect to inquiring into the nature of their own practice. . . . Most importantly, they are no longer willing to let the administrative class define themselves as the exclusive experts in the content of the curriculum and as the sole decision-makers about who is fit to teach it" (pp. 97–98).

The question of whether highly educated workers will have autonomy and discretion or whether they will be subject to industrial-style routines is critical in this generation. At the societal level, knowledge gains power, and to some it becomes a substitute for capital (Drucker, 1993; Toffler, 1990). But whether the production of knowledge equates to decent jobs is an undecided issue.

In the industrial era, successful mass organization was possible because for the first time it became feasible for unions to apply leverage to large employers. They did so by understanding the productive environment in which they were working and by connecting workers to the common good and organizing around its three primary characteristics: the division of labor, the way work was organized, and the way quality was produced.

CONNECTING TEACHERS TO THE COMMON GOOD

The educational progressives were successful, in part, because they were able to connect education to perceptions of the common good. The transformation of schools was at the center of things. "Proponents of virtually every progressive cause from the 1890s through World War I had their program for the school. Humanitarians of every stripe saw education at the heart of their effort toward social alleviation" (Cremin, 1962, p. 85). In similar fashion, education—preschool through graduate school—now appears as the basic industry of the knowledge society (Kerchner, 1995). If knowledge and its manipulation creates wealth and influence, the institutions charged with knowledge creation obtain the same status in the coming society that railroads, steel making, and auto manufacturing had in the era that is now closing.

The question is how to link teaching to the common good. In the nineteenth century, the common school was not to be a school for the common people, but a school common to all the people. It was to embrace both rich and poor and to provide an educational experience as good as, and perhaps even better than, that provided by private education. It expressed the Jeffersonian belief that democratic institutions depend on a knowledgeable citizenry able to make intelligent decisions in their personal lives, in their civic engagement, and in their economic choices. It also was to be an engine for social mobility, enabling persons from every social stratum and background to realize their own potential, and thereby to contribute to national economic prosperity (Cremin, 1962).

In this century, expanding the base of elementary and secondary education produced the human capital, and thereby the growth in economic resources, to allow for the extension of the pyramid upward. Universal primary education, for example, made possible the provision of high-quality secondary education to students who desired and qualified for it. The extension of compulsory education through the middle grades strengthened further the quality of high schools and made possible an expansion of postsecondary education. Expanding the base of students entering college, in turn, improved the quality of graduate education. It was at once a sorting machine, an expression of egalitarian values, and an institution for national economic progress. The structure and logic of the system, in other words, is predicated on the most fundamental of democratic beliefs: namely, that a society that expands the scope of opportunity accorded to ordinary men and women will be more prosperous than one that restricts choice to an elite.

In many ways the problems we have to solve are the same as the progressives did—extending education, increasing mobility, providing connections between education and the economy, and creating social harmony.

UNITING MIND WORKERS

Unions of knowledge workers will not fit comfortably within the frameworks of industrial unionism, or within industrial assumptions about how schools should be structured and operated. By the early 1950s, a relatively stable web of rules surrounded U.S. industry's growing production of standardized products for mass production. Workers were usually narrowly trained, and jobs were similarly specialized. Quality was created by standardizing products and routinizing work. The system created both growth and stability through relatively permanent employment and opportunities for promotion. Increasingly, workers stayed with a single employer for long periods of time, often for an entire career, and thus rights to a particular job and prospects for promotion within the firm became very important.

This industrial union setting essentially replaced an older tradition of craft work and occupational unions. In the craft tradition, unions played a much more active role in the training and allocation of labor and were often involved with management in organizing production (Cobble, 1991; Locke, Kochan, and Piore, 1995). The new industrial arrangements produced well-paid jobs, and rapidly raised manufacturing workers to middle-class economic status. The post–World War II economic boom and the rapid rise in educational aspirations were fueled by this cycle of virtue.

Starting in the 1970s, the set of institutional arrangements broke down under the pressure of increased competition and globalism, shifts toward high technology, and the movement of jobs from manufacturing to service sectors. As a consequence, there have been movements toward new forms of work and organization.

Considerable attention has been given to how knowledge worker unions might be organized. Cobble (1991, 1994) studied craft-based waitress unions (no longer in operation) and found within them an approach to organizing the vast numbers of service workers whose work may move among many employers. Heckscher (1988) observed the extent to which employee guarantees have been achieved through legislation and by means outside of collective bargaining, and advocated "associational" forms of unionism less tied to contracts. Our own earlier work created a mosaic of practices we called *professional unionism* from the bits of reform in school districts around the country, showing that it was possible but difficult to organize unions around improving schools (Kerchner and Koppich, 1993). However, any vision of future unionism requires organizing around and gaining access to the sources of power in the society and within the particular institution, in this case education. In the industrial era, unions gained power by attaching themselves to the three key decisions required of any organization: how the work was divided up, how productivity was achieved, and how quality was assured and assessed. These same three functions remain, but they are expressed differently, and thus they require different patterns of organization. The vision of a union of knowledge workers is a vision that understands and builds upon changes in the processes of teaching and learning.

The Division of Labor

Industrial organizations were built on specialization. Only by dividing the task of making a whole product into many parts was the organization capable of coping with rapidly expanding technical knowledge. Specialization found its way into industrial-era schools, which invented the forms we know well: separated subjects, grade levels, and departments, teaching specialties, clear boundaries between the curriculum and an extracurriculum. These demarcations were reproduced in teachers' work. "Grade Eight English Teacher" came to define a job assignment, a knowledge domain, and—through unionism—a property right.

INDUSTRIAL-ERA SPECIALIZATION.   Unions gained power by organizing around specialization and job classification. Through union contracts, teachers gained a protected property right to particular jobs. The correct classification of teachers in jobs became the mechanism for unions to claim work for members of the bargaining unit and to settle teacher-versus-teacher disputes over who was entitled to a particular position. Seniority and certification clauses provided an objective means of showing which teachers were entitled to hold which positions. Unions guarded and advanced seniority rights that, in effect, made more preferred teaching jobs an accrued property right. At the same time, they were vigilant about the assignment of teachers "out of position," into jobs for which they did not hold the nominally required certification. One of the longest-running areas of union-management dispute has been the hiring of teachers on "emergency" or special credentials.

Union power is threatened when the boundaries of existing job classifications are breached and when schools provide different treatment to teachers of the same classification. Thus unions have historically opposed differentiation among teachers in pay and privilege. Merit pay is viewed more as a source of favoritism than a means of rewarding performance. Unions argue, with strong logic, that the production of learning is so atomized among teachers that rewarding one teacher when achievement soars does not capture the combined effort of a whole school. Even the rewards that the unions create for their leaders are subject to criticism from their own members. Union officers released from full-time teaching are frequently criticized for ceasing to be real teachers or having cushy jobs. To teachers, equity came to mean sameness.

KNOWLEDGE-ERA FLEXIBILITY.   A knowledge-era division of labor builds on flexibility and thus inherently threatens union power built on specialization. The phrase "flexible specialization" describes manufacturing processes designed to be highly responsive to changes in customer needs. The product or process may be specialized, but the worker stays flexible. Rather than production lines creating an endless stream of nearly identical items, the new vision is of groups of workers coming together around unique problems, solving them together, and moving on. Rather than being rigid, assignments are highly variable, and projects are frequently assigned to teams of workers who decide among themselves exactly how to perform a given task.

The image of flexible specialization arose first in manufacturing: the Volvo Kalmar plant in Sweden, the General Motors–Toyota NUMMI plant in California, and the fabled Saturn plant in Tennessee. But as the instructional core of schooling starts to change, we see the instinct toward flexibility and teamwork reaching into education. Individualized instruction, inclusiveness or mainstreaming in special education, and the teaming inherent in new approaches to middle schools—each breaks down old occupational boundaries, and in so doing becomes an item of controversy.

ORGANIZING SCHOOL INNOVATION AND PRODUCTIVITY.   When work is highly flexible, unions are able to gain power because only teachers and teams of educators have the capacity to link the creation of new knowledge about school practice with distribution of fiscal and human resources. In small, autonomous schools it is possible to depart from complex management schemes and more easily return to hands-on, face-to-face school operations. It is in the creation of a knowledge of practice that teaching lays claim to the title of profession. Small, autonomous schools aid this development by confronting teachers with the need to make their schools work better. No one else is going to do it for them.

Chapter Seven explores the idea of building a contractual relationship around schools. The primary school site instrument we have in mind is called an enterprise compact. The name and function were introduced by Bluestone and Bluestone (1992) in their investigation of labor relations breakthroughs in the auto industry. As they put it, "A *contract* is essentially adversarial in nature, representing a compromise between the separate interests of each party to the agreement. In contrast, a *compact* is fundamentally a cooperative document, providing for a mutual vision and joint system for achieving common goals that foster the general well-being of all stakeholders in a given endeavor" (pp. 24–25). While these agreements are largely foreign to our labor relations tradition, they are as old and as American as the

Mayflower Compact in which the colonists pledged to "combine our selves together into a civil body politick . . . for the generall good of the Colonie" (quoted in Bluestone and Bluestone, 1992, p. 25).

The Shape of Organizations

Industrial-era organizations work around *economies of scale:* bigger is better. They seek economies of scale by making the organizational pyramid both taller and fatter; everything the organization needs is included within its boundaries. Under this logic, newspaper publishing companies bought forests and paper mills and movie studios bought theaters to show their productions. School districts, as we have seen, both consolidated and brought all manner of supplies and services under their corporate umbrella. Schools found themselves in the construction and maintenance business, besides providing nursing, food service, police protection, and warehousing.

INDUSTRIAL-ERA SCALE.   To belong to an industrial organization was to be an employee. Having a job meant that you were part of the organization, and job consciousness became the key to union organization. Unions organized around a set of employees, not around the production process itself. Thus teacher unions organized teachers as people with jobs and essentially ignored the act of teaching and the process of learning. Above all, industrial union organization became job conscious. Unions were in business to protect members' positions and to enhance the conditions under which they worked. Other than representing the reemployment rights of laid-off teachers, the union had little connection with persons attached to schools by means other than through employment. Parents, for example, were frequently viewed as enemies from whom teachers were to be protected.

As a consequence, unions became highly attached to the centrality of the employment relationship. "Wages, hours, and conditions" became more than a phrase in bargaining statutes; it was the organizing principle of the unions. How long teachers worked, how many classes they taught, and how many children were assigned to a classroom served as the basis for the work-effort bargain in the labor contract and also became the device for maintaining employment security.

Under these conditions, the union was highly threatened by efforts to bring in resources from outside the bounds of the organization. Just as unions opposed technological substitution for human capacity, they also opposed outsourcing work to private contractors and using casual or part-time labor that was inevitably purchased at lower rates, except on the condition that the full-time employees, who were considered the authentic members of the organization, were protected from displacement. In exchange for employment security, unions ceded to management control over work processes, products, and quality. Defining the organization and designing the work became management's job.

KNOWLEDGE-ERA SCOPE. Knowledge-era organization challenges these keys to union influence by organizing around *economies of scope* rather than economies of scale. Economies of scope occur when an organization is able to accomplish a broader range of tasks without increasing the size of the organizational pyramid. The one-room school embodies high economy of scope—a single teacher with a great range of tasks. Modern equivalents, we suggest, are self-managing schools that are relatively small and autonomous.

ORGANIZING AROUND CAREER STABILITY. For unions, the instability of public school organizations creates the opportunity to create *career control* at the institutional level. If employment is fluid, then unions need to function as the means through which employees get hired. If schools are to be autonomous, and teachers may in the course of a career work in many of them, pensions and benefits can no longer be attached to a single school. Unions need to work toward career structures that allow teachers maximum flexibility in the labor market.

Unions create career stability through intervention in the labor market. From the days of the guilds, unions served as market intermediaries, protecting their members' economic and social interests. In this situation, the balance between protection and a productive relationship is among the most difficult to achieve over time, which is one of the reasons that we have witnessed historic reinvention of unionism around emerging modes of production.

No aspect of American unionism is more pronounced than its job consciousness, its sense of justice about who is entitled to work and under what conditions. The issue of employment permanency is an important one in this decade, just as it was in the 1930s when industrial unionism energized workers. The old pact between companies and employees, the idea of lifetime employment and a secure pension in exchange for employee loyalty, has been effectively voided. It could not withstand the pressures of international competition any more than the corporate paternalism of the 1920s could withstand the Great Depression.

We are seeing a new type of employment relationship emerging, one that is in many respects paradoxical. "Postindustrial technology demands involvement and commitment from employees, but the competitive market and corporate restructuring now deny to all but the most sheltered firms the means for assuring job security and predictable treatment on which employee commitment depends" (Brody, 1993, p. 263). One gains a picture of a highly organic organization that changes rapidly with conditions and combines and recombines itself with fluidity. In this setting, employment is also likely to be fluid—no more forty years and gold watch.

ORGANIZING AROUND OCCUPATIONS, NOT EMPLOYERS. In this setting, the unions' historical strategy of building a set of rights around a particular job is challenged, and the unions have two possible avenues of action. One is to fight at each of the boundaries over such issues as the redefinition of teacher work, contracting out, the use of interns, substitution of volunteers or employees of other organizations and agencies. The other is to begin to organize around career security rather than job security.

By *career security*, we mean that union members would be buffered from the winds of organizational change through a series of mechanisms that would allow members to move relatively easily from school to school, from job to job, and from one type of economic relationship to another. This form of representation has a rich history in craft and occupational unions of nonfactory workers—longshoremen, agricultural laborers, janitors, and musicians—which strove for control over hiring through strong closed-shop language and union hiring halls. They "stressed employment security rather than 'job rights' at an individual work site and they offered benefits and privileges that workers could carry with them from employer to employer" (Cobble, 1991, p. 421).

Chapter Eight examines the labor market for teachers in detail and sketches our ideas for:

• A career ladder where teaching is on the top rather than the bottom rung

- An incentive system so that teachers would have both psychological and financial ownership of their jobs
- A scheme for portable pensions and benefits
- An electronic hiring hall that makes movement between schools, cities, and states easier

Organizing Around Quality

Quality in industrial-era organizations is controlled though *standardization and routinization* of rules and practices within organizations. Designing quality in this way allows lower-skilled workers to produce complex goods of high quality simply by following rules and procedures. The same idea of rules and procedures is incorporated in the organization's control and management system. When organizations become large, the rule of policy substitutes for direct supervision. Rules are also copied from other organizations. Schools that have followed this mode of organization make the assumption that the way to solve quality problems is to create teacher-proof curricula and to enforce their use with management systems. Categorical programs, which operate on the basis of compliance, make the same assumption.

INDUSTRIAL-ERA ROUTINES. However, the eventual pattern is that following the rules becomes a substitute for the original idea of quality, rather than a means of achieving it. Organizations then become rule-bound, as schools often are. Unions didn't cause this to happen, but the structure of union contracts and the force of union representation behind their enforcement clearly adds to the rule-boundedness of schools and to the implication that following the rules is the first duty of school leaders. Novelty and innovation are generally discouraged. Both unions and employer organizations maintain "model" contracts and judge labor relations practitioners according to how they performed against an ideal rule and structural system rather than judging labor relations by its contribution to organizational performance.

In a rule-based environment, teacher unions seek *fair treatment* for their members through the universal and evenhanded application of rules. The unions' job, or indeed the job of employees, is not to create quality but to faithfully undertake the routines and procedures that others have designed. Unions gain substantial power through monitoring the uniformity of rule application, when those rules affect the conditions of employment or the ways in which employees are compensated, evaluated, or assigned to duties. Due process requirements give unions great influence in evaluation disputes largely because the rules themselves are so complex that school administrators most frequently run afoul of them, thus creating grounds for a challenge of decisions adverse to an employee.

In terms of substantive quality, however, unions are left with blunt weapons, incapable of responding with much grace to individual workplace problems. Experienced administrators and union leaders frequently find themselves searching for ways to amend, bend, or reinterpret rules so that teachers can get what they want and so that useful work can get done.

When this rather mechanical world fails to work, its legitimacy is threatened. The educational quality crisis in the United States threatens the entire institution of public education with radical reformation, and neither unions nor managements organized around rule enforcement can do much about the problem. The quality crisis also complements the growing social tendency to see education as a matter that should be governed by individual preference and taste, that is, that people are entitled to the education they want as opposed to the education any public agency decides they should have.

KNOWLEDGE-ERA OUTCOMES.   Knowledge-era organizations attach quality to outcomes rather than procedures. They can be highly adaptive in how work actually gets done, and because they make quality goals explicit, they can also deal with changing ideas about what quality is or should be.

In a knowledge-era division of labor, quality depends on workers' understanding what quality is in any given situation and knowing how to create and authenticate it. In industrial-era education, school districts could try to build in and teacher-proof quality with a prescribed curriculum that required only that teachers enact a series of steps. In the knowledge era, by contrast, quality requires that teachers deeply understand and be able to articulate what quality is. Drucker argues, "Knowledge employees cannot, in effect, be supervised. Unless they know more than anybody else in the organization, they are to all intents and purposes useless" (Drucker, 1993, p. 65).

The next three chapters consider the ways in which teacher unions can pull the levers attached to creating quality in schools. Chapters Three and Four consider the ways in which teaching work will change in response to the movement from behavioral to cognitively based learning. And it considers how unions can link classroom realities to national standards and curriculum policy. We argue that both the existence of national standards and their content are important. It is crucial that standards reflect what educators know about how people learn, as well as society's expectations about what people will need to know and do in the twenty-first century.

Chapter Five takes up the crucial issue of what unions can do to create and enforce quality standards in teaching. Peer review of teachers emerged in the 1980s as bold experiments by several unions and school districts. We believe that peer review serves an essential quality lever for schools, not just as a better means of teacher evaluation. Creating a means by which teachers can describe their craft changes the conversations teachers have among themselves and the ways teachers interact with parents, students, and school administrators.

PART TWO

The Quest for Quality

CHAPTER THREE

Improving the Craft of Teaching

~~~

eacher unions can wrap their hands around three powerful levers for changing educational quality. The first of these levers is the definition of teaching work itself: Who does what and how. The second is the setting of national curriculum and performance standards. The third is setting and enacting peer review for teachers. However, none of these quality levers can be pulled effectively unless teacher unions first address the process of learning itself. Without knowing what creates learning and how to create schools around learning, teacher unions cannot organize teachers around their essential function.

As we argued in the preceding chapter, fundamental change in education systems begins with changes in the instructional core of transactions between teachers and students. Who goes to school and for how long? What do they study and how are they taught? What is a good result? These are the questions that structure classrooms, schools, teaching jobs, and ultimately the ways unions represent teachers.

The changes in organization that we see in schools mirror those in the larger economy, as do the changes in sources of power. For unions generally, this change represents a deeply troubled time of downsizing, globalization, declining real wages, and most particularly suspicion about institutions. For many labor relations writers, the current era calls to mind the 1920s, when craft unionism was in retreat, management was strong, and mass manufacturing made craft organizing ineffective (Kochan and Osterman, 1994; Heckscher, 1995). We think the more apt parallel is to the 1880s and 1890s, when large-scale industry was in its infancy, workers throughout society were being displaced, and frustration combined with nativism in reaction to the largest wave of immigrants the country had ever seen. As we have seen, the ensuing revolution in practice and thought produced the current institution of public education. And while the political battles raged over control of the public schools, another and quieter revolution was taking place in the ways in which people thought about learning and practiced it. It is this revolution that deeply affected the nation's idea of educational quality and led to the subsequent realignment of the instructional core of education. Thus before discussing teaching work and the standards for students, we need to examine how the movement from industrial to knowledge-era societies changes the nature of learning itself.

INDUSTRIALISM AND BEHAVIORISM

The characteristics of traditional industrial workplaces were well matched to behavioral ideas of learning. In the industrial world, these practices were consistent with how work was organized for lower-skilled jobs and with the requirements of narrow specialization that characterized higher-skilled technical and managerial positions. However, as we have discussed, the nature of work is changing. The demand for analytical and problem-solving skills is increasing for jobs at all levels, and the percentage of workers needed for higher-skilled jobs is increasingly rapidly. Despite the increases in low-skilled service jobs that are so visible to educators, the dramatic increases are on the highly skilled level, and certainly public policy needs to favor the connection between high skills and high wages. Just to put the matter in historical perspective, in 1900 roughly 20 percent of the workforce was professional, technical, or white collar. By 2000, more than 70 percent of Americans will earn their living through jobs in these classifications.

The rise of industry and the decline of agrarianism in the United States coincided with a change in the psychology that underlay both schooling and industrial management. Both teaching and management as we know them reflect the triumph of behaviorism over what in the nineteenth century was called introspection. At the turn of the century, just as psychology and the other human sciences were being recognized, a group of aggressive young scientists, mostly Americans, staked out the territory that was to shape society during this century (Gardner, 1985, p. 11).

Behaviorists established two propositions. First, science ought to be public and observable. "No subjective ruminations or private introspection: if a discipline were to be a science, its elements should be as observable as a physicist's cloud chamber or a chemist's flask" (Gardner, 1985, p. 11). Second, science ought to focus on behavior. The mind became a black box. Rather than acting because of their ideas or mental constructions, individuals reacted to external stimuli. The tradition of Pavlov, Skinner, and Thorndike held that behavioral models could explain not only what people did but also how they learned.

Behaviorist learning theory emphasized arranging and manipulating a student's world so that teachers would create the desired stimulus-response chains. "Teachers would present lessons in small, manageable pieces (stimuli), ask students to give answers (responses), and then dispense reinforcement (preferably positive rather than negative) until their students become conditioned to give the right responses" (Bruer, 1993, p. 8). This view of the world is perhaps best captured by the homemade sign we encountered on a classroom door: "Knowledge dispensed; bring your own container." It is a view that emphasizes coverage and prescribed curriculum, practice and repetition.

Since World War II, what became known as the *process-product* view of teaching transformed behaviorism into a template for teaching. The logic was that all teachers could become effective if they would just do what teachers who were found to be effective did. The voluminous research on teaching has come close to codifying good teaching (see Good and Brophy, 1986). Good teachers frequently present information through lecture and demonstration. They get feedback, and they supervise student work. Consultants and staff development experts such as Madeline Hunter (1985) have turned these practices into a sequence of steps. While useful as a training device, however, the reproduction of "perfect lessons" leads to a petrified one-best-system approach when schools and districts build it into their evaluation schemes for teachers and thus into their official description of good teaching. The policy apparatus of most schools thus misses the beauty and artistry of teaching.

Management had a parallel application. It was thought that copying the behaviors of successful managers would transfer success from organization to organization. From the 1920s principles-of-management movement to the current search for excellence, the assumption has been that following the same behavioral steps will recreate good organizations (Peters and Waterman, 1982). In schooling, this practice reduced research about the differential effects of inner-city London schools to the effective-schools mantra for American schools (Rutter, 1983). It is this worldview that cognitive science has come to challenge, both in schools and in organizations.

The history of the effective-schools movement presents a good example of the differences between the ways cognitive construction and behavioristic approaches are applied. Resting on the work of Rutter (1979), Brookover and colleagues (1982), Edmonds (1981), and others, the effective-schools message was widely welcomed following the "school doesn't matter" interpretations of the Coleman Report (Coleman, 1977) and Jencks's *Inequality* (1972) in the 1970s. Effective-schools researchers found that the patterns of use of school resources mattered a great deal, and they revived hope that schools could be useful bodies for social intervention in the lives of inner-city children.

Edmonds (1981) reduced the research to five principles, and these took on a shorthand character of their own as they were incorporated into school reform programs:

- *Instructional leadership:* Principals pay attention to the quality of instruction.
- *Academic press:* Schools have a broadly understood instructional focus.
- *Order:* Schools provide a safe and orderly environment.
- *High expectations:* Teachers convey the expectation that all students will obtain at least a minimum level of mastery.
- *Accountability:* Pupil achievement is the basis for program evaluation.

Within months, the elements of a description of schools found to be effective were translated into programs for rescuing failing schools.

Some of these programs were created to increase time-on-task, raise teacher expectations, and institute discipline programs for students. While some of the programs built on effective-schools principles attended to the creation of strong organizational cultures or common beliefs, most didn't. Brookover's admonition that an effective school learning climate consists of "collective norms, organization and practice" often went unheeded (Brookover and others, 1982, p. 8). Most reform programs continued to treat schools and teachers as mindless black boxes.

THE CHALLENGE OF COGNITIVISM

Cognitive science challenges the black box view of learning. Rather than storing facts, the mind creates representations of reality. It stores and uses these mental representations, which we recognize as a system of symbols, to solve problems. Since World War II, cognitive science has developed an increasingly complex representation of the mind's operations. Studies of experts and novices as they solve problems reveal the complex *schemas* or associative structures that link knowledge and data together into networks of related information. Chess experts, for example, see their opponents' pieces in groups; novices see them one at a time. These images are extraordinarily powerful and important to learning because of our severe limitations on short-term memory, as Miller (1956) suggested in the title of his 1956 essay, "The Magical Number Seven, Plus or Minus Two."

Because our capacity for processing information is highly limited, our ability to solve problems rests largely on the mental representations or schemas we have developed. Thus a glance at something rustling in the bush evokes a classification system that distinguishes robin from canary while ruling out bears and snakes. The relationship between working memory and long-term memory makes it possible to integrate bits of current data with long-term sense-making schemes, using not simply facts but facts integrated into patterns, as shown in Figure 3.1. Our senses present us with problems for active consideration by our working memory. Our ability to solve problems, however, rests largely on our ability to recall schemas or patterns of information from long-term memory. It is there that associated chunks of information are stored: knowledge of problem-solving procedures, as well as associated facts. Yes, facts matter. Cultural literacy, or literacy in any other domain, is impossible without them; but what

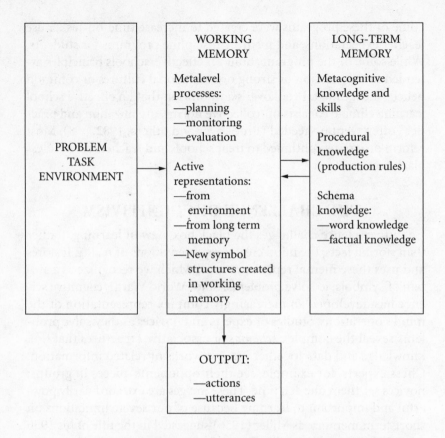

Figure 3.1.   The Standard Picture of Human Cognitive Architecture.
Source: Bruer, 1993, p. 24.

matters most to the solution of higher-order problems is the capacity to associate patterns of facts with one another.

Although short-term memory is highly limited in the number of representations of reality it can hold, long-term memory is thought to be virtually unlimited. But unlike a computer, which has a digital address for each chunk of information, human memory functions through an associative structure that links bits of information together. Cognitive science has validated what William James knew over a hundred years ago: "When we wish to fix a new thing in either our own mind or a pupil's, our conscious effort should not be so much to impress and retain it as to connect it with something else already there" ([1900] 1909).

Cognitive approaches to education become relevant when one moves from simple to complex tasks, exactly the point where the American education experiences break down. Using the National Assessment of Educational Progress as a reference, we see high levels of competence in basic numeracy and literacy. Increases in basic skill levels correspond to the political and organizational attention given to basic skills over the last twenty years and suggest that long-term gains can result from focused educational policy. But many fewer examinees can solve high-level, complex problems. Only 7.5 percent of high school students could draw correct conclusions using detailed scientific data. Fewer than 5 percent of seventeen-year-olds could integrate specialized information and state their own views about what they had read (Bruer, 1993, p. 5). Behavioral training can produce additions to human memory that can be reproduced on tests of basic skills, but it helps little with the *ill-defined problems* characteristic of higher-order cognitive tasks and real-world applications.

With ill-defined problems such as writing an essay, we begin to have an idea of the solution only after we start solving the problem. Most everyday problems and virtually all creative tasks in work, higher education, and civic life are ill defined. Teaching is one of these ambiguous problems. "Teaching a classroom lesson presents an ill-defined problem that the teacher has to solve on the spot, where every student-teacher interaction can change the teacher's goals and choice of operators" (Bruer, 1993, p. 32). Good teachers have a quality of "double-mindedness," the ability to carry out a task while trying to define it at the same time, a dynamic of putting things together that goes beyond the structure of the lesson and makes a mockery of the plan filed with the principal's office (Mitchell, Ortiz, and Mitchell, 1987).

COGNITIVE LEARNING AND THE NEW ECONOMY

If the cognitive sciences suggest that behavioral approaches to learning are misdirected, so too does the economy. As Berryman and Bailey (1993) note, "What makes these developments so powerful is that our new understanding of both work and learning seems to imply very similar directions for reform" (p. 370). Berryman (1992, 1993) writes about the five mistaken assumptions of education as it is currently structured, how these assumptions were consistent with the industrial economy, and how they now place students, and the country, at risk. Table 3.1 sketches these assumptions in parallel for education and industry.

1. *Transferability.* The first mistaken assumption is that people routinely transfer learning from one setting to another, that learning in school meant that you were smart outside, and that failure to perform in school signaled probable failure elsewhere. Cognitive scientists show that transfer between domains represents a huge educative problem and that a great deal of educational strategy needs to be directed to taking knowledge and applying it in different domains. In industrial society, this mattered relatively little because jobs were in themselves so limited that workers had little need to transfer skills and insights from one type of problem to another. In the knowledge society, it counts heavily.

2. *Passivity.* The second mistaken assumption holds that learners are essentially passive. This assumption fits the industrial notion of hierarchy and also fits the traditional idea that education's function was to transmit a body of fact or a cultural canon. However, even assuming that the passive student is actually learning, passive learning diminishes the capacity to explore, discover, and invent. It limits the ability to do what the knowledge society demands most: to create and synthesize.

The cognitive revolution has enormous implications for the definition of quality and the organization of teaching. In behavioristic teaching, the learner can be passive; school is even arranged to encourage passivity. Cognitive approaches to learning require experimentation and engagement. Teaching settings—classrooms, laboratories, playgrounds, communities—become more situationally responsive, the curriculum and the teaching process more fluid. These schools have to devolve more authority and responsibility to individuals and teams of teachers, and teachers need to be more knowledgeable and better educated.

The structure of behavioristic learning is hierarchical. Learners follow a teacher's script through a set of lessons that place the teacher in control; the lessons themselves assume that one set of facts of a body of knowledge needs to come before another. Cognitive approaches to learning allow branching and networking. They begin with a student connecting existing knowledge to that which is being studied. This

	Characteristics of Ineffective Learning	Characteristics of Traditional Workplaces
1	Limited Transfer	Narrowly defined jobs and tasks
2	Learners are passive vessels • Reduced exploration • Dependence on teacher • "Crowd control" problems	Passive order-taking in a hierarchical work organization; heavy supervision to control workers
3	Strengthening the bond between stimuli and correct response	Emphasis on specific responses to a limited number of possible problems (deviations from the expected are to be handled by specialized service personnel)
4	Emphasis on getting the right answer • No attempt to get "behind" answer • Little learning from mistakes • Little emphasis on how to think about problems	Emphasis on getting a task done rather than on improving its subsequent performance
5	Decontextualized learning	Focus on the specific task independent of its organizational context

Table 3.1. Ineffective Learning Environments and Traditional Workplaces: Parallels.
Source: Adapted from Berryman and Bailey, 1992, p. 71.

type of learning is possible only through inquiry and suggests that passive learning is no learning at all.

   3.   *Conditioning.* The third mistaken assumption is that learning mostly consists of strengthening the bonds between stimulus and response. This assumption led curriculum makers to break down subjects into small, disconnected items and subskills without much thought to understanding the whole. There were strong parallels between this behavioral method of schooling and the way in which Taylor's scientific management fractioned work in industry. Neither school nor work was supposed to make sense.

   4.   *Superficiality.* The fourth assumption is that the right answer counts most, thus encouraging superficial learning and discouraging experimentation and problem solving. This tendency in schooling parallels the industrial tendency toward short-term task completion rather than encouraging workers to solve underlying problems.

Contemporary work processes including self-managing teams and quality self-management won't work on superficial answers; the employees involved need to understand how processes work.

5.   *Disconnection.* The fifth mistaken assumption holds that learning is independent from context. Behaviorists thought that by disconnecting learning from application they were creating more rigorous knowledge that would be available for general application. Dewey doubted this seventy-five years ago, and his point has been underscored by contemporary research. Whether in first grade or in medical school, connection to context makes learning effective. Creating context is not 1960s-style relevance or shallow vocationalism, either—establishing a link between lived experience and school or work is what makes it possible for the learner to use rather than merely recite or reproduce the material being learned. Changing occupations and modes of work make context construction all the more important.

In the knowledge society, abstractions and representations of reality become important. Just as cognitive psychologists create symbolic representations that mirror the brain, everyday occupations increasingly use and manipulate symbols. Reich (1991) coined the phrase "symbolic analysts" to describe the people who control and analyze distant situations based on their understanding of abstract symbol systems. Those persons hold a range of occupational titles from research scientist to lawyer, consultant, film editor, journalist, marketing strategist, and even university professor. "They simplify reality into abstract images that can be rearranged, juggled, experimented with, communicated to other specialists, and then, eventually, transformed back into reality" (Reich, 1991, p. 178). While they may sit in front of computer screens, their tools are the building blocks of cognitive construction: mathematical algorithms, psychological theories, legal principles. From spreadsheets to video images, these workers have the capacity to create and manipulate virtual realities. They intertwine invention and calculation. And they make up the most affluent 20 percent of the workforce.

The cognitive problem of creating knowledge essentially returns the focus of education to the classroom, to the activities of learners rather than legislatures. It raises anew the learning problem addressed by Dewey as the country moved from an agrarian society to an industrial one, namely how to create a context in which children could learn naturally. The principles of Dewey's school frame the problem that has to be solved today:

- Instruction focused on development of a student's mind, not on coverage of subject matter. The emphasis was on learning how to learn rather than on recitation.
- Instruction had a context, started with active projects, was integrated, and resulted in a substantial project.
- Instruction began in the learner's world, and the teacher made connections between the student's background and experience and the more abstract and disciplinary knowledge (Farham-Diggory, 1990).

Almost all the contemporary reforms have returned to these principles: Theodore Sizer's Essential Schools, Henry Levin's Accelerated Schools, the Central Park East Academy in New York. "Practicing any art or any science means circling around a subject, trying this and trying that, asking questions that simply cannot be answered in a trivial way," says Sizer (quoted in Cushman, 1994, p. 1). Each of these schools works on the basis of strong internal values, connections between the school and the surrounding environment, and a clear organizational identity. What is significant in this context is that leading examples of successful learning have largely been originated by teachers, either acting alone or cooperating with university-based scholars. Although they may have made use of computer technologies, the successful examples were not packaged by computer software manufacturers or textbook publishers or state departments of education.

One need look no further than the examples of labor-management invention over the past decade. Those settings that intensified bureaucratic routines made only shallow reforms. Those that invoked command-and-control changes met resistance (Fowler, 1988; McNeil, 1988). Those that involved teachers and first-line administrators actively in reworking their schools, and provided the institutional stability to protect them, made better progress (Bascia, 1994; Kerchner and Koppich, 1993; Shedd and Bacharach, 1991).

LINKING UNIONS AND QUALITY

Teacher unionists care deeply about children and about learning, and many are also gifted teachers. But under industrial approaches to organization, quality assurance was management's work, except under the logic of "what's good for teachers is good for kids." In the knowledge era, organizing around quality becomes both educationally necessary and organizationally potent for unions. As the instructional core of education changes and schools become more autonomous, teachers become the most logical guarantors of quality standards and the processes that cause them to come about. In such a setting, unions cannot avoid responsibility for defining and defending quality standards for schools, students, and teachers.

Organizing around quality challenges the industrial-era assumptions of both labor and management. Unions assumed that decent pay, safe working conditions, and freedom from administrative tyranny would free teachers' natural instincts to produce high-quality schools. Management assumed that it could engineer quality through curriculum scope and sequence, school scheduling, and assignment of teachers to jobs. Both assumptions were wrong.

In education, as in manufacturing, industrial-era organization runs up against severe limits. When the quality expectations of schools are ratcheted up, as they have been, and the existing system struggles but fails to meet those expectations, a genuine institutional crisis exists. When people are working hard—and we cannot doubt either the sincerity or the intensity of the reform movement over the past decade— and the system is not meeting societal expectations, a genuine institutional crisis exists (Walton, 1986). Intensification will not produce the results needed, and incremental change is so painfully slow that it loses external support before it can either produce results or create organizational learning.

Public education in the United States is not provided by the lamebrained and the lazy. Most teachers work devilishly hard; stress and burnout are much more a threat to the teaching corps than incompetence or inattention (Johnson, 1990). Most principals and superintendents put in work weeks that would crush all but the toughest corporate executives, and at a fraction of the pay. Television commentator Robert McNeil had it right when he concluded a program on teaching by saying, "No matter who you are, you don't work as hard as these teachers."

Exhortations to work harder and plans to lengthen the school day or school year without reference to the quality of the schooling involved do no good. They invite comparison to a forceful quality control lesson that W. Edwards Deming, the American father of Japanese industrial processes, provided for his seminars. He gave attendees little scoops and led them to a large bowl full of red and white balls, telling them to scoop out white balls—good production—and leave behind all the red balls, which represented process defects. Participants had to keep score, and Deming constantly harangued them to work harder and pay more attention to quality. Of course, it didn't work. As statistics would suggest, over time each group of participants produced a rate of red-ball errors approximating the percentage of red balls in the bowl. Deming's object lesson is that workers can't produce quality when the system itself is broken. In education, it is the system that is broken, not the teachers.

Like most humans, teachers have responded in the wrong way to system failure. They close their doors and work harder. The extent of their systems thinking is to blame (usually silently) the teacher in the grade before them for not adequately preparing the students. The movement from industrial to knowledge era offers teachers and unions a unique opportunity to organize around quality by defining it and enforcing it in the workplace. We believe there are three mechanisms for creating quality in education that are readily accessible to teacher unions and capable of being influenced by them:

- Rethinking the work of teachers and preparation for teaching
- Creating standards for student performance
- Assuring quality in classrooms through peer assistance and review

WHAT UNIONIZED TEACHERS MUST DO DIFFERENTLY

Rethinking teaching work is the toughest change of all. Shifting the instructional core of education requires great shifts in what students learn, what classrooms are like, and what teachers do. The changes involved occur at such a fundamental level that we often overlook them or mistake their ordinariness for simplicity. Ball and Cohen (1995) illustrate how subtle and difficult the changes are. Moving from a traditional exercise (in which a student can get the so-called right answers by reproducing the examples) to an exercise crafted to reveal student thought processes requires that teachers encounter great uncertainty—they must follow students' patterns of sense making rather than simply determine the rightness or wrongness of answers. Exhibit 3.1 illustrates the issues involved in creating the new type of problem.

Traditional Exercise:

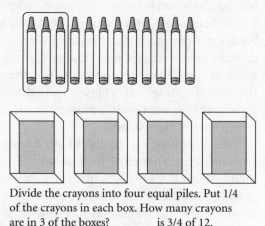

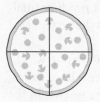

Shade 3/4 of
the pizza

Divide the crayons into four equal piles. Put 1/4
of the crayons in each box. How many crayons
are in 3 of the boxes? _____ is 3/4 of 12.

Teacher Reframing

3/4 of the crayons in Mrs. Rundquist's box of a dozen crayons are broken. How
many unbroken crayons are there?

The teacher created this simple problem because she noticed that many students
thought a fraction was always less than one. The same concept is taught in the traditional exercise above, except that all the students display is their answer, not the
process they used to get it. In this case, the teacher watched the students solving the
problem in groups and then asked students to explain their logic. Most of the students would have gotten the right answer on a traditional question, like the one
above, but they would not know what 3/4 means. To get the right answer to the
pizza question, a student only has to know that the 3 "on top" means that one
colors in three sections. For the crayon diagram, they simply have to follow the
example.

Exhibit 3.1.   Traditional and Cognitive
Approaches to a Fraction Problem.

Source: Ball and Cohen (1996)..

The teacher created the reframed problem in Exhibit 3.1 after noticing that many students thought a fraction was always less than 1. The traditional exercise in the exhibit addresses the same concept, but the students only display their answers, not the process they used to get them. Worse, the structure of the problem allows students to answer without knowing what the underlying concept means. For the pizza, they only need to know that the 3 on top of the fraction means they should color three of the sections; for the crayons, they only have to follow the example and count the results. After presenting the reframed problem, the teacher watched groups of students solving the problem and then asked them to explain their logic. The students came away with a flexible understanding of the concept that they could use even when they had no convenient little pictures to follow.

The last century's experience teaches us that these changes are formidable. Many programmatic attempts disappear without a trace. Progressive education lost its battle with behaviorism, team teaching went away and came back again, whole language teeters between popularity and damnation. Changes that persist tend to be structural in nature (longer school days, class hours, or lists of subjects), create new constituencies (special education), and be easily monitored through testing or compliance requirements (Tyack, Kirst, and Hansot, 1980).

Thus it is not surprising that the attempts to change teaching that have been part of labor relations initiatives during the past decade have been both halting and controversial. Projects have gone from the flush of media enthusiasm to premature obituaries and a declaration, like that of Rochester teacher union president Adam Urbanski, that "real reform is real hard" (Kerchner and Koppich, 1993, p. 3).

Meier (1995) says that teachers need to make three changes, more or less all at once: "change how they view learning itself, develop new habits of mind to go with their new cognitive understanding, and simultaneously develop new habits of work." (p. 140). "Habits of the mind" underlay the Central Park East Schools that Meier and her colleagues founded. They served as central organizing ideas for the curriculum, the set of standards the school put together, and ultimately for the organization of work in the school.

At Central Park East, students learn five habitual approaches to information they encounter (Meier, 1995, p. 50):

- *Ask about evidence:* "How do we know what we know?"
- *Examine multiple points of view:* "Who's speaking?"

- *Search for patterns and connections:* "What causes what?"
- *Understand supposition:* "How might things have been different?"
- *Consider consequence:* "Who cares?"

Habits of the mind serve as organizing ideas for teachers and also as ways of introducing students to the world of ideas. Central Park East Secondary School students who go on to college write of their usefulness. They "set us apart as special" wrote one student (Meier, 1995, p. 157). In similar fashion, mental apprenticeships have become part of other programs of cognitive construction. The O'Farrell Community School in San Diego constructed the "O'Farrell Way," a mixture of mental sets and interpersonal expectations that guide the school. Students and teachers use it as a benchmark for their own work.

These processes are not easy ones, which is one of the reasons that their institutionalization is so important. Cognitive construction, like every major curriculum change, will be a multigeneration project, subject to opposition, fits and starts, ideas about practice that don't work, parents who don't understand, and recalcitrant teachers who don't subscribe to the new idea. Part of the solution lies in differentiating among types and styles of schools, departing from the one-best-system idea of school organization; we treat this organizational question in Chapters Six and Seven. But before raising questions about school organization and governance, we must first consider explicitly what teachers need to do differently in their work. The conceptual literature on workplaces and the experiences of teachers in breakthrough schools suggest three major differences in teaching work: teaching becomes more complex, it involves more interaction among adults, and it becomes more explicitly involved with the process of generating knowledge.

Teaching Becomes More Complex

Historically, the design of work has been driven by the twin tendencies of complexity and rationalization. Early industrialization rationalized work as machine tending replaced craft work and technology generally deskilled work (Hage, Powers, and Henry, 1992). Later stages of industrialization added complexity to rationalization. The scientific management revolution, with which the last major institutional change in schooling was so identified, created specialties. For each new industry or product, scores of occupational specialties appeared. In education, for each classification of child a corresponding classification of teacher was found. Frequently, licensure and certification, separate job classifications, and sometimes separate bargaining units followed.

Currently, one can find impulses toward both rationalization and complexity. Teachers have massively resisted rationalizing efforts to teacher-proof the curriculum or to focus teaching work roles solely on basic skills. Teacher test protests in Texas and Tennessee, which were discounted as simple intransigence, were seen by those involved as a strong voice against the dumbing down of teaching. In Texas, McNeil (1988) reports that "the best teachers in the state saw 'reforms' threaten their ability to develop meaningful teaching styles and substantive curricula as authority of schooling became more and more distant" (p. 201). In Tennessee, frustration and low morale led to the politicization of the teaching force (Fowler, 1988). Countertendencies are found in efforts such as Harvard's Project Zero, in the CHART humanities projects supported by the Rockefeller Foundation, John Goodlad's educational renewal network, and in the work of Ann Lieberman and Linda Darling-Hammond in the National Center for Restructuring Education, Schools, and Teaching—and in virtually every school-based labor relations initiative. Among schools that have reorganized themselves around cognitive approaches to instruction, there is little doubt that teaching has become more complex.

First, teaching is more complex because it is less routine. Research on classrooms continues to show that instruction is mostly teacher centered and focused on low-level tasks involving the acquisition and memorization of facts and concepts. "Only in the later years of schooling, and then only in the higher-ability groups, are students exposed to challenging intellectual tasks. . . . As the goals of education shift toward a focus on higher-order thinking and problem solving, teachers must design classroom instruction around tasks that are complex and authentic in nature. Moreover, teachers must learn to use indirect methods of instruction that allow students to witness the thinking of others and have to use instructional grouping strategies in which diverse learners work cooperatively on common tasks, thus extending the learning resources of the novice-level students." (Rowan, 1994, pp. 127–128).

In knowledge-era schools, there is a dramatic increase in the amount of behavior that is not rule-bound. There are fewer scripts to follow as scope-and-sequence curricula give way to problem diagnosis and treatment. Lesson presentation gives way to indirect instruction. Phrases such as "student as worker; teacher as guide" and "the sage on the stage is replaced by the guide on the side" capture the role shift within teaching.

Getting students to build powerful cognitive schemas requires that teachers understand the schemas students are using, particularly when they are wrong. In multidigit subtraction, for example, student errors frequently fall into patterns; students are following a procedure, but it's the wrong one (Bruer, 1993). Teaching consists of discovering error patterns and treating them as bugs in the student's program rather than as dumbness or inadequacy. Diagnosing student bugs differs markedly from the traditional presentation and illustration of subject matter or even the careful grading of papers.

Writing is also a matter of schema building, one applied to particularly ill-defined problems; "a writer is a thinker on full-time cognitive overload" (Flower and Hays, 1980, p. 33). While any form of writing instruction is labor intensive, diagnosing the inadequate schemas of bad writers and replacing them with effective ones is extremely taxing work, even more so when the writing task involves a student's creation of knowledge and engagement in communication rather than recitation of facts.

School as we know it, and teaching as we define it, is not set up to carry out these tasks. Virtually every study of teaching begins with a plea for association similar to this one from Liz Woods in Philadelphia, which launches *The Empowerment of Teachers:* "There is no way I can say it strongly enough. In a typical school you are isolated, cut off from everyone. The rest of the culture outside the school doesn't give a damn about you or the kids you are trying to teach. The school system itself almost regards you in that way. You are in the place where the bells are ringing, but the people who are calling the signals for schools are in places where they can't even hear the bells" (Maeroff, 1988, p. 1). Even though Woods—and more than two million other teachers—belong to strong labor organizations, she and her colleagues have somehow been unable to develop workplaces built around collaboration and teamwork.

Second, teaching is more complex because it is more personalized and individualized. Industrial-era schooling handled diversity through tracking, arranging a curriculum in broad bands and sorting students according to assumed capacity for schoolwork and ascribed position in life. Scientific management moved schools from Henry Ford's adage—"The customer can have any color he wants so long as it's black!"—to the old General Motors idea of sorting on a social hierarchy from Chevrolet to Cadillac.

Virtually every recent instructional change challenges these classification schemes: mainstreaming in special education, literature-based curriculum, cross-discipline teaching, theories of multiple intelligences. Each cuts against the simple classification of students and produces more complex teaching work. Some are counterintuitive; detracking, for example, requires that the teacher engage in more differentiation among students, not less. A heterogeneous classroom may bring together students with different backgrounds, learning styles, and displayed abilities. But the job of the teacher is not to present one lesson to all the students; it is to make subtle changes in teaching so that students with different attributes can learn in the same physical and social space.

Special education is a particularly good example of increased complexity and the challenges of individualization in action. Setting aside for a moment the more serious physical, neurological, or social classifications and concentrating on the broad category of learning disabilities, we see individual prescription embedded in curriculum design. A diagnosis of a student's learning problems and a prescription for learning become part of an individual educational plan that is shared with special education teachers, support personnel such as psychologists, the child, and his or her parents. These individual educational plans are much more complex in their creation, and much more time-consuming in their formality, than are the curricular and tracking arrangements used to classify groups of learners.

Third, teaching becomes more complex because it involves a broader range of roles. Industrial work was premised on the benefits of specialization, benefits that organizations are now questioning. The knowledge era may well be distinguished by much less specialization (Clegg, 1990). Collapsing specializations and expanding training across jobs is a common denominator of modern organizational change, from auto assembly plants to fire stations. When General Motors and Toyota joined forces to reopen the Fremont, California, assembly plant, they reduced thirty-three job classifications to three. When fire departments across the country were restructured, firefighters found themselves doing much more than fighting fires. Many of their duties and much of their training involve medical assistance, emergency preparedness, rescue work, and maintaining civil order. Likewise, when schools began to restructure in the 1980s, teachers added counseling, crisis intervention, family mediation, and dispute resolution to their repertoire. Education's adaptation of what manufacturing calls flexible specialization calls for teachers to respond to ambiguous situations by taking on more activities.

Teaching Becomes Less Isolated

Historically, teachers interacted with many students but relatively few adults. Kidder's title, *Among Schoolchildren* (1989), was an apt description of the social conditions under which teachers worked: "After spending most of six hours alone with children in only one room, a teacher needs to talk to another adult, if only to remind herself that she is still an adult" (p. 22). Knowledge-era adaptations allow teachers to work with other adults, many more adults: other teachers, parents, social service providers other than teachers. This interaction helps develop a language of professional practice, but it also punctures a safe, self-made cocoon of individual practice.

Teachers working together in academic teams or in school organization and governance represent a profound change in work roles. Teachers engage in highly intense interactions in situations where authority is ambiguous and where answers are not clear. As in similar situations, such interactions increase the emotional intensity and the potential for interpersonal conflict (Malen, 1992).

In redesigning the institution of education, teacher unions in particular need to confront the reality that their purpose is not to make teachers happy in any superficial way. As Meier (1995) put it, "It's not enough to worry about some decontextualized quality called 'teacher morale' or 'job satisfaction.' Those words, like 'self-esteem,' are not stand-alones. What we need is a particular kind of job satisfaction that has as its anchor intellectual growth. . . .High teacher (or student) morale needs to be viewed as a by-product of the wonderful ideas that are being examined under the most challenging circumstances" (p. 142).

One of the ways in which teaching gains intellectual substance— and withstands the frustrations of change—is to link teachers with one another. Telecommunications and teacher-centered organizations such as professional development centers create webs of teachers throughout the country who consider themselves peers. Many educational reform efforts depend on such networks. The Coalition of Essential Schools uses what it calls a "national faculty" of teachers drawn from schools that do coalition work. Likewise, teachers create vertical linkages within school districts. School restructuring breaks down hierarchy and inserts teachers into educational policy and governance roles.

Teaching Becomes Explicitly Connected to Knowledge Generation

Postindustrial work is largely defined "in terms of information gathering, problem solving, and the production of creative ideas" (Hage, Powers, and Henry, 1992, p. 11). For teaching, postindustrial work means making explicit the relationship between what teachers do and the creation of knowledge. The increased role of research and development and of colleges and universities is explicitly recognized as part of the knowledge-era revolution, but the role of elementary and secondary schools is less well recognized. Yet if teaching is the creation of cognitive constructions in students—mind work—it is explicitly knowledge creating, as much as the work of a theoretical physicist.

Teachers have a type of practical knowledge, a know-how, that is reflected in the intelligent activities of the classroom (Pring, 1993). "Teachers may not be able to articulate that practical wisdom, but the fact that practice outpaces theoretical explanations, or even an accurate description of that practice, does not entail that this is not practical knowledge" (p. 4).

It is precisely the critical reflection that raises teaching from craft to profession. Reflection transforms the craft culture of teaching into a professional culture—an understanding based on the verbalization of the principles implicit within a social practice and on the incorporation of those principles within a tradition of criticism. This is professional judgment—that is, judgment based on the tacit knowledge that comes from experience and from acknowledgment of a distinctive relationship between teacher and learner within a particular social tradition. Recognizing that teaching creates knowledge has three important implications for teacher unionism. First, it requires that teachers consciously become part of a learning organization. Second, it requires that they grapple with questions of productivity. Third, it requires that they recreate teaching as knowledge work.

BUILD A LEARNING ORGANIZATION.   The term *learning organization* suggests that schools gain knowledge of practice from reflection on their own processes rather than from replication of model programs and practices mandated by higher authorities. Thus for educators and unionists building schools, change becomes purposeful innovation rooted in knowledge of local successes and failures rather than compliance with rules and regulations (Senge, 1990).

Although most teachers and their leaders would applaud freedom from external mandates, schools have generally not organized themselves as structures that consciously engage in practices of continuous improvement, in part because doing so implies substantial increases in teacher responsibility and out-of-classroom time. The idea of organizations as brains is an appealing metaphor, but a difficult organizing principle (Morgan, 1986).

Suppose school labor relations started to take the metaphor of schools as brains seriously. "Would it be possible to design organizations so that they have the capacity to be as flexible, resilient, and inventive as the functioning of a brain?" (Morgan, 1986, p. 78). Interest in cybernetics and the capacity of self-organizing groups runs parallel with cognitive approaches to learning, but applying such thought to how teaching is organized is new territory. The last decade has been bracketed by the publication of reconceptualizations of teaching work. The Carnegie Forum on Education and the Economy volume *A Nation Prepared: Teachers for the 21st Century* (1986) spawned widespread discussion and was a useful support for ongoing labor relations changes in leading districts around the country. But the Carnegie report, like scores of similar initiatives, immediately became controversial by focusing on school organization and governance. As principals told us, "We liked this school reform stuff fine when it was based on the effective schools idea, but this Carnegie business doesn't leave much room for us."

Movement toward a high-trust–high-discretion workplace requires that teaching and school management change in tandem, and labor relations is one of the few mechanisms available that allows such a signal change. The changes advocated by the National Commission on Teaching and America's Future (1996) would allow simultaneous recovery.

LAY THE GROUNDWORK FOR PRODUCTIVITY.   The controlling face and the personal eccentricities of Frederick Winslow Taylor are recognized by historians of education. His motives and social allegiances are less well recognized. Politically, Taylor leaned to the left rather than the right, but he understood that industrial capitalism could become enormously productive and that the social fissure over meager spoils, which threatened to tear the country apart in the late nineteenth century, need not happen. Taylor's solution was a vast increase in productivity—and productivity indeed began to climb at a rate of 3.5 percent to 4 percent a year, doubling every eight years. Since Taylor began his work at the turn of the century, productivity has increased fifty times (Drucker, 1993).

Now, the service sector of the economy faces a productivity crisis similar to that which occurred in manufacturing a century ago. When education, medical care, and other services were small and manufacturing was growing, service productiveness mattered little. It was essentially a matter of cost control. But for the last fifty years, demand for services has increased wildly, and one of the clear pressures on the knowledge society is to increase the productiveness of services.

Without a sophisticated knowledge of productivity, efforts to rationalize services quickly turn ugly: contracting out work to low-paid part-time workers, speedups, and predatory deregulation. In most of public education, productivity is reduced to increasing class sizes or holding the line on teacher wages. In classrooms, productivity is often reduced to coverage: finishing more curriculum units and grading more tests. There are few serious discussions about how schools might actually create more learning with fewer dollars, and the critical literature on educational production functions has consistently been unable to find an association between system inputs and educational outputs (Hanushek, 1986). Still, we know that resource allocation *within* schools means a great deal. A long and credible literature on effective schools and an equally distinguished one on teachers' work shows dramatic differences in educational outcomes associated with how schools are organized and how teachers expend their efforts. (For a review of these developments, see Rutter, 1983.)

When resource allocation decisions move to schools, either through decentralization or the uncoupling of school districts, it becomes extremely important that teachers understand the link between their actions and educational productivity. Discussions of productivity, which have historically been administrators' work, now become the work of everyone in the school.

Meanwhile, the conventional wisdom about how to increase productivity is changing. When mass manufacturing was the culturally dominant organizational form, the conventional wisdom was to seek gains in productivity through specialization and increases in scale. By engineering the work at the upper levels of management, high levels of productivity could be reproduced throughout a large organization. As discussed in Chapter Two, it is becoming apparent that productivity can also be achieved through what are called economies of scope: educating more broadly competent people and using a greater range of their talents. For school reformers, and particularly for teachers, this change in the conventional wisdom about productivity can be enormously liberating—it suggests that the capacity to change schools for the better can lie within schools and within decisions that can be made by teachers themselves.

In a knowledge society, we have come to understand, productivity is advanced in three ways. The two most familiar are *invention*—the development of breakthrough ideas and processes—and *exploitation,* or adaptation of knowledge generated elsewhere. But *continuous improvement* creates change from within by following the Japanese tradition of Kaizen. "Every artist throughout history has practiced Kaizen, that is, organized continuous self-improvement. The aim of Kaizen is to improve each product or service so it will become a truly different product or service in two or three years' time (Drucker, 1993, p. 59).

Organizing teaching work around continuous improvement requires that teaching days and interactions allow for discussion of both student and adult performance. Teachers will need easy-to-use indicators they believe in, and discussions of indicator systems, such as Bryk's (1993), become important. Teachers will need to be able to compare alternative programs, and teacher professional development will need to include easy-to-use cost-effectiveness methods (Levin, 1983, 1988).

Linking teachers to productivity also requires rethinking the linkage between teaching and computer technologies. It comes as no surprise to most teachers that microcomputers have not lived up to their revolutionary promise; training and software have lagged far behind equipment purchases. But there is little doubt that access to and proper use of technology can have a major productive effect on learning. Access to learning tools at home is strongly associated with high-achieving schools, and while computers and other learning tools are highly associated with family income, the price of learning tools is dropping rapidly while the price of human services is increasing (Perelman, 1992, p. 191).

Finally, productivity requires that teachers come to grips with how learning is produced in schools, as well as with the educative functions of students, parents, and the community. Economies of scope imply that every person in a student's life, including that student, becomes part of an educational system. Teacher aides, janitors, cooks, secretaries, and security workers all become part of a student's educational system, in addition to computers, video, film, books—and other students. Throughout the educational process, teachers must continuously recognize what students learn and can teach.

Particularly with the use of relatively easily created microcomputer software, straightforward estimates of cost-effectiveness are within the grasp of any team of teachers or local school council. Some of the analytic power that has historically allowed administrators to reach decisions can easily become the province of teachers (Levin, 1983).

RECREATE TEACHING AS KNOWLEDGE-CREATING WORK. The final change that teachers must make is to recreate their occupation as knowledge-creating work. To do so implies that teachers will teach other teachers as an expected part of their work.

Changing teaching work in this way requires embracing professionalism and at the same time changing its meaning. Schön (1983), Fullan (1991), and others recast the definition of profession, discarding the notion of hegemony over clients. Drawing on the practice of architecture, town planning, music, and science, Schön invoked the concept of reflection-in-action, learning from one's interaction with clients. A reflective professional "gives up the reward of unquestioned authority" in exchange for more substantive knowledge, and enters into a "continuing practice of self-education" (Schön, 1983, p. 299).

For the cognitive science revolution to change learning as it needs to, teaching needs to serve as the linchpin in a network that includes both basic and applied scientists and parents and other members of the critical public who traditionally distrust educationists.

Educational research, often dismissed by teachers themselves, is so woefully underfunded and its practitioners so politically powerless that without an effective coalition with classroom teachers important research into learning is unlikely to be recognized or heeded, much less encouraged. In 1988, the Department of Defense spent $39 billion on research and development, the National Institutes of Health, $5.5 billion, the National Science Foundation, $1.6 billion, and the Department of Agriculture $1 billion. The same year, the Department of Education spent about $130 million, about 0.5 percent of its budget (Bruer, 1993, p. 294).

Research into learning will not be successful until teachers become part of the enterprise in ways that go beyond translating theory into practice. As Bruer (1993) notes, "Researchers know about (say) the cognitive capacities of children, but often lack the rich understanding of the audience that comes from daily classroom experience" (pp. 295–296). Collaborative research becomes a union issue because collaboration involves time and redefines a teacher's work life.

CONCLUSION: TIME, MONEY, AND BELIEF

In his book about the auto industry, *The Reckoning* (1986), David Halberstam tells the story of how America lost sight of quality. In the post–World War II period, the country was so big, and the demand for its products was so huge, that output itself was more important than quality. Until the 1970s, it was much the same in education. Just building a system that could house the increasing numbers of students that wanted to march up the educational pyramid represented a huge undertaking. Quality in these terms largely meant *inputs* to the system: buildings, teachers, equipment, curriculum. Quality control through curriculum essentially asserted that a relatively uniform process could be created that teachers could use to produce satisfactory outputs, just as factory workers were trained in uniform assembly procedures. Under these circumstances, unions gained power by their ability to insist on the fairness with which inputs were distributed. Did all employees work under the same set of rules? Did they all have the required training?

By the 1980s, however, education began to focus on quality *outputs,* and the more closely outputs were inspected, the more difficult the time schools had producing them. Tightening control over inputs through teacher testing and scope-and-sequence curricula didn't seem to help much. Intensification didn't produce quality, and the debate—which still rages—began over what quality is and how to produce it. In this setting, unions gain power, influence, and social utility by their ability to define quality and to organize teaching around it.

Ultimately, rethinking teaching will require changes in time, money, and—most important—beliefs. Teaching as we know it and unionism as we know it are belief systems, codified and carried by law and tradition but belief systems nonetheless. To change what teachers do, it is necessary for teachers to change what they think they should do. In this area, unions have both a historic role and high credibility—for however much external critics of education decry the power and hegemony of union leadership, they must recognize that virtually all the union leaders were elected by teachers. When union leaders embrace change, teachers listen. They do not always agree, but they listen.

On a research trip to Jefferson County, Kentucky, we encountered a teacher working well after the sun was down to create instructional materials for her class for unwed fathers—a high school English course adapted to the social conditions of young men who under normal circumstances had little to do with the children they had fathered. "Why are you doing this?" we asked. "Why are you working so hard?" The teacher spoke about the kids and their needs, but then she added: "It's partly the union; June Lee [then-president of Jefferson County Teachers Association] is a hero to teachers in this state. If she says that it's OK to change how we work, then it's OK."

CHAPTER FOUR

Upgrading Educational Standards

~~~

In addition to recasting teaching work, unions can link themselves to quality education by becoming clear and articulate about student standards. Doing so will require real leadership, for most teachers see national or state standards—and the tests that come with them—as intrusions into their domains and as incomplete indicators of what students know. Most teachers would check "none of the above" if offered a choice among existing tests. One finds evidence of this opposition in the ethnographic research on teachers and teaching as well as in the policy positions of teacher unions. The NEA's policies in opposition to standardized testing "mandated by local, state, or national authority, and the uses of competency testing" essentially abdicate responsibility for quality. While there is much wrong with existing tests, and unions need to be in the forefront of correcting them, a blanket policy of opposition places organized teachers on the wrong side of history. Exhibit 4.1 gives the text of the NEA position. (Note that all NEA policies are reviewed annually.)

We believe standards are necessary, and unions should lead the institution of education in setting them. And we believe that the question of what standards ought to be institutionalized in unions is an

NEA Resolutions on Standardized Testing and the Uses of Competency Examinations.

D–18 Competency Testing and Evaluation
The National Education Association believes that competency testing must not be used as a condition of employment, license retention, evaluation, placement, ranking, or promotion of licensed teachers. The Association also opposes the use of pupil progress, standardized achievement tests, or student assessment tests for purposes of teacher evaluation. (Adopted 1969, 1987)

B–52 Standardized Testing of Students
The National Education Association opposes standardized testing that is mandated by local, state, or national authority. The Association also opposes the use of these tests to compare one student, staff member, school, or district with another, especially when the threat of loss of prestige, control, or resources is attached.

The Association urges affiliates to work to eliminate the use of standardized tests and high-stakes testing whenever they currently exist. Instead, affiliates should advocate the design and use of a variety of developmentally appropriate assessment techniques that are bias-free, reliable, and valid. These assessment measures must be viewed within the context of a continuum of educational strategies for the individual student. Such assessments are best developed on site as an integral part of an instruction plan. (Adopted 1978, 1994)

Exhibit 4.1.   NEA Resolutions on Standardized Testing and the Uses of Competency Examinations.

ongoing process, one not solely the province of the national leaders. Standards are necessary because they define the central mission of education and, in the larger sense, the evolving concept of American nationhood. Standards say what we value. They also serve as a means to regain public confidence in the institution of education.

STANDARDS AND NATIONHOOD

We can expect a furious battle over educational standards—what they are, how to measure them, and how to reflect those measurements in schools. Questions of culture, equity, and workability join in the same decisions. If history is any guide, the debate will be ongoing and as hard fought as the debate over the federal government's role in education. (See Ravitch, 1983, for a description of prior school wars.) In a sense, the immediate objects of the debate—whether there should be one standard or many competing sets of standards, whether the standard-setting agency should be part of the federal government or should rest outside it, whether truth, beauty, and artistic judgment can be captured by tests—are all minor issues compared with the audaciousness of a national discussion about what we ought to expect our children to learn. This is the issue that defines the instructional core.

The debate, which began as a discussion among educators, and which has pushed the art and science of curriculum and test construction, is now highly politicized. While the standards movement has generated little steam with teachers in general, it has activated the Christian Right and other wellsprings of conservative thought. Even pushing against national standards has the effect of continuing the debate over what standards should be and who should set them. The question is not now likely to disappear. Nor are the shortcomings of the existing crapshoot—the system in which students take the Scholastic Assessment Test and similar exams that have consequences on their futures but that by design are unconnected with what they study in high school (Jennings, 1995).

Politically and socially we are in a new stage of nation building. The question of unity and diversity needs to be debated in a forum that allows the application of values and beliefs to the political process within a shell of constitutional democracy. Just as nation building requires statements of rights, it also requires statements of belief about what is important in its own culture and ideals. While standards may have instrumental value in raising expectations for cognitive achievement, their primary national meaning is as an expression of what society should provide for its children. Standards help do this because once standards are adopted, society takes on an obligation to create pathways for children from all circumstances to reach those expectations. National standards thus serve to guide the way for local political and policy action.

High standards are an act of civic belief. As Theodore Sizer notes: "Most Americans do not care about rigorous high school education and thoughtlessly accept, for example, the convenience of the massive employment of teenagers on school days and the exquisite entertainment of Friday night football, however it may undermine the players' academic progress. Leaders lie, misuse facts, deliberately distort. The country happily tolerates mediocrity and the conviction that anything which sells must be good. High educational standards are impossible without high civic standards" (1992, p. 115).

Enacting standards nationally also makes practical sense. National standards and associated means of assessment can buffer individual schools and their teachers from debilitating local conflicts over the same issues. National standards will help prevent vicious local battles over texts and lessons, fights that should be avoided. Because national organizations can institutionalize standards, local democracies do not have to return to first principles at every Tuesday's school board session. If they do, schools will not prosper and students will not learn. The battle over standards is important, and it is also important to keep the battle away from individual schools and classrooms.

The questions of who establishes standards and whether there might be more than one standard are important but secondary. Our history has been to use nongovernment agencies for setting standards and running testing programs, the pattern established by the College Board, the Educational Testing Service, and the regional accreditation agencies. However, as we can see from the debate over the Scholastic Assessment Test, lodging standard-setting outside government is no assurance that task will be executed without controversy; it just means that those controversies tend not to be immediately politicized in congressional campaigns.

STANDARDS AND CREDIBILITY

Elementary and secondary education has a credibility problem. The general public doesn't believe that grades or diplomas are good indicators of student achievement. As a consequence, arguments about school quality almost always rest on a unique quality or special ethos of a school, such as those Lightfoot (1983) or Hill (1990) describe, *and* validation by an external referent such as test scores or college attendance percentages.

In what may be circular logic, employers proclaim they don't trust school standards in hiring new nonsupervisory employees. In a recent survey, employers said they gave much more weight to attitude, communication skill, and previous work experience than they did to teacher recommendation. Years in school count more than what students did, what courses they took, or how hard they studied. "Is there any doubt," asks Shanker (1995), "that the word gets back to students who are still in school that these things don't count? And if they don't count, why should students work hard to get good grades or attend schools with reputations for high standards rather than easy ones?" Shanker adds that in Germany and Japan, both teacher recommendations and the external examination scores count heavily in employment decisions.

STANDARDS AND EXPECTATIONS

Standards serve as a signal mechanism. American culture has tolerated relatively low standards in comparison with other countries. Teachers ought not be scapegoats in a system that forces them to compromise what they know to be decent standards. Consider Sizer's protagonist, a high school teacher named Horace: "Horace believes that each student should write something for criticism at least twice a week—but he is realistic. As a rule, his students write once a week. Most of Horace's students are juniors and seniors, young people who should be beyond sentence and paragraph exercises and who should be working on short essays, written arguments with moderately complex sequencing and, if not grace exactly, at least clarity. A page or two would be a minimum—but Horace is realistic. He assigns but one or two paragraphs" (1984, p. 17).

Horace and his colleagues can't go the standards battle alone. They require a combination of powerful external supports to build a culture of quality within schools. Teachers' influence in creating higher expectations in their classrooms is more likely to be successful if high standards are supported and rewarded in educational and social policy.

We know that setting standards changes behavior in schools, for both good and ill. One sees this clearly at the basic skills level where passing proficiency tests is required for high school graduation, and at the advanced placement level where successful performance may exempt students from beginning-level college courses. In both cases, intense classroom activity is spent in preparation for the tests, and in both cases achievement has markedly increased.

Between 1983—when *A Nation at Risk* came out—and 1990, the percentage of high school students who completed a curriculum recommended by the National Commission on Excellence in Education increased from 2 percent of all students to 17 percent. The recommended course of study includes four years of English, three years each of social studies, science, and mathematics, two years of a foreign language, and a semester of computer studies. If foreign language and computer studies are removed from the list, then 40 percent of students complete such a core curriculum, up from 13 percent just seven years earlier.

It is startling to realize that in 1975, 19 percent of seventeen-year-old black students had reading achievement below the National Assessment of Educational Progress's 200 level, in which students "learned basic comprehension skills and strategies and so can locate and identify facts from simple informational paragraphs, stories and news articles." But the good news is that by 1988 the score distribution had shifted upward. Only 3 percent of black students tested at the NAEP 200 level, and the percentage scoring at 300 or above had increased from 8 percent to 26 percent. At the 300 level, students "can comprehend complicated literary and informational passages," among other skills (Linn and Dunbar, 1990, p. 137).

Advanced Placement exam taking also continued to increase—by 270 percent in the decade 1983–1993. The percentage of Advanced Placement examinations taken by students of color has increased from 20 percent to 26 percent, meaning that students of color take the AP exam with nearly the same frequency as white students. This examination is significant because it connects to challenging subject matter and is externally graded.

The history of reform over the last forty years strongly suggests the truth in the maxim, "What gets tested gets taught." Thus unions that represent teaching face a sophisticated task of making tests that are fair and reasonable—that ask questions students have had the opportunity to learn to deal with.

STANDARDS AS AN INDICATOR SYSTEM

Union members, not just national leaders, need to be involved in standard setting and test creation because, once adopted, standards rapidly transform into indicators of school success or failure (Bryk and Hermanson, 1993). Over the last decade, state and federal policymakers have developed a powerful thirst for performance indicators as an inexpensive way to drive reform and as a means to demonstrate the efficacy of their efforts. However, it is one thing to espouse an indicator system and another to construct one. The gap between "academic aims and available measures" (p. 455) can threaten good teaching, particularly when what is measured is only a narrow swath of a school's concern either for cognitive achievement or for social integration. Teachers need to be able to advocate for indicator systems that place value on democratic ideals and practice, self-expression, and commitment.

Improvement Requires Useful Data

A good indicator system enlightens a school (Bryk and Hermanson, 1993; Weiss, 1977). It broadens the understanding of school problems and, in a reasonably tolerant political setting, provides information about how the system is doing. It is not enough that newspapers publish comparative school data; schools need to be able to use information to improve. Data have to be available in forms that teachers can use (LeMahieu, 1986), and they have to be available in forms that the public, media, and politicians are less prone to misuse.

Social data are always open to multiple interpretations, but the problems of "casual modeling" by armchair observers are particularly difficult in education (Bryk and Hermanson, 1993, p. 471). The ability of a public official or newspaper writer to proclaim loudly that something does not work, and the tendency to rank schools based on superficial and often static data, create substantial problems for educational change and reform. One of the union's less glamorous roles needs to be the support of independent analysis and publication of data about schools. It is a courageous step to take; not all data will make teachers look good, so teacher organizations must be looked upon as credible and reliable sources of achievement data just as they are viewed as the primary source of information about teachers and their work lives.

Educators have recoiled from what they call superficial indicator systems, such as the wall charts that gained currency in the last decade. But there has been little effort to construct a substitute or to attach accountability to results. Sophisticated indicator systems exist in concept, but not yet in reality. In the early 1990s, a National Center for Education Statistics study panel (Special Study Panel on Educational Indicators, 1991) designed a complex set of indicators that could be used to evaluate education from institution to individual. The idea was to collect parallel data on learner outcomes and school and societal characteristics associated with student success. In this way, both schools and communities would know where to put their efforts first.

In addition to learner outcomes, the NCES indicator system would contain measures of school quality, the readiness of students when they entered school, social support for learning, the relationship of schools to the economy, and social equity. Figure 4.1 shows the six areas and the concepts to be measured. "Without such a system, reform cannot be sustained because, lacking a reliable means of charting progress, it will have to rely on inadequate data and poorly conceived analysis" (Special Study Panel, 1991, p. 6).

Unfortunately, the education indicator idea fared poorly in Washington. It is still alive, however, as it has caught the interest of educational reformers in cities around the country. Bryk and Hermanson foresee indicators arranged as a "data pyramid" with key aggregate "how are we doing" indicators suitable for use in a newspaper graphics box or on the evening news. The second level would include expanded statistical information that could be used by policymakers and others. The third level would include rich case study information, program evaluation, and school and classroom material (1993, p. 470).

Unions Link the Top and Bottom

Teacher union involvement at the national policy apex of education has the capacity to link the capitol to the classroom. The unions are perhaps the only institution with the ability to reconcile the instinct for using testing as a device for micromanagement and the instinct for teacher empowerment as a way to create knowledge-building institutions (Porter, Archbald, and Tyree, 1990). These tensions occur regularly. In New York, the state adopted a "Compact for Learning," exhorting schools toward teaching for understanding, teaming, and

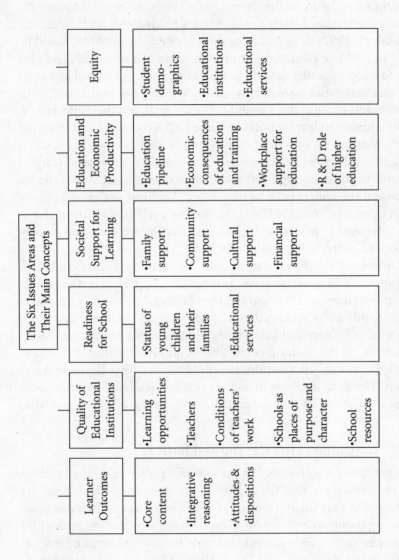

Figure 4.1 Proposed Educational Indicators System.

Source: National Center for Educational Statistics, 1991, p. 28.

The Six Issues Areas and Their Main Concepts

Learner Outcomes
- Core content
- Integrative reasoning
- Attitudes & dispositions

Quality of Educational Institutions
- Learning opportunities
- Teachers
- Conditions of teachers' work
- Schools as places of purpose and character
- School resources

Readiness for School
- Status of young children and their families
- Educational services

Societal Support for Learning
- Family support
- Community support
- Cultural support
- Financial support

Education and Economic Productivity
- Education pipeline
- Economic consequences of education and training
- Workplace support for education
- R & D role of higher education

Equity
- Student demo-graphics
- Educational institutions
- Educational services

cooperative learning while simultaneously supporting a Regents exam and courses that emphasize none of those attributes (Darling-Hammond, 1993).

As Darling-Hammond notes, criticism of current systems as too rigid and passive mirrors past criticisms. "Indeed, with the addition of a few computers, John Dewey's 1900 vision of the 20th Century ideal is virtually identical to current scenarios for 21st Century schools" (1993, p. 755). Thus contemporary visions of creating communities of teachers require that teachers first create indicator systems that are capable of assuring a critical public that teachers pay attention to educational outcomes and are constantly working on improvement.

One of the things that unions can do is join the chorus of outrage at how bad most of the current tests are and how little they measure. Unions ought to be willing to engage tough-minded tests and substantive international comparisons such as the NAEP, even if the results make educators look bad. At the same time, unionists can campaign for reduction in the sheer number of tests and the preparation time involved in testing, as well as for elimination of tests that have outlived their usefulness.

THE BUCK STOPS HERE

At some point America's teachers need to invoke Harry Truman's aphorism and say they will own the problem of standards. It's fine to understand that the problems of schools and teaching are deeply contextual, that our society is deeply unfair, and that fates are quirky. But context *defines* the problem; it is not an excuse for not solving it.

Teachers are justified in their position that they can't go it alone; families and communities have to shoulder the responsibility for the condition of children. Everyone is afraid of being held accountable for that which they can't control, but commitment to quality will make teachers and their unions stronger rather than weaker. The public is much more likely to be tolerant of teachers for organizing around quality improvements, even if progress is difficult, than it is of being offered nostrums.

The NEA's 1994 statement on accountability puts the problem in context and rightly suggests that the entire education community has a stake in quality. But it is silent about what the union will pledge to do unilaterally in pursuit of higher standards.

The NEA is a huge organization with a big budget and staff. It can organize a presidential campaign; why can't it organize school quality? One would have been much more comforted by a statement such as: "The NEA pledges to organize around higher student achievement. The NEA will create a system of indicators of school accountability at the national and state levels. It will offer training to its local affiliates in how to gather and interpret indicator data at the local level. It will publish indicator information annually. Where changes in the way teachers work, are trained, or are rewarded will help increase student achievement, the NEA pledges to support those changes."

CHAPTER FIVE

Evaluating the Work of Peers

The third way unions can link themselves to educational quality is through developing and assuring quality among teachers. Peer review is probably the most powerful demonstration that teachers create and display a knowledge of practice. In the twenty or so school districts that have tried it, teachers have found that peer review brings higher standards to teaching. It significantly changes the conception of teaching work by recognizing the importance of engagement and commitment as well as skill and technique. It recognizes a legitimate role for teachers in establishing and enforcing standards in their own occupation. For unions, it represents both a radical departure from established industrial norms and a rediscovery of traditional craft union and guild functions. Under peer review, the union's role balances protection of individual teachers with protection of teaching. As Albert Fondy, president of the Pittsburgh Federation of Teachers, notes, "A union is not conceived with the primary mission of protecting the least competent of its members" (Kerchner and Koppich, 1993).

Peer review is still unusual—particularly explicit union involvement in hiring and dismissal decisions—but dramatic examples exist.

It is still controversial in many quarters, but as Rochester Teachers Association president Adam Urbanski says, "Peer review is only controversial where it hasn't been tried" (Kerchner and Koppich, 1993, p. 158).

Peer review started in 1981 when the Toledo, Ohio, schools and the Toledo Federation of Teachers added a one-sentence clause to their contract. The teachers agreed to police the ranks of their veterans in return for the right to review new teachers. Since then, peer review has spread among progressive districts within the American Federation of Teachers, and the Toledo idea has been examined seriously in scores of other locations. (In spring 1995, Toledo briefly suspended peer review as a result of a dispute between the Toledo Federation of Teachers and the district. Reinstatement became a prime negotiating item, and the agreement reached in fall 1995 reinstated peer review effective fall 1996.) Cincinnati, Rochester, and Pittsburgh have adopted differing forms of teacher involvement in evaluation and assistance. The National Education Association still officially opposes peer evaluation, but privately—and increasingly publicly—its leaders are urging adoption of peer evaluation as part of a larger agenda of teacher education and career development. One district, Columbus, Ohio, has adopted a peer review plan, and in a number of districts teachers have begun to engage in less judgmental forms of peer coaching and assistance. Jefferson County, Kentucky; Glenview, Illinois; and Greece, New York, all have such programs.

HIGHER TEACHING STANDARDS

Peer review brings higher standards to teaching in two ways:

- Peer review systems generally have more resources and thus put forward a more thorough system of evaluation than conventional, administratively driven evaluations.
- Peer review systems link good teaching and professional development.

The traditional evaluation system is very constrained, capturing only a small portion of a teacher's work. Less by design than by experience and operation, peer review comes to tap a broader portion of teacher's work. It recognizes the need for excitement and commitment in teaching, for situational responses to classroom circumstances.

A More Thorough System

Most teacher assessment is what McGreal calls "common law" evaluation. Assessment is undertaken to meet state mandates or community expectations of good practice. About 65 percent of the country's school districts use this type of evaluation (McGreal, 1983, p. 9). Typically, these systems involve short observations of teaching by principals, a checklist of desired characteristics, and some kind of form for recording information. A conference may follow the observations, and teachers typically have the right to comment on a principal's assessment of them.

These so-called hit-and-run evaluations have been the subject of criticism for so many years that it is at first surprising that they continue as the primary means of assessment for continued employment. Common law evaluations are usually summative and top-down, requiring very little involvement on the part of teachers themselves. Moreover, they are mostly universalized, with the same standard criteria being applied to all teachers—novice or veteran, probationary or master.

Common law evaluations persist partly because they are *easy* to use. They require very little expertise in evaluation methods—most principals have relatively little (Wise, Darling-Hammond, McLaughlin, and Bernstein, 1984)—and a principal can squeeze the quick observation method into an already overcrowded schedule. Common law evaluations also persist because they are visible. They fill the public's need for an accountability system.

Common law evaluations establish *working treaties* between teachers and administrators. Many if not most schools operate within a culture of independence between teachers and principals that says, in effect, "Parties bring to each other the taken-for-granted, good faith assumption that the other is, in fact, carrying out his or her defined activity" (Meyer and Rowan, 1978, p. 101). This arrangement has the effect of signaling employees that they are free from substantive oversight and harsh criticism.

Peer review systems are not inherently better than administratively driven ones. As one unionist said, "What's the big deal about peer review? It's just teachers carrying out the same lousy evaluation system that administrators used." However, in practice peer review changes the character of evaluation.

Anecdotal evidence suggests peer review is tougher than administrator review. In the years that the Toledo internship program has been operating, approximately 6.4 percent of the new teachers resigned, were not renewed, or were terminated for inadequate performance. In the five years before the internship program began, when evaluation was done by administrators, only one new teacher was terminated (Lawrence, 1985).

There is no evidence to support the proposition that teachers would soft-pedal evaluation to save the jobs of colleagues. Quite the contrary. More than administrators, other teachers bear the burden of incompetent colleagues. "To see someone that bad being called a 'teacher' just like I am lowers my stature and self-esteem," said one teacher. Teachers know who's good and who's not so good. In Toledo, the veteran teachers who were subjected to the intervention process were so notorious that they were referred to as "the local legends."

Peer review is able to be tougher and still maintain standards of fairness because it is also much more extensive than traditional common law evaluation. The review plans used in Toledo, Ohio, and Poway, California, assign between ten and twenty novice teachers to each supervising teacher. Assistance and evaluation is the supervisors' full-time job. For new teachers, who must gain tenure or leave within two to three years, this intensification means getting more help and a closer look at what expert teachers do.

Most evaluations by principals consist of one or two formal sessions during the year plus a few drop-ins. Principals also factor in parent complaints and the buzz around the school concerning new teachers. In contrast, we asked a supervising teacher in Poway about a new teacher whose contract was not renewed.

RESEARCHER: How many times would you say you were in this person's classroom?
TEACHER: *(Laughs.)* Lots. From the first semester until we had the review board in the second semester, I put in approximately seventy hours. . . .
RESEARCHER: Did all the novices have your home phone number?
TEACHER: You bet. Some of the best conversations were at night when [a teacher is] thinking, "Gosh, you know, *tomorrow*."
RESEARCHER: And they would call you up?
TEACHER: Sure . . . maybe a couple of times a week.

The supervising teacher also kept a journal with each new teacher so they could pass comments back and forth without disturbing the flow of the classroom day. She said, "A teacher might write, 'Would you watch Joey the next time you come in? It's a behavior problem, or an inattention problem or something I don't understand.' It helps me be an observer for the teacher."

Another teacher talked of having visited a novice's classroom fourteen times during the year, including spending two whole days there. The extensiveness of interaction between novice and expert teachers shifts the focus of evaluation from the structure of a lesson to the teacher's entire practice: how students are regarded as they enter and leave school, how the teacher handles interruptions and circumstances that cause deviation from previous plans, and how the school day and semester come together with coherence.

In both Poway and Toledo, undertaking peer review meant that the district and union were willing to spend enough money to run a substantive evaluation system. In each district, assistance and evaluation cost approximately $2,000 per new teacher. Unions in both districts negotiated hard to get and keep the money to run the program.

In Toledo, maintaining the peer review program and other union-initiated improvements led to the brink of strike in 1991. In Poway, the union and management financed peer review with $100,000 of California lottery receipts that they had negotiated to be set aside for school improvement. The Poway program, threatened by the 1992 California education finance cutbacks, was the first item restored after the legislature and governor resolved their budget impasse.

Linking Evaluation and Growth

Peer involvement in teacher review tends to extend the functions of evaluation. In looking at four leading districts, each of which had some aspect of peer involvement, Wise noted, "Evaluation is not just an ancillary activity; it is part of a larger strategy for school improvement" (Wise, Darling-Hammond, McLaughlin, and Bernstein, 1984, p. viii). Evaluation supports and is supported by other activities of the school. "Peer review forces teachers to define good teaching," says Miles Myers, executive director of the National Council of Teachers of English and former president of the California Federation of Teachers. "Teachers have to be able to express good teaching in language that other teachers understand and accept." When teachers develop a language of good teaching, it is frequently different from the official language of the school district.

Evaluation has two classic functions: accountability and improvement, as shown in Figure 5.1. Most discussions of evaluation center on the accountability function—the need to assure minimum standards and to remove incompetent teachers. Teacher evaluation is tied to personnel decisions involving renewing contracts and granting tenure for new teachers, recognizing teacher mastery and advancing teachers in districts with career ladder schemes, and initiating disciplinary or dismissal proceedings against poorly performing teachers. Negative personnel decisions have historically brought forth the union in defense of the affected teacher.

In any given year, the vast majority of teachers are not threatened with dismissal or nonrenewal. What teachers doing an acceptable job need is an evaluation system that addresses their needs to grow in work, to gain skill and recognition, and to expand the scope of their responsibilities. For these teachers, evaluation should take on a staff development role. An evaluation system ought to provide formative assistance with teaching technique and in subject matter. Evaluation's coaching or mentoring role is frequently neglected, and, as we shall see, one of the by-products of union involvement is increased attention to this role.

Most discussions of evaluation involve teachers as individuals, but teacher evaluation also has an organizational dimension. Whole schools also get evaluated. Schools routinely face review from accrediting agencies. Teachers, as peers, play a role in these evaluations, serving on accrediting teams and engaging in self-studies of their own schools. Historically, unions have not been greatly involved in this aspect of peer evaluation, nor have they generally recognized its significance. However, within the last decade, the negative evaluation of schools has attracted substantial attention. Schools and entire school systems have been placed in receivership. Unions have started to take a role in working with troubled schools.

In Dade County, Florida, the Little River Elementary School was threatened with closure and reorganization by then-superintendent Joseph Fernandez. The faculty and principal asked for a chance to set things right themselves. They created a plan to revitalize the school, activated parents, hired bilingual community workers, designed uni-

	Improvement	Accountability
Individual	**Staff Development** •Assistance with technique or subject matter •Identify personal or occupational goals	**Personnel Decisions** •Tenure or reemployment •Discipline or dismissal •Recognition, advancement
Organizational	**School Improvement** •Strategic planning •School or district staff development	**School Status** •Accreditation •Receivership

Figure 5.1.   Functions of Teacher Evaluation Systems.
Sources: Costa, Garmston, and Lambert, 1988, p. 148; Wise, Darling-Hammond,
McLaughlin, and Bernstein, 1984, p. 11.

forms, and strengthened their own teaching (Kerchner and Koppich, 1993).

Peer review does not automatically move toward including artistic and professional standards, but it has that dynamic. Peer review systems are created with a mixture of formative and summative evaluation. They are different from administratively executed evaluations because they are more intensive and more extensive. A typical administrative review takes an hour or two a semester. Most administrators will say that's all the time they can afford, and the due process system is sometimes contractually constructed to make more frequent or substantive review difficult. In contrast, peer review systems involve intense interactions between the teacher being reviewed and the teacher doing the reviewing. Peer review entails not simply a different person doing the reviewing but a different system.

HOW PEER REVIEW PROGRAMS WORK

The broadened meaning of evaluation can be seen in the peer review programs themselves. The Toledo Intern and Intervention Evaluation Programs operate for both individual accountability and development. The intern program serves to socialize new teachers, while the intervention program serves as a vehicle for teachers to improve their schools by eliminating veteran teachers whose performance is so bad that it has become disruptive to the school's functioning.

The Intern Program

Since 1981, all teachers new to the district have been required to participate in the Intern Program for two years, regardless of prior experience, unless exempted by the joint management-union Intern Board of Review. The board comprises four district and five union appointees. It takes six votes to carry an action on the board, but there has never been a party-line 5–4 vote. During the ten years since its inception, 1,141 teachers—40 percent of the teachers now employed in the district—have completed the intern program. Seventy-three of them, or 6.4 percent, resigned, were not renewed, or were terminated.

The intern program hinges on the work of a cadre of *consulting teachers*. During an intern's first year, supervision and evaluation is entirely within the cadre's jurisdiction. The responsibility for supervision, evaluation, and goal setting is the province of the intern's consulting teacher. The intern's principal has the responsibility to inform the consulting teacher about the intern's conformance to district and school policies pertaining to such matters as attendance and discipline. In the second year, full responsibility shifts to the intern's principal.

During the first year, interns and consulting teachers work together on a continuous process of mutual goal setting and follow-up conferences based on detailed observations in the intern's classes. Working as a team, the two analyze the intern's in-class work and set practical goals for improvement during the first two years of employment.

Consulting teachers are experienced faculty who apply and are screened by the current supervising teachers and recommended to the board of review for selection. They are released from all teaching for three years, and at the end of that time, they return to their regular classroom assignment. Supervising teachers are forbidden to apply for administrative jobs.

The number of consulting teachers varies each year depending on the number of interns. Each consultant, who supervises up to ten interns, has final responsibility for presenting the board of review with recommendations regarding maintaining or rejecting continued employment of the interns under his or her jurisdiction. The board almost always follows the consulting teacher's recommendation.

The Intervention Program

The intervention program focuses on experienced teachers whose teaching performance is unacceptable: "The Intervention Program in the Toledo Public Schools is a cooperative effort between the federation and the administration designed to assist non-probationary teachers who have been identified as performing in a way so unsatisfactory that improvement or termination is imperative" (Toledo Public Schools and Toledo Federation of Teachers, 1991, p. 35). In the ten years since the program was initiated, thirty-five teachers have been placed in the intervention program. In twelve cases, improvement allowed teachers to continue. In twenty-three cases, the teachers were either dismissed or left the district voluntarily.

The identification process that results in a teacher being placed in the intervention program has been designed to prevent abuse by either the district or the federation. It contains a set of checks and balances in which both the principal and the union building representative must concur that a teacher should be assigned to intervention. Refusal by either union or management means that the teacher in question will not be placed in the program.

Once a teacher is placed in intervention and a consultant teacher is assigned, an intervention plan is drawn up. The plan includes the purpose of the intervention, the role of the consultant in the process, the kinds of help that may be offered, and the length of the intervention. However, because each intervention is unique, no standard methods for raising teacher performance have been adopted. The consulting teacher is free to use a variety of methods to help teachers raise performance to a satisfactory level (Toledo Public Schools and Toledo Federation of Teachers, 1991, p. 38). However, the consulting teacher reports frequently to the board of review to justify actions taken and to appraise progress made. Thus while the consulting teacher is free to use whatever helping means seem appropriate, the Intern Board of Review stimulates the consulting teacher to think deeply and critically about the needs of the person in intervention and to act creatively to bring about improvement.

The approaches used with teachers in intervention have been as varied as teachers' needs. One burned-out teacher simply asked for a nonteaching position with the district's grounds maintenance staff. After negotiations with the two unions, the transfer was made and both the teacher and district officials are pleased. Others voluntarily entered new work outside the district. Some were dismissed. Twelve teachers successfully improved their work and have returned to the classroom. But the important matter is that in ten years, thirty-five poor teachers have either left the district or improved as a result of the cooperative work between the district and the union. Most important, this represents a major change from the traditional protective stance of unions to a position in which the union works with administration to improve or remove the least effective members of the teaching force.

Alternate Evaluation

The Poway (California) Unified School District and the Poway Federation of Teachers have adopted and modified the Toledo evaluation plan, and they added to it a striking variation from convention.

During the 1990–91 school year, the district and union began an alternative to conventional teacher evaluation (Poway Unified School District, 1991). The program is open to teachers with five years of experience, and teachers may elect this program with site administrator approval. (Some teachers who transferred to new schools and who thus had new principals were denied approval.) This program is also operated by the joint union-management governing board. As with the other programs, there is a trust agreement memorandum between union and management establishing the program (Poway Unified School District and Poway Federation of Teachers, 1990).

Alternative evaluation begins with a teacher-made goal statement and evaluation plan that may include a collaborative group of teachers, self-evaluation, portfolios, peer coaching, classroom action research, or participation in structured staff development. It may also include a modification of the standard principal observation evaluation system (Poway Unified School District, 1991, p. 3).

Listening to the Governing Board

Poway governing board meetings followed a clinical case model. Consulting teachers presented the evaluation of each teacher and the review board probed and queried. In the ensuing conversation, the review board came to function not simply as a body that rendered decisions about continuing employment, but as an organizational subunit that triggered administrative action, redefined the role of the union, and sharpened and amplified the definition of good teaching in the district.

THE CASE CONFERENCE.   Let's take a closer look at one review meeting in action. The conference began with the case of a first-year teacher who was having difficulty. The consultant presented a summary recommendation on the district's standard evaluation form: A decision on second-year employment should be delayed. Several more visits were necessary. The consultant presented her worksheet showing the various times she had visited the classroom. The teacher in question was enthusiastic and popular with the students. But the teacher showed very little interest in preparing for class. Lessons were haphazard and demonstrated little of the craftsmanship emblematic of good teaching. The teacher had made improvement following a correctional conference at which the consulting teacher and principal were present. But the supervising teacher and the principal were both concerned that the teacher would not continue to develop without the pressure of external evaluation. The board voted continued vigilance.

The conference continued with cases of stellar young teachers who were performing above levels that would be expected, and a routine was established in which consulting teachers would present a case, administrators would check off teachers as not needing additional scrutiny, and file folders would be closed upon recitation of the magic words "meets district standards."

This scenario was repeated several times until, as the case folder was being shut, one teacher added, "meets district standards . . . but something about this teacher bothers me." Heads rose from their paperwork as the consultant teacher said, "This [twenty-four-year-old] teacher is like fine white wine that has begun to go to vinegar. She teaches like someone over sixty."

A remarkable discussion followed. The district's evaluation form, modeled after a Madeline Hunter lesson plan, does not mention joy, enthusiasm, or engagement in teaching. The Hunter method of teaching had been the district standard, widely taught through in-service education courses; the presentation of lessons with all appropriate steps had been the basis of classroom observations, originally by principals and then by consulting teachers. The district's evaluation form did not consider situational adaptivity or receptivity to new ideas, but all agreed that these qualities were what made good teaching. In effect, that afternoon the criteria for being a good teacher in Poway changed. The review panel recognized the artistic dimensions of teaching.

NEW ROLES FOR TEACHERS AND ADMINISTRATORS.   Through witnessing the review board in action, it is possible to see substantial deviations from expected roles among unionists and administrators. Administrators, initially wary of teachers as evaluators, came to trust the teachers' judgments. In one case, a principal had recommended a novice for a first-year teaching award based on a single observation of the teacher's classroom and the normal kinds of principal-teacher interactions. The consulting teacher disagreed, and carefully presented evidence of repeated interactions with the teacher. The district administrators agreed with the teacher.

In another situation, William Crawford, the union president, remarked of a candidate, "I'm a little worried that she is not taking an interest in the classes we offer" (Kerchner and Koppich, 1993, p. 171). "We" in this case was the district, which offered noncredit, voluntary, and unpaid training and development classes. The idea of a union leader suggesting participation in uncompensated activities as a mark of good teaching cuts against the industrial expectations. Thus peer review becomes important not because it transfers responsibility for teacher evaluations from administrators to teacher peers—all the systems of peer review include administrators on peer review panels—but because it changes expectations of teachers. It changes their own knowledge of pedagogy.

RADICAL AND TRADITIONAL UNIONISM

Organizing around quality and enforcing it with peer review is both radical and traditional. It departs from industrial assumptions about worker protection and the sources of union solidarity. In what Kochan (1984) calls *job protection unionism,* the role of labor is to protect an individual's right to a specific position. In teacher unionism, this has traditionally meant vigorous defense of members involved in discipline and dismissal proceedings. The union's role is not to make an independent judgment of a person's fitness or capability, but to vigorously represent him or her in the series of adversarial proceedings required by procedural due process.

The guild and craft traditions, which preceded industrial organization, considered workers as members of communities. Even today, craft unions wield control through apprenticeship and job placement programs. It was craft solidarity, not organizing power, that empowered craft workers (Heckscher, 1988, p. 23). In most craft situations, development and enforcement of standards became part of what unions did and still do. It is the case with white collar unions such as engineers (Kuhn, 1970) and also, as Cobble (1991) reports, with much more common occupations such as waitressing: "Culinary unionists assumed responsibility for 'management' tasks such as hiring and discharge of employees, the mediation of on-the-job disputes, and the assurance of fair first-line supervisory practices. In a sense workers in the culinary industry had instituted a form of self-management" (p. 426).

We believe teachers have little to lose and much to gain from organizing around the quality dimensions of teaching work. Peer review is capacity building for teachers and unions. It creates an important building block for using unionism as a means to make schools themselves perform better, a subject to which we turn in the next chapter.

PART THREE

New Union-Management Agreements

CHAPTER SIX

Reforming the Districtwide Contract

F lexibility, creativity, the ability to adapt to changing circumstances, and an ethic of continuous improvement are hallmarks of successful modern organizations. Indeed, successful organizations develop a passion for quality and improvement. As they seek—or create—opportunities for growth, these organizations are highly responsive to the needs of their customers and clients. Individuals, work teams, and small operating units gain substantial autonomy about how work is to be done and how resources are to be used. Public education has only begun to adopt this organizational spirit.

The evolution of school districts as centralized bureaucracies has created a structure—and an organizational demeanor—that stymies rather than supports change and innovation. School districts function generally on the command-and-control model, or its only slightly kinder and gentler cousin, monitor-and-compliance. The job of district-level personnel is to ensure that schools hew faithfully to local, state, and federal rules, regulations, and statutes. It is hard to imagine finding a school district that could match the efficiency of a Federal Express office, the innovativeness of a Saturn plant, or the entrepreneurial corporate culture of a Hewlett-Packard division.

Teachers' contracts—districtwide agreements between teachers, as represented by their union, and local school boards—developed in response to centralized educational decision making. As power and authority accrued to school district headquarters, so, too, did unions consolidate their efforts, in master contracts, to influence the terms and conditions of employment of those they represent. Viewed in this light, the centralized collective bargaining agreement appears as a rather rational development.

Nonetheless, conventional wisdom holds that teachers' contracts are a principal impediment to educational improvement. We agree—to a point.

Collective bargaining agreements apply a districtwide template to teachers' conditions of employment. The same set of professional rules of engagement applies equally to all teachers in a given school district, regardless of assignment, circumstance, or qualifications. Under the terms of most teachers' contracts, flexibility is discouraged and support for innovation is tepid at best.

Yet while we may lament the limiting educational effects of centralized, rule-driven contracts, we are also persuaded that the processes and procedures that govern an enterprise's work must be arrived at by means of an orderly and well-understood system. In this chapter, we describe how such a system might look and operate.

We propose that the all-inclusive districtwide contract be replaced by a slender central agreement setting forth consensually achieved educational goals and providing the basic procedural architecture for those matters that ought to be decided at the district level. Much of what is currently determined in centralized collective bargaining agreements would shift to individual schools, where decision-making processes and procedures would be enshrined in the school-level educational compacts discussed in Chapter Seven.

PROTECTION THROUGH STANDARDIZATION

To understand the new system we propose, it is useful to briefly explore the three premises that underlie contemporary bargaining arrangements. The first premise deals with the nature of contracts.

Premise 1: Contracts are the vehicles through which the union protects its members from arbitrary actions by the employer.

To ensure that their members receive equitable treatment from the employer, the union, through the contract, develops uniform districtwide policies and standardized procedures. Three typical contract areas—salary setting, defining the salaried workday, and achieving common organization of students for instructional purposes—illustrate this point.

Establishing Compensation Rates

Salaries for nearly all of this nation's two million teachers are structured around the "standard single salary schedule." This pay-setting formula is designed to mute variations in teachers' demonstrated knowledge and expertise.

The standard single salary schedule became widespread in the post–World War II baby boom era, when teachers were in short supply. The pay formula abolished what had previously been separate compensation rates for elementary teachers (who were mostly women) and secondary teachers (who were mostly men), substituting a single salary rubric for teachers at both levels. In addition to unifying compensation schemes, the unitary salary schedule was designed to remove the possibility of political or professional favoritism influencing salary setting.

Constructed as a two-dimensional matrix, the schedule allows teachers to advance vertically by virtue of longevity in the district, and horizontally with accrued course credits. Uniformity is achieved by compensating at the same rate all teachers with like time on the job and equivalent numbers of postbaccalaureate credits.

Defining Salaried Time

Additional standardization is achieved through contract provisions specifying the number of days per year and number of hours per day for which teachers will receive compensation. Typical of contract provisions in this domain are the following:

> "The academic teaching year shall consist of no more than 184 teaching and non-instructional days" (Collective Negotiations . . . San Diego, 1992–1995).

> "The . . . teacher workday shall begin at 7:25 A.M. and conclude at 2:15 P.M." (Collective Bargaining . . . Pittsburgh, 1988–1992).

"No teacher shall be required to be in school more than ten (10) minutes before the students' official day begins" (Master Contract . . . Hammond, 1990–2001).

To be sure, many teachers work far more days and hours than their contract authorizes. However, by defining the bounds of salaried time, the contract endeavors to ensure that the employer cannot *require* that some teachers devote more days and hours to professional duties than do others.

Grouping Students for Instruction

Developing districtwide formulas to achieve common organization of students for instructional purposes, through the class size provision of the contract, is another means of standardizing teachers' working conditions. Reaching agreement on a class size provision is often one of the most contentious areas of bargaining. The goal of the union typically is to secure class size maxima, limits beyond which class sizes for individual grade levels and subject areas may not be increased. Management's objective generally is to restrict contract language to class size *goals,* numbers toward which the district will work, rather than limits to which it is required to adhere.

Inviolate class size maxima are rare. Contract language more often occupies the middle ground, with class sizes stated as variable averages. The contract between the Pittsburgh Federation of Teachers and the Pittsburgh public schools, for example, states: "The following shall constitute what are *reasonable* class sizes for all schools," with class sizes—which may vary up to six students on the high or low side— then specified for the elementary and secondary levels. Standardization is achieved by precluding class sizes from deviating beyond the contractually set bounds.

PRESERVING INDIVIDUAL RIGHTS

Employing the contract as a means to ensure fair and evenhanded across-the-district treatment of teachers leads to the second premise of collective bargaining.

Premise 2: The contract serves as a statement of the accrued rights of individual teachers.

The contract establishes teachers' terms and conditions of employment by detailing the rights of those whose professional lives are governed by it. In effect, the contract serves as a kind of handbook of accumulated job benefits, responsibilities, and exemptions.

The notion of the contract as a statement of individual rights is reinforced by the document's dispute resolution mechanism. Grievances—disagreements between union and management regarding the application or interpretation of contract provisions—are adjudicated through a quasi-legal set of progressively higher level due process hearings. Decisions about sustaining or denying grievances are based solely on determinations about whether or not a teacher's contractually guaranteed rights have been violated.

CONFLICTING INTERESTS

The contract is not designed to encompass institutional welfare. It is not meant to enumerate the goals of the educational program or define the purposes for which that program is established. Instead, it relates purely to individuals and their place in the institution. This conception of the contract as bible of individuals' conditions of employment gives rise to the third premise of collective bargaining.

> Premise 3: Union and management have inherently different, and conflicting, interests.

Conventional bargaining assumes employees desire secure financial and work rule arrangements, achieved by garnering as many resources as possible for personal benefit and constraining the employer's ability to alter or increase workload. The employer's goal is to retain authority over educational policy and operational decisions, matters such as hiring personnel and allocating resources. Stated another way, collective bargaining assumes that "bread and butter" issues of compensation, benefits, job security, and general conditions of employment are properly part of the employee's concern—and that the mission of the institution and the content and conduct of the work are not.

This presumed bifurcation of union-management interests is reinforced by the statutorily restricted scope of contract negotiations. State laws define those issues about which union and management can bargain and those about which they can not. The phrase typically used to describe both the sweep and limits of scope is "wages, hours, and working conditions." Salaries, benefits, and transfer policies, for example, are bargainable. Curriculum and education goals typically are not. The statutorily defined separation of interests contributes to adversarial union-management relations as both parties spar over how to maximize the gains each seeks.

DRIFTING TOWARD CHANGE

Labor scholars describe two modes of bargaining, *distributive* and *integrative* (Walton and McKersie, 1965). In distributive negotiations, the parties see the bargaining table as laden with items each side wants to claim, or preserve, for itself—money, rights, responsibilities, power, and authority. Bargaining is about dividing up the spoils and carrying them away.

Integrative bargaining focuses on union and management seeking common roads for mutual benefit. The parties treat each other as professionals, and consciously consider those issues that are important to both and the trade-offs with which each side can live. It is this conception of negotiations that has given rise to a set of modern bargaining reforms.

Collaborative Negotiations

For the better part of a decade, we have witnessed some visible efforts in a few bold school districts around the nation both to alter the adversarial union-management relationship and to widen the bargaining envelope. Dampening conflict generally has been patterned on the principles of win-win bargaining.

Popularized in *Getting to Yes* (Fisher and Ury, 1987), the "win-win" approach promotes collaborative union-management negotiations. "Hard on the problem, not hard on each other" is win-win's functional slogan, employed by teams of union and management adherents who work through the process of identifying common goals and "inventing options for mutual gain" that allow both sides to claim victory.

For some districts, *collaborative bargaining*—the generic name for win-win and its multiple spin-offs—has come to be viewed as an end in itself. Achieving an enhanced level of union-management cordiality is the proudly hailed goal, as negotiations then proceed along the usual path of topics with rather predictable results.

Other districts have understood that the reason to change the form of the relationship is not simply to alter the tenor of discourse. In fact, union-management relations, while they do not need to be steeped in animosity, are likely to involve conflict from time to time as teachers assert rights and responsibilities lodged firmly in traditional management domains. These districts have endeavored to confront the more vexing—and ultimately more important—issues of what kinds of educational decisions are being made, the operating level at which they are struck, and the cumulative impact of these decisions on issues of student achievement. The resulting reforms have generally proceeded along three paths: joint union-management committees, educational policy trust agreements, and contract waivers.

Expanding the Portfolio

Joint union-management committees are designed to expand the portfolio of the negotiated agreement. They embody both more collegial and more professional union-management relationships and provide an opportunity for teachers and administrators to move substantive discussions of educational policy and practice beyond the legally restrictive scope of the contract.

Pittsburgh, Pennsylvania, established a joint committee to oversee the district's school-based management undertaking. In Cincinnati, Ohio, the union and the district removed the thorny issue of resolving class size disputes from the contract grievance procedure and placed it in the hands of a joint committee. In Poway, California, the peer review system is overseen by a committee composed of union and management representatives.

Dade County, Florida, employs joint committees to carry out many of its reform initiatives in the Miami area, including school-based shared decision making. The San Diego, California, contract lists eleven joint committees that focus on a range of topics from administration of health and welfare benefits to professional growth programs. Rochester, New York, has a joint committee to oversee its career-in-teaching program. Under the unique labor-management constitution in Glenview, Illinois, much of the district's decision making on instruction, personnel, and finance takes place in joint committees.

Trust agreements are another means of expanding the envelope of union involvement in educational policy formation and implementation. Legally binding bilateral trust agreements sit outside the contract and are designed to deal with issues that arguably fall outside the scope of bargaining (particularly important when discussions of legally allowable scope are likely to eclipse discussions of substance) or are better handled in an arena less formal than contract negotiations and with an outcome less rigid than a contract. A four-year California experiment involving twelve school districts resulted in union-management trust agreements covering issues such as peer review, professional development, and school site collaborative management and decision making.

A few contracts have established procedures that enable individual schools to request exemptions, or waivers, from specific portions of the agreement for school-determined educational reasons. For example, say a school wants to experiment with some very large classes and some quite small ones. Doing so would violate the class size provision of the contract. A waiver provision allows the school to request relief from that portion of the agreement.

Contracts that include waiver provisions require that the school seeking the waiver submit a written request to a team of designated central union and management representatives. The team considers the request and makes a decision, which is binding on the school. The waiver, if granted, is limited to the school requesting it, and is in effect for a specified period of time.

Waiver provisions have not been widely adopted. Indeed, even while waivers offer the possibility of flexibility for school-developed programs, the language of the waiver provision itself may be quite limiting. Schools (or groups of teachers), for example, are often prohibited from seeking exemptions from transfer, salary, and evaluation provisions of the contract.

TINKERING AT THE MARGINS

Joint committees, trust agreements, and waivers are designed to loosen the constraints of the contract without losing the purpose of collective bargaining. However, we believe that these reforms (some of which we have participated in and even led), no matter how faithfully conducted and thoughtfully executed, have failed to move unions and districts much beyond the educational reform starting gate. Reduced in most instances to sporadic flirtations with flexibility, they have generally been fairly timid, focused on single issues, and hamstrung by much of the same sort of tight procedural language and bureaucratic machinery that characterizes the contracts themselves.

Trust agreements and joint committees expand the range of union-management discussion, but they are, themselves, centralized pacts. Negotiated at the district level, these union-management arrangements still tend to focus on preserving equity and extending teacher rights. Waivers, the clearest effort to decentralize decision-making authority, are enmeshed in their own web of rules.

Moreover, waivers, trust agreements, and joint operating committees sit outside the regular education structure. They thus have about them a perpetual air of impermanence. Generally accorded about equal status as other pilot projects in a school district, these reform approaches tend to be seen by teachers and administrators as temporary educational aberrations. The bureaucracy continues to operate as if little had changed. In the inevitable test of wills between change and the status quo, change invariably blinks first.

The problems these bargaining reforms endeavor to solve in practice are not the fundamental issues of educational quality and student achievement. Yet, despite the rather modest nature of these reform efforts—none really threatens the basic form and purpose of the negotiated agreement—even they have not spread very far very fast. Rhetorical flourishes and noble intentions of the 1980s and early 1990s notwithstanding, education labor relations remains much the same as it has been for the past three decades.

We thus return to the beginning of this chapter. In our judgment, public schools need to adapt to educational purposes some of the fundamental characteristics of successful firms. They need to be entrepreneurial, innovative, and flexible, and to adopt an ethic of continuous improvement. Rethinking collective bargaining agreements is a place to begin.

TOWARD A NEW SYSTEM

We propose that the comprehensive districtwide contract be replaced by two new forms of written union-management agreement—a slender district-level contract and a much more encompassing school site educational compact. These agreements would have the effect of recognizing the union as an equal participant in educational improvement, refocusing negotiated agreements on institutional rather than individual welfare, and placing significant educational decision-making authority and responsibility in the hands of schools.

The new central agreement, which would provide a kind of bare-bones philosophical and operational architecture, would be structured around educational goals toward which union and management would agree all schools would strive. The document would also contain a few basic wage and working condition provisions, many of which would be subject to school site modification. More comprehensive agreements would be forged at local schools in the school site educational compacts described in Chapter Seven.

Theoretical Roots

We borrow the notion of the modern-day workplace compact from the work of Irving and Barry Bluestone. In *Negotiating the Future* (1992), the Bluestones write: "A contract is essentially adversarial in nature, representing a compromise between the separate interests of each party to the agreement. In contrast, a *compact* is fundamentally a cooperative document, providing for a mutual vision and a joint system for achieving common goals that foster the general well-being of all stakeholders in a given endeavor" (pp. 24–25).

The term *compact* has both substantive and symbolic meaning here. The agreement would be developed at individual schools by the administrators, teachers, and support staff who work there. Rather than serving as an enumeration of accrued employment rights, the educational compact would represent a social contract between the school and its community.

The parties to each agreement—union and management in the case of the districtwide contract, the school community in the instance of the site-based compact—would reach decisions based on their assessment of a common vision of education and common goals for the district or school. Both the central contract and the site-based compact would adopt as their organizational and operating framework improving the quality of the educational enterprise. To permit a focus on continuous improvement, all issues of educational purpose and policy would be expected topics of discussion.

In the Union's Interest

Why, a reader might reasonably ask, would a union have an interest in this model? After all, it places additional burdens on the organization for "value added" quality, for visible and measurable educational improvement, and for accountability for results. It requires union and management to develop entirely new patterns of professionalism through the assumption of mutual responsibility for the overall health of the educational enterprise. While this system of interlocking agreements potentially could place the union in the position of accepting a considerable share of public kudos if educational improvement swings upward, it also creates the risk that a downward achievement spiral would be attributed to union involvement in traditional management domains.

We have suggested some of the reasons for these changes under the general theoretical umbrella of creating a new institutional structure to meet the changing education needs of twenty-first-century society. There is a more pragmatic explanation as well, one that lies at the heart of unions' historical raison d'être.

Kochan and Osterman offer a compelling explanation in *The Mutual Gains Enterprise* (1994). They write that when Michael Bennett, the United Auto Workers president at a Saturn plant, was asked why his local would enter into a radically different labor-management arrangement with General Motors, he responded that his people needed Saturn to make a success of the plant. For Saturn to succeed, he said, the union had to begin to recognize its responsibility, along with management, for *both* the economic and the social performance of the company.

Saturn needed economic results to demonstrate its ability to meet the challenges of increasingly stiff competition. This meant doing things differently in this new auto plant to achieve greater levels of efficiency, higher rates of productivity, and a better car.

At the same time, the needs of the workforce also had to be met. Bennett knew, he says, that accomplishing his two-pronged goal for his members—long-term employment stability and secure financial futures—was inextricably tied to Saturn's economic success. He could only produce what he wanted for his members if the auto plant produced the kind of car the American public wanted to buy. Involvement in Saturn's planning and business decisions became a sine qua non for the union.

The Bluestones echo this new approach in describing the kinds of trade-offs both sides need to make and the bargains they need to strike. Labor, they write, must "take on greater responsibility for productivity and quality." In exchange, "management assumes a greater obligation to provide employment security" (p. 25).

We believe this philosophy has much to recommend it to teacher unions. By structuring union-management agreements around principles of quality and innovation, focusing on the continued vitality of the schooling enterprise, and offering reasonable employment security in uncertain times, the union can simultaneously help to infuse a new dynamism in the system of public education *and* enhance the professional opportunities available to its members.

THE NEW CENTRAL AGREEMENT

For many of the provisions of the new central contract, as well as for many of the components of the school-based educational compacts (described in the next chapter), we draw on examples from currently operating union-management agreements and ongoing education reform experiments. In other words, while much of what we suggest may appear radical and even extreme, elements of it already exist.

The new districtwide contract would enunciate newly conceived joint union-management obligations. Six basic provisions, many of which would be available for school site modification, would compose the contract: a statement of union-management responsibility for improving education, a basic pay and benefits structure, a system for professional development and assessment of professional performance, a basic calendar for the school year, a statement of union and employment security guarantees, and a mechanism for resolving contractual disputes.

Joint Responsibility

This contract provision would offer a clear statement of the union's and district's mutual intention to assure the continued health and ongoing improvement of the educational enterprise. Both parties would commit to actions that further the district's educational mission. The agreement would be embedded in an underlying assumption that union and management share a *common* purpose in improving schooling.

An initial statement of mutual obligation might be structured along the lines of the preamble to the 1990 contract between the Rochester school district and the Rochester Teachers Association: The union and the district, it states, "are dedicated to undertake the purposeful change necessary to restructure schools. A commitment to change means a willingness to reconsider and alter traditional relationships, organizational structures, and allocations of personnel, resources, time and space to advance student achievement and enhance the life of the school as a center of learning and productivity."

Here, the union and district state their commitment to school change *as a means for increased student achievement.* They assert, up front in the contract, that conventional ways of doing labor relations business will give way to new modes of interaction and decision making as teachers and administrators work toward continuous educational improvement.

Another means by which union and management can state their mutuality of purpose is offered by the Glenview (Illinois) constitution. The constitution is an impressive union-management invention that has replaced the traditional contract (Kerchner and Koppich, 1993).

The labor accord between the Glenview Education Association and the Board of Education of the Glenview Public Schools is functionally structured around a statement of educational principles, expanded professional roles for teachers, and enhanced school site operating authority. Much of the heart and soul of a traditional contract—transfer and grievance procedures, salary and benefit schedules, leave of absence policies, evaluation protocols—is included as the bylaws to the constitution. In other words, Glenview has taken the issues that typically form the sum and substance of a union-management agreement and turned them into a set of operating rules designed to enable the union and the district to meet their educational goals.

The educational principles enumerated in the Glenview constitution (1989–1992, p. 3) read, in part:

- We recognize that the primary educator of all children is the family unit. We are committed to encourage and provide opportunities for informed and meaningful parental involvement in the District's educational process.

- We recognize that the standard by which we evaluate all our efforts is whether these undertakings advance the well being of children entrusted to us. We are committed to this standard.

- We recognize the great responsibilities involved in the educational process. We are committed to holding ourselves and each other accountable in these matters by processes that will assess fulfillment of mutually determined goals and objectives.

Rochester and Glenview offer examples of language and concepts that might be adapted to statements of union-management joint educational responsibility. As a means of establishing a clear course and direction for this joint action, the union and the district together would establish measurable educational goals, focused on student achievement, toward which all schools in the district would strive. Achievement could be defined in multiple ways. For example, goals might be designed around levels of academic performance, school attendance and completion rates, rates of student participation in extracurricular activities, levels of parent and community participation in schools and school-related activities, and the like.

Goals would be specific enough to be measurable, but not so specific as to limit schools' ability to adapt them to the needs of their particular student populations. And these educational goals would serve as a public statement to the community of the union's and district's commitment to continuing educational improvement and their willingness to be held accountable for the results of their efforts.

Dealing with Nonperforming Schools

A significant element of union-management joint responsibility for educational quality would be the development, in the context of the contract, of a quality review procedure for nonperforming schools. Teachers and administrators would publicly acknowledge that, under an agreed-upon set of circumstances, schools could be declared *nonperforming* and subjected to progressively more intense district intervention, up to and including full district takeover.

Nonperformance could be established in three ways. First, a school could experience some sort of a catastrophic event that made it impossible to operate the educational program. Second, a school might be declared nonperforming if it was unable to reach agreement on its educational compact. Since the compact essentially establishes the plan of operation for the school, failure to construct such a plan after an agreed-upon period of time would prevent the school from fulfilling its educational obligations. Third, schools that did not meet established educational goals could be declared nonperforming. The contract would spell out procedures for certifying schools as nonperforming as well as processes by which the district would assume responsibility for such schools.

Salaries and Benefits

Critical to the new central agreement is a transformed salary schedule and a new kind of benefits plan and structure. Compensation would be based on teachers' demonstrated knowledge and skills. In essence, pay would focus on a "value added" orientation. What does the individual professional add to the needed repertoire of his or her own classroom as well as to the school as a freestanding educational unit?

Pension and benefit plans would no longer be the property of individual school districts (or, in the case of retirement plans, individual states), but instead would be independent and portable, thus affording teachers added flexibility to pursue professional opportunities.

THE NEW SALARY SCHEDULE.   We have already discussed the uniform pay structure, the standard single salary schedule, which currently governs compensation for most of America's teachers. In a bureaucratic, centrally driven system of education, which measures productivity on the basis of inputs to the system and values professional training (credentials and courses) as a proxy for expertise, the standard single salary schedule serves both to reflect a kind of pay-for-performance and to provide teacher-to-teacher equity throughout a given school district.

The standard single salary schedule, however, is a mismatch with the kind of education system we envision in this book. A school-based and results-oriented system—one that relies on employees' innovative spirit and entrepreneurial skills—requires a different compensation structure. A system that focuses on measurable student achievement goals and schoolwide improvement, what might be called an achievement-based design for education, is better served by a pay formula that offers teachers financial remuneration tied to their demonstrated achievement of various skills and levels of expertise that can assist the school to fulfill its purposes.

We propose, then, that a new pay structure for teachers be established. Not merit pay, however. We do not suggest here a compensation scheme along the lines of merit pay plans, because merit pay breeds the kind of individual competitiveness destructive to teamwork and cooperation. It assumes that merit can be fairly and objectively judged—that somewhere there exists a blueprint for effective teaching. Finally, merit pay schemes are limited. Typically, only a select number of teachers can be designated as "meritorious" and receive the added compensation (Murnane and Cohen, 1986).

Rather, building on experience in industry, we propose that the new teacher salary schedule be constructed around salary incentives for knowledge and skills. This sort of performance-based pay would both offer teachers multiple ways to increase their salaries and encourage teachers as they assume new roles and responsibilities in their schools (Conley and Odden, 1995). Much of the developmental work for this new salary structure has been undertaken by Professors Allan Odden and Carolyn Kelley at the University of Wisconsin–Madison.

The new schedule would be constructed, like the present one, as a two-dimensional matrix. Vertical columns would correspond to longevity increments, but perhaps no more than ten. (The standard single salary schedule contains as many as twenty longevity increments.) Horizontal rows would correspond to knowledge and skill blocks.

Teachers would receive added compensation for demonstrating the acquisition of any or all of three types of skills—*depth, breadth,* and *vertical* skills. Depth skills would reflect levels of expertise in particular functional or disciplinary areas, for example teaching itself or teaching a particular subject. Breadth skills would reflect expertise in areas such as curriculum development, counseling, and professional development. Vertical, or management, skills include those necessary for school-based educational systems. This block of skills would encompass, for example, budgeting, personnel management, and leadership (Conley and Odden, 1995; Kelley and Odden, 1995). Compensation, then, would reward the development of content, pedagogical, and management knowledge and skill (Kelley, 1995).

A skill-based pay system would accomplish several essential purposes. It would more accurately reflect an assessment of professionals' contributions to school-based educational improvement. It would enable individual teachers to be rewarded for accomplishment without breeding unnecessary and unproductive intraschool professional competition. It would be equitable in that all teachers who demonstrate the requisite skills would be entitled to salary advancement. Finally, it would provide an incentive to remain in teaching since new skills would translate to new professional responsibilities and added financial compensation.

As part of the districtwide contract, then, the union and district would jointly agree on both the skills that would offer higher compensation for teachers and the method for assessing these skills. The decision as to which skills would produce pay increments would be based on the union's and district's assessment of district needs.

SOME OPERATING EXAMPLES. Skill-based pay is already beginning to make its way into a few teachers' contracts. Some districts, for example, have added certification through the National Board for Professional Teaching Standards as a means by which teachers can earn salary advancement. National Board certification requires peer-reviewed, performance-based demonstrations of professional accomplishment. Broward County, Florida, offers its Board-certified teachers an additional $2,000 per year. Rochester, New York; Cincinnati, Ohio; and Minneapolis, Minnesota, are among other districts that provide pay differentials for National Board certification.

Robbinsdale, Minnesota, through a contract provision titled "Skill-Based Compensation," provides up to $14,000 in salary increments ($5,000 of which may be earned by achieving National Board certification) to teachers who submit an approved skills portfolio. A committee of teachers, administrators, and community members is charged with reviewing and scoring the contents of the portfolios. The union and district have established a scoring rubric to equate salary increments to particular portfolio contents and have agreed that the scoring rubric may change as district needs and goals change.

Among the most ambitious performance-based pay plans is that negotiated in Douglas County, Colorado. The Douglas County contract enables teachers to qualify for additional pay based on the acquisition of designated skills, assumption of additional school- and district-related responsibilities, and their schools' achievement of measurable educational goals.

JOINT SALARY BOARD. Once the basic salary schedule is established, its ongoing maintenance would be overseen by a joint union-management salary board. This board's responsibilities would be to ensure that salaries remain appropriately competitive, offer reasonable compensation for the professional skills the union and district have jointly agreed are most desirable, and ensure that fair means are used to adjudge teachers' acquisition of those skills. The board would review the salary structure annually, make internal adjustments as warranted, and report to the district's school board.

The work of the salary board will require a delicate balancing act. The districtwide schedule would represent minimum or basic rates of pay that could be enhanced by individual school sites. Thus if the board sets the districtwide salary bar too high, schools will be constrained in their ability to allocate resources as they see fit. On the other hand, the board will need to take into account the risk that teachers might seek employment outside the district if minimum salaries are not maintained at a competitive level.

BENEFITS.   Teachers currently are captives of their state pension and district benefit plans. Accepting a professional opportunity in a new district or a different state often requires wrenching considerations—lost retirement earnings and altered, sometimes reduced, health care and other insurance coverages. We propose that the new labor relations configuration minimize these issues by establishing statewide systems of health and other insurances and a nationwide pension system for teachers. Portable pensions and benefits become an important part of creating a labor market for teachers in which teachers are not captives of individual school districts and districts are not the sole source of employment security. This topic is covered in more detail in Chapter Eight.

Professional Development

Professional development in education generally has a bad name—and deservedly so. School district–administered staff development for teachers typically flies in the face of research findings about what constitutes good ongoing professional education (Little, 1993). Most is decided on by district officials rather than teachers. Most is structured as one-shot presentations or workshops with little follow-up and coaching. Most is conducted by outside "experts" rather than by teaching professionals themselves. In the case of professional development that comes in the form of college-level courses, these classes may bear little or no relationship to the teacher's professional responsibilities.

But perhaps the greatest failing of current staff development configurations is that they tend to reinforce existing patterns of schooling and conventional conceptions of teachers' roles. In a fluid system that places high value on flexibility, innovation, and entrepreneurship, professional development needs to serve the function of enabling employees to continuously adapt to new—and often unanticipated—circumstances. Districts and schools, in other words, need to ensure that teachers have the requisite skills and training not only to meet immediate job requirements but also to prepare for professional demands that will evolve over time (Kochan and Osterman 1994).

In the bargaining model we propose, the majority of professional development would be school-based. As part of their central agreement, however, the union and the district might choose to join forces on some development dimensions. For example, the National Board for Professional Teaching Standards might be the focus of some districtwide professional development efforts (particularly if certification by the National Board carried with it added financial compensation for teachers). Together, the union and district could offer courses to assist teachers to prepare for National Board certification. Or they might, as have districts in several states, set aside funds to reimburse teachers who achieve Board certification for the fees required to undergo the process.

RETRAINING. In addition, the district and union might take the long view, extrapolate the district's future needs, and determine areas of anticipated teacher shortage. Joint professional development programs might then be organized for the purpose of retraining willing teachers who would develop new professional skills and competencies designed to meet the district's future educational needs.

Cincinnati has initiated such an effort for teachers who are laid off. The current contract between the Cincinnati Federation of Teachers and the Cincinnati school district provides that the district will reimburse a significant portion of the tuition expenses for teachers who return to school to earn new teaching certificates in areas of need, as jointly determined by the union and the district. Teachers who complete retraining certification are guaranteed reemployment with the district.

The principal purpose of districtwide statements about and programs for professional development is to reinforce joint union-management expectations for and commitment to teachers' ongoing professional growth. This is an additional tacit signal that the teaching career is not static, and that learning is a continuous undertaking for those who teach as well as for those whom they teach.

ASSESSING PROFESSIONAL PERFORMANCE. Professional performance would be based on a system of peer review, such as that described in the previous chapter. Peer review—the process by which teachers assess the professional competence of their colleagues—is an essential component of the process whereby the union can assume responsibility for the quality of the teaching profession.

The districtwide contract would delineate the procedural components of peer review. What does the system look like? How does it operate? Who participates and under what circumstances? What are the criteria—the elements of good teaching—that frame the process?

The peer review system would be governed by a board of professional practice. This board, composed principally of teachers, would act on recommendations from the peer evaluators for mandatory professional development or termination. As part of this process, the board would review the evidence submitted by reviewers, including reports of classroom observations, portfolios of teachers' work, and information regarding steps taken by reviewers to assist the teachers in question to improve their professional practice. The board would also offer the teachers under discussion an opportunity to respond to reviewers' recommendations before it renders a final and binding decision.

INSTANCES OF PROFESSIONAL MALFEASANCE.   The board of professional practice would have a second important function. It would be authorized to hear appeals from decisions made by school principals to remove individual teachers for dereliction of duty. This is designed as an important safeguard, both for teachers and for schools.

Instances of professional malfeasance that do not fall into the peer review net perhaps will be rare, but they will occur. The board of professional practice provides a means by which to deal with them.

A teacher, for example, is habitually late for work, or consistently exhibits inappropriate professional behavior. This teacher is not eligible for the peer review sequence for another year, but the principal believes the teacher must be removed from the school or classroom as quickly as possible. The principal would submit to the board his or her reason for requesting removal of the teacher. The board would hear the principal's case, listen to the teacher's response, perhaps conduct an independent investigation, and render a decision.

School Year Calendar

Schooling in America has been labeled a "prisoner of time." A 1994 report by the National Education Commission on Time and Learning asserted, "Unyielding and relentless, the time available in a uniform six-hour day and 180-day year is the unacknowledged design flaw in American education" (p. 13).

This report takes an interesting cut on the time issue. It does not, as have so many reports before it, assert that a key to improved education lies in increasing the absolute number of days students spend in school. Rather, the National Commission finds that the principal problem is that American schools devote so little of the time they have to fundamental academic learning. "On average," states the report, "students can receive a high school diploma if they devote only 41 percent of their school time to core academic learning. . . . French, German and Japanese students [in their last four years of school] receive more than twice as much core academic instruction as American students" (p. 25).

The National Commission report points to the need to consider time a flexible resource, to be molded to suit different educational venues and purposes. What do students need to accomplish during their in-school hours? Do all schools, and all students, require the same configuration of hours per day and days per year of instruction? What kind of time do teachers need to plan and consult with one another? How might that time best be "captured" and how might it be structured? Will the time needs of professionals vary from year to year and from school to school?

We believe that the current lockstep approach to the school calendar, ensuring that all students are in school the same number of hours per day and days per year, impedes essential school flexibility and adaptability. Therefore, rather than specifying a rigid school year calendar, the new districtwide contract would establish instructional time minima. The contract would specify only the days during which schools typically would be expected to be in session. Individual sites, through their educational compacts, would be free to modify this calendar by increasing the number of school days and establishing their own hours of operation.

Union and Employment Security

Agreements ensuring organizational security for the union and employment security for teachers would contribute to both a stable work environment and a ready supply of qualified labor. And they would do this without imposing undue restrictions on either school site flexibility or professionals' ability to market their services.

UNION SECURITY. The union security provision of the contract would have the effect of preserving the institutional integrity of the union as the agency that supplies competent professional labor to the district.

The agreement would acknowledge the union as the sole source supplier of teachers for the district. To secure a teaching position, employees would sign up with the union's electronic hiring hall and be notified of schools that have openings matched to the teacher's interests and skills (See Chapter Eight for more detail on the hiring hall.)

An additional dimension of union security is that all teachers would be required to pay fees to the union. We recognize that this requirement is likely to generate controversy. We believe, however, that if the union is the organization that sets and maintains quality professional standards, provides retraining, and acts as the clearinghouse for multiple kinds of employment opportunities, teachers should—and will be willing to—pay a fair price for these services.

EMPLOYMENT SECURITY.   We differentiate here between employment security and job security. Employment security—the right to a teaching position in the school district, assuming satisfactory performance—would be assured by a no-layoff provision in the contract.

Job security—the right of a teacher to remain at a particular school—would not be a contractual guarantee. Decisions regarding teacher assignments—who stays at a school, who comes to a school, what an individual's particular responsibilities are at a school—would rest with school staffs and would be based on the school's particular needs. A position would not be construed as an individual's property right, and seniority would not be the deciding factor in determining a teacher's school assignment. The principle that would underlie staff selection and assignment would be the welfare of the school as an institution. A teacher who leaves or is displaced from an assignment would have recourse through the union hiring hall (described in Chapter Eight) to seek a new position better suited to his or her skills and talents.

Dispute Resolution

As we noted earlier in this chapter, negotiated mechanisms to resolve disputes assume that the contract is an enumeration of individual rights. Settling disagreements about the application of particular contract provisions involves determining whether or not the employer has violated one or more of the conditions of employment of an individual teacher.

The means for adjudicating disputes in the new districtwide contract would be suited to the new purpose of the agreement. In other words, dispute resolution would focus on preserving the integrity of the educational institution and the goals it is attempting to achieve. Thus this new formulation of the grievance procedure would strive to balance institutional welfare—ensuring the district and its schools can achieve their educational goals—with individual rights—ensuring that the system does not treat individual teachers in an arbitrary or capricious manner.

Here, again, we can point to a few instances of districts and their unions attempting a different interpretation of dispute resolution. More often this is accomplished by removing particular topics from the grievance venue than by changing the purpose of the adjudication procedure. The Cincinnati contract, for example, provides that the decisions of its class size committee, a joint union-management group that makes decisions regarding application of the class size provisions of the contract, are final and not subject to the grievance procedure.

The Glenview constitution establishes the union-management District Coordinating Council to monitor the labor accord. Among the responsibilities of the district-level council is to hear and act on appeals to the actions of a building-level council or district committee or subcommittee. The constitution states, "The decision of the District Coordinating Council shall be final and binding. . . . No concerns, complaints, or appeals regarding the actions, inactions or deliberations of any Local School Council, Building Council, District Committee or subcommittee or the District Coordinating Council shall be handled through the grievance procedure" (p. 8).

RESOLVING DISTRICTWIDE DISPUTES. For purposes of adjudicating disputes regarding the districtwide agreement, the union and the district jointly would select an individual (or a group of individuals) to serve as a kind of permanent umpire. Disagreements that are not resolved through informal district and union discussions would be submitted to the umpire, who would act much as an arbitrator does. The umpire would listen to both parties to the dispute and would render a decision designed to resolve the disagreement.

There would, however, be an essential difference between the roles and responsibilities of the permanent umpire and those of the conventional labor arbitrator. An arbitrator typically is an outside neutral, acceptable to both labor and management but not necessarily known by either side to the dispute.

The arbitrator generally is not familiar with a particular school district or its contract, and his or her decision is required to be based solely on the language of the written labor-management agreement. The arbitrator, in other words, attempts to determine if the language of the agreement, or of the provision in dispute, is "clear and unambiguous." Arbitrators' rulings are based on the words as written. Few arbitrators venture onto the slippery slope of attempting to interpret the parties' intent in the absence of clear language.

The permanent umpire under the new set of operating rules we propose would have a different relationship to the district and a different function from that of an arbitrator. The umpire would be knowledgeable about the district and familiar both with and to the parties to the dispute. This individual would have an intimate familiarity with the district's established educational goals and a feel for the district, its schools, and its personnel. The umpire would be authorized to render a binding decision that would take into account the obvious language of the disputed contract provision, the intent of the parties in developing it, and the extent to which a particular resolution contributes to or inhibits the parties' ability to achieve their mutual educational purposes.

SOLVING SITE DISAGREEMENTS.   Since many of the key educational decisions would be reserved to schools, the majority of disputes regarding agreement interpretation and implementation likely would revolve around the school-based educational compacts. For purposes of resolving school-based disputes that are not resolved at the school site, the union and the district would agree to create a system of binding arbitration in which the arbitrator, or arbitration panel, would function as a kind of "court of equity." Arbitrators would be selected by and mutually agreeable to both union and district officials as well as to representatives of those who signed the educational compact.

As with the permanent umpire who would resolve central disputes, the arbitration panel that would take up school-based disagreements would not, in determining an equitable solution to the dilemma, be constrained by the specific contract language. The panel would have a clear understanding of the vision and goals of the district and the purposes and expectations of the school at which the dispute arises. The panel, in rendering its judgment, would take into account the concerns of the parties to the dispute as well as the welfare of all of the stakeholders at the school. In other words, the panel would be authorized to balance issues of individual teacher equity with issues of general school welfare.

The new, slender version of the districtwide contract would thus have the effect of focusing district-level union-management negotiations on a few central features of the employment relationship. Most of the decisions that lie at the heart of teaching and learning would shift to the schools.

CHAPTER SEVEN

Establishing School-Based Compacts

The new districtwide contract serves to frame the basics. The real power of the system, however, lies in allowing the heart of the educational enterprise to be shaped by the people who must make it work—the ones at each school site. Rather than ironing out the details once for everyone, as the current system does, we picture a new kind of document, an educational compact that each school site would prepare and administer. By means of the compact, employees would gain the right to make essential workplace decisions. In exchange for this new authority, the parties to the compact would assume responsibility for the educational performance of the school.

We are mindful that contemporary efforts to devolve decisions to school sites have a rather checkered history. Debates about school governance structures have often eclipsed discussions of standards, curriculum, and student achievement. Roles have remained muddy and teachers and principals have found themselves in a kind of professional netherworld. The crucial question of accountability—of how to link measurable outcomes and improved program quality to rewards and consequences for action—has more often been a query begged than addressed.

The system we propose here, we believe, confronts the challenges of many school-based management operations. Critical education decisions, not just about the time bells ring or the way in which a school deploys its very limited fund of discretionary dollars, but about matters such as hiring and evaluation of personnel, curriculum and instruction, and allocation of the majority of the school's operating resources, would become the province of schools through their educational compacts. Moreover, schools would be held responsible for the results of their actions. Accountability would be assessed against the district's and the school's measurable educational goals, and rewards and consequences would flow accordingly.

USEFUL EXAMPLES

A number of districts and their teacher unions have taken important steps to move crucial education decisions to schools. The language from their contracts can inform the development of educational compacts.

The Glenview constitution (1989–1992, p. 6) establishes a "building council" at each school and defines the selection, role, and function of this group as follows:

> Each building shall establish a Building Council which, collaboratively with the principal, shall determine how the school can best achieve the goals and expectations established by the [district school] Board, the Local School Council and the building staff. The Building Council shall develop policies and/or procedures related to the organization, budget and educational program for each respective school. These policies and/or procedures may address scheduling, student assignment, recommendations concerning staff selection, staff assignment, and other professional matters as may be appropriate and shall be consistent with District goals and expectations. The structure of the Building Council shall be left to the discretion of the staff and the principal in each building.

The contract between the Hammond (Indiana) Teachers' Federation and the Hammond school district, which has a decade-long life (Master Contract, 1990–2001), provides a set of guidelines for "school-based restructuring." The guidelines authorize each school to establish a planning team that "shall develop programs/practices . . . which are consistent with and which lead toward fulfillment of both the City of Hammond's and the individual school's goals and objectives." Planning teams are empowered to make the following kinds of decisions:

- Developing educational priorities for the building, based on the district's priorities, taking into account the special needs of students
- Developing new programs to meet the needs of the school's population
- Developing scheduling to meet instructional objectives
- Allocating a building's resources to best meet the needs of the students
- Determining professional development programs to meet faculty needs
- Restructuring the school to meet the needs of students in the twenty-first century

Implementing these contract provisions requires that teachers assume new and expanded professional roles. Implicit in this is the recognition that teachers cannot function in isolation behind the closed doors of their classrooms, that meeting the educational challenges they face in their schools requires collaboration with colleagues, as well as willingness to accept negotiated solutions to problems.

CONSTRUCTING THE COMPACT

The site-based compact would be legally binding and enforceable. The document would feature statements of principles, an annual plan of operation, guidelines for school operation, and procedures for making decisions about matters such as time, staff, and resource allocation. The questions that would undergird development of the compact and the decisions that emanate from it would be, "What is in the best interest of the institution?" and "What policies, procedures, and strategies will best promote enhanced student achievement?"

The compact would be an enabling document, sufficiently flexible so as to be amenable to modification as the need arises. As much as anything else, the compact would represent a statement of a school's principles and purposes. In order to ensure that the compact was structured in a manner designed to help the school reach established educational goals, the school district would retain authority to approve compacts.

The basic components of the educational compact would include the following: a statement of educational philosophy and student performance targets, mechanisms for resource allocation, procedures for hiring, means for achieving salary decisions, procedures for class and course organization, programs for professional development and assessment of professional performance, a statement about quality assurance and community support, and a dispute resolution plan.

Philosophy and Student Performance Targets

The first part of the compact would be a statement of the school's operating mission and principles. In effect, this provision would provide an opportunity for the school staff and community to mutually determine the fundamental philosophy and educational underpinnings of the institution. The purpose of this section would be to reach consensus on the answer to the question, "What does our school stand for?"

This section of the agreement might also contain language that reinforces the collective responsibility of all the compact's signatories for achieving continuous student improvement. This would reframe the central contract's statement of joint responsibility, which asserts the mutual purpose of the union and the district in achieving common educational objectives, in terms meaningful to the individual school.

A set of measurable student performance targets would be another component of this compact provision. Keyed to the student achievement goals enunciated in the central union-district pact, the compact targets would be tailored to the school's clients and mission. Targets would be more specific than goals, but would, like the goals, focus on measures of student achievement.

Compact-enshrined targets would serve as a set of "quality indicators" for the school. Annually, the school would assess and make public the degree to which it was making progress toward reaching the targets and achieving the districtwide goals. The school would also be obliged to study, attempt to understand, and explain to the wider school community conditions or impediments that might, in any given year, prevent the school from reaching its anticipated targets.

Resource Allocation

The vast majority of fiscal resources (roughly 90 percent) would be controlled at the school site. Resources would be allocated by the district to each school on a per-pupil basis. In other words, each school would be able to anticipate its fiscal resources based on its student enrollment. The union and district might determine, at the district level, to develop a weighted allocation formula for special needs students (for example, limited- and non–English speaking pupils, those with physical and mental handicaps, and so on).

The principal purpose of the per-pupil allocation arrangement is to prevent the central district office from skimming resources from schools. Insofar as schools are able to predict their student populations, they ought to be able to predict their revenue streams.

Parties to the school-based educational compact would establish procedures by which to determine resource allocation priorities. How many teachers do we need this year and in what fields? Should we invest in new computer equipment? Should we target resources to developing a new science program? Here is where the staffing rubber meets the professional road.

Should a school collectively decide that an individual teacher's skills, while perhaps valuable in past years, no longer meet the needs of that school, the staff would have the authority, based on the school's mission and educational targets, to replace that teacher with another staff member (another teacher with different skills, an administrator, a classified employee). The displaced teacher's seniority would not provide an extra advantage in terms of remaining at the school. Instead, that teacher would contact the union via the electronic hiring hall and seek a position more clearly suited to his or her particular professional skills.

All school-based resource allocation decisions would be stated in terms that clearly link resource distribution to efforts to further the educational program of the school. While individual schools might use their entrepreneurial talents in the search for additional resources (loaned executives from business, community volunteers, financial donations from parents, and so on), their budget from the district would be set, and schools would be required to live within their financial means.

Hiring

Hiring would be a school site function. The school would develop procedures by which to make decisions regarding the numerical and job-specific composition of the staff as well as mechanisms for adding and deleting staff positions. Hiring decisions would be grounded in judgments about the welfare of the educational program and school-determined priorities regarding resource allocation.

The union hiring hall would send prospective teachers for interviews at schools with advertised position openings. In general, the hiring hall would screen only for proper certification; union officials would make no judgments regarding the fit of applicants for particular openings unless specifically requested to do so. School staffing decisions would be made according to the procedures outlined in the site's educational compact. As previously stated, seniority would not be a factor in deciding an individual teacher's suitability for a particular teaching opening.

Internal assignments, in other words, teachers' specific placements and duties at their schools, would also be school-based decisions. Schools would determine the division and allocation of duties and responsibilities based on the school's needs. Such needs change, and it is likely that the particular tasks each teacher performs might be somewhat different from year to year.

Salary Decisions

Teachers' pay would be structured along the lines outlined in the chapter on the districtwide contract. Salary would be based on demonstrated knowledge and skill. The districtwide salary schedule, however, would serve as the baseline. Schools would be free, within the limits of their available resources, to offer teachers additional financial compensation.

Added compensation might be paid as a kind of "signing bonus" to induce a particularly well-thought-of, or well-suited, teacher to come to a particular school. Or a school might decide to award added dollars to a teacher or a group of teachers who have made an especially significant contribution to the school in reaching its performance targets.

If teachers received financial compensation above that to which they would ordinarily have been entitled by virtue of their placement on the salary schedule, those added dollars would not be permanently attached to their pay scheme. The money would become a one-time bonus, renewable at the school's discretion. Determination of the distribution, if any, of added salary to teachers or groups of teachers would be made at the school site using the procedure established in the compact.

Allowing schools to supplement teachers' basic compensation serves an essential purpose. Namely, it enables schools to compete for teachers' services, and then tangibly reward those professionals whose contributions measurably advance the school toward fulfilling its mission and achieving its performance targets.

We are aware that the option to award some teachers added financial compensation over others might appear to enhance the kind of unhealthy interpersonal competition that would constrain teachers from cooperating with one another. We believe that in practice, however, this system would have a different result. Namely, it would have the effect of enhancing the ability of individual teachers or groups of teachers to be entrepreneurs, to market their specific complement of skills and talents to schools seeking these attributes. Advantage, we believe, would accrue to collective rather than individual efforts.

Class and Course Organization

We have asserted that the ways in which schools are organized for teaching and learning must undergo fundamental changes. School flexibility—the ability to adapt to the diverse and changing needs of students—is critical to improved educational achievement. The educational compact would provide schools with the kind of structured freedom requisite to a more effective educational organization.

Schools would be free to determine the length of the school day, the number of days school would operate (though they would not be able to fall below the minimum specified in the districtwide contract), and the organization of time. Fifty-minute periods might give way to extended class blocks in high schools. Elementary schools might structure their day so as to allow teachers to team teach. Class sizes would float depending on the school-determined needs of the educational program.

The educational compact would acknowledge time as a flexible and precious resource. The agreement would contain a set of school-determined procedures detailing the ways in which decisions about the allocation and use of time would be made. The actual specifics of such decisions would be subject to continual review and possible alteration, as the needs of the school warranted.

Professional Development and Professional Performance

Each school would determine a regular, ongoing program of professional growth and development tied specifically to increasing teachers' capacity to improve student educational performance so as to meet school-developed targets and district-promulgated goals.

The compact might, for example, include a set of school-specific incentives, supports, and rewards for teachers who become certified through the National Board for Professional Teaching Standards. Or it might designate particular areas of needed staff knowledge and skill and establish a program designed to help teachers acquire them.

Performance assessment would be accomplished by means of the peer review system previously described. Schools would adhere to the districtwide peer review scheme, although they might contribute additional components of professional accomplishment that they elect to assess.

The peer review system would serve as the regular professional appraisal system. Cases of negligence of duty, in which a teacher who is not part of the immediate evaluation cycle is said to be derelict, would, as previously discussed, be referred to the board of professional practice for adjudication.

Quality Assurance and Community Support

The educational compact is not simply a bargain among school staff members. It is also an agreement with the school's public, a statement of mutual obligation and commitment—thus it represents both professional accountability and *public* accountability.

Teachers would agree to guarantee the quality of the educational program. They would agree to act in the service of improved student achievement, to make every reasonable effort to meet measurable educational goals, and to continually upgrade and assess their own professional practice so as to contribute to the welfare of the school.

In exchange, parents and the community would commit to support teachers and the school. Support might be achieved in various ways. Parents, for example, would agree to encourage students at home, assist students to the degree possible with homework, attend parent conferences and back-to-school events, and, to the extent their schedules permit, volunteer at their children's schools. In addition, parents and the broader community would commit to enhancing and preserving the fiscal viability of schools.

We believe that by including this kind of provision directly in the educational compact, parents and the broader community are included as partners in the educational program. Partnership does not simply imply some form of modest participation in school or schooling activities. Rather, this arrangement requires a mutual and symbiotic commitment of educators, parents, and the full school community in ensuring student success.

Dispute Resolution

The agreement would include a set of procedures to resolve compact interpretation or application issues that fall into contention. While we believe there would be few of these, it is possible that internal disagreement might arise, for example, over the way in which the hiring procedure was implemented, or the process by which dollars were allocated to various school programs and functions.

The first step of this dispute resolution mechanism would involve an informal meeting among the aggrieved parties to try to resolve the situation. Should this not result in resolution of the disagreement, the issue would be submitted to a school-based panel that would act as a sort of "court of competent jurisdiction." Like the permanent umpire in districtwide disputes, the school-based panel would, in developing a proposed solution to the problem, take into account the welfare of the school and the furtherance of its educational mission *as well as* the rights of the individual or individuals who are asserting that they have been wronged.

Disputes that are not resolved at the school level would be submitted to the district-based permanent umpire for final adjudication.

CHANGING RULES, ROLES, AND RESPONSIBILITIES

The educational compact places authority squarely with individual schools, following the now-honored dictum of successful firms that decisions ought to be lodged "closest to the client." It provides a system of accountability in which schools are judged on the basis of the degree to which they meet district-established measurable educational goals and their own locally determined student performance targets.

The compact, when combined with other elements of the new collective bargaining system we outline, enables schools to be entrepreneurial while remaining part of a whole-district organizational structure. It enables teachers to market their services, to select schools whose philosophy and operating design are most in sync with their own, and to create the kinds of roles in schools that will render teachers true professionals.

The compact, in short, contributes to a system of education that marries many of the most dynamic elements of the public sector with many of the most admired dimensions of the private sector.

A NEW SYSTEM FOR NEW PURPOSES

Collective bargaining invests in the union the obligation to enhance and protect the rights of its members. It implicitly invests in management the responsibility for the health of the educational enterprise. What is missing from this equation is an expression of the common aspirations educators hold for the students and the communities they serve and the means by which to fulfill the purposes of the institution. The system we propose—slender central agreements shaped by consensually arrived-at and measurable indicators of student progress, and school-based educational compacts that focus authority and responsibility nearest to students—makes union and management responsible to each other, to the system of education, and to the public that system serves. To carry out those school site functions, however, unions also need to be organized around those aspects of teaching as an occupation that take place outside the school. The next chapter turns to organizing a labor market for teachers that is both efficient and responsible.

PART FOUR

Institutionalizing the New Union

CHAPTER EIGHT

Strengthening the Market for Teachers

~∞~ Intervention in the labor market has always been a prime union function. From the days of the guilds forward, unions have served as market intermediaries, protecting their members' economic and social interests. Craftworker and artisan unions, guilds, and professional associations also protect the market by keeping out shoddy goods, bad services, and incompetent persons. Unions thus become part of the market solution to obtaining an adequate supply of qualified workers: the visible fingers of the unseen hand.

Along with other market regulations, unions form a useful social and economic ecology that ultimately matches workers and work. But the ecology is fragile, and history requires it to adapt. Particularly in times when the means of production change, the ecology of the labor market becomes unbalanced, which is one of the reasons for the historic reinvention of unionism around emerging modes of production described earlier. When work changed from craft to industry, so too did unions. As work becomes increasingly knowledge intensive, unions face a new challenge and must adapt to survive.

Productivity in industrial organizations was built around economies of scale and increased worker specialization. Central purchasing, architectural planning, curriculum development and alignment, and the uniformity of control made it possible for schools to function in rather modular fashion. Principals, teachers, and other workers could be shifted from one school to another relatively easily and plugged into work that looked more or less the same.

The literature on knowledge-era organizations suggests that the new market puts a premium on flexibility and economies of scope: the ability to switch easily from task to task and to integrate work across boundaries. These qualities of responsiveness are also necessary for dynamic schools, but they are the very qualities that cause problems for existing bureaucratic and union structures. Here, we suggest rearranging the teacher labor market, and the union role in it, to make teaching simultaneously self-advancing and socially productive. We attempt to strike a balance between the two legs of unionism: workers' rights of self-determination and society's need for institutions that are both productive and just. Historically, both legs are necessary. Maintaining this balance will require several major changes in the teacher labor market.

Classically, organizations were defined by their boundaries. One was either a part of the organization or not, and employee status set the boundary. One either had a job and was a part of the organization or didn't have one and wasn't. This relationship is beginning to break down as the organization we know as school operates with part-time employees who are part of the organization, but not entirely, contractual services where people perform vital functions but are not on the payroll, consultancies where people perform highly strategic activities but only for a short period of time, volunteers or community resources from other organizations and agencies where valuable service is rendered by a provider who may never have an economic relationship to the school.

One gains a picture of a highly organic entity that changes rapidly with conditions and combines and recombines itself with fluidity. In this setting, employment is likely to be fluid. As a result, the union's historical weapon of building a set of rights around a particular job is challenged, and the union has two possible avenues of action. One is to fight at each of the boundaries: redefinition of teacher work, contracting out, the use of interns, substitution of volunteers or employees of other organizations and agencies. Or the union can begin to organize around career security rather than job security.

While the structure we outline is also workable in multischool districts, it anticipates radical decentralization, charter schools, vouchers, or any other highly decentralized system. We assume that the individual school becomes the primary employer. The elements of the new labor market are:

- Organize around career security rather than job security.
- Make choice a weapon in the fight to reform schools.
- Create an electronic hiring hall that allows teachers to switch jobs or to relocate easily.
- Develop a career ladder that begins with apprenticeships or classroom aide jobs for novices and extends through career teaching positions.
- Create a system of portable pensions and retirement benefits that make job switching easier.
- Redefine tenure so that free speech and civil rights protections apply for all teachers, and so teachers gain economic security with experience.
- Create the means for teacher ownership of their jobs and their intellectual property.
- Endorse teacher certification systems that link with career development.
- Achieve a legitimate and secure place as a representative of both teachers and teaching.

ORGANIZE AROUND CAREER SECURITY RATHER THAN JOB SECURITY

No aspect of American unionism is more pronounced than its job consciousness, its sense of justice about who is entitled to work and under what conditions. The issue of employment permanency is an important one in this decade, just as it was in the 1930s when industrial unionism energized workers. In the thrall of international competition, the old pact between companies and employees—the idea of lifetime employment and a secure pension in exchange for loyalty and obedience—has effectively been voided. It could not withstand the pressures of greed and globalism any more than the corporate paternalism of the 1920s could withstand the Great Depression.

Employment instability historically associated with blue-collar production work is now visited upon educated, white-collar workers—not simply the ebb and flow of business cycles in aerospace, engineering, or advertising, but structural shifts in employment that put "the royalty of workers" on the streets. Corporations are eliminating two million jobs a year, and the list of companies eliminating employees now includes those with long-standing no-layoff practices: IBM, Xerox, AT&T, GTE, General Electric (Rifkin, 1995, p. 3). In 1993 alone, BankAmerica turned twelve hundred full-time positions into part-time jobs carrying no benefits. Only 19 percent of the jobs at the country's second largest bank are now full time, and 60 percent of the workers work for less than twenty hours a week and receive no benefits (Rifkin, 1995, p. 190).

Our public policy has tolerated levels of unemployment and underemployment that would have evoked a crisis response thirty years ago. Moreover, changes in employment have been structural rather than cyclical.

When firms restructure, jobs go away. Although we may be building a leaner and more competitive society, the transition costs have not at all been fairly distributed, falling as they have disproportionately on the weak and marginally employed.

Although union protections have not been without effect, the unions have shown surprising inability to stem or even much direct the tide of job relocations and plant closings. It seems highly unlikely that the answer to our employment security problem lies in a return to corporate giantism any more than it lies in a return to the Fordism of the 1920s. Instead, it means attempting to secure decent careers rather than individual jobs. By career security we mean that union members would be buffered from the winds of organizational change through a series of mechanisms that would allow members to move relatively easily from school to school, from job to job, and from one type of economic relationship to another.

This form of representation has a rich history in the craft and occupational unions of nonfactory workers—longshoremen, agricultural laborers, janitors, and musicians—who strove for control over hiring through strong closed-shop language and union hiring halls. They "stressed employment security rather than 'job rights'" at an individual work site, and they offered benefits and privileges that workers could carry with them from employer to employer (Cobble, 1991, p. 421).

We believe we are seeing the emergence of a new type of employment relationship that is in many respects paradoxical. "Postindustrial technology demands involvement and commitment from employees, but the competitive market and corporate restructuring now deny to all but the most sheltered firms the means for assuring job security and predictable treatment on which employee commitment depends" (Brody, 1993, p. 263). Career security is a means of resolving this paradox, and we believe that it is wise for both unions and employers to reconsider the role unions need to play in employment security.

The traditional approach to employment security has been tenure granted by school districts, creating an expectation of continuing employment. While tenure has not protected teachers from dismissal in times of financial stress or declining enrollment, teachers have been protected from displacement by technology or school reorganization. But maintaining job security under districtwide contracts comes under severe pressure when schools restructure, and existing security arrangements are even more greatly challenged when the instructional core of education changes. Rather than attempting a war of attrition around existing positions, we believe stronger, more institutionally useful unions will result from organizing around a career in teaching rather than a single job.

As public agencies find themselves under increasing pressures in what essentially continues to be a depression economy, there will be enormous pressure to rationalize and cut costs. The impact can be dramatic. Michael Hammer, the father of the corporate reengineering movement, estimates that corporate restructuring typically involves losing about 40 percent of jobs and sometimes as much as 80 percent of middle management (Rifkin, 1995).

Government employment has historically been a bastion of stable employment, and indeed its stability was one of the factors that compensated for what were historically low salaries. However, given the disappearance of high-paid manufacturing jobs and the successes of public sector unions, government jobs are no longer relatively poorly paid, and the bureaucratic rigidity of government programs combines with the pay levels of employees to form an attractive target.

Outsourcing and part-time employment have increased at all levels of government, and both political parties have endorsed the "reinventing government" thesis. Indeed, locally driven school site reforms frequently involve restructuring jobs so that work can be accomplished with part-time workers or other less-well-paid people.

These are profoundly disturbing changes. Osborne and Gaebler (1992) badly miss the seriousness of the labor market changes when they say: "Public employees do not have to be the victims of entrepreneurial government. . . . The total number of jobs created by such governments does not change very much; some of the jobs simply shift to private firms and community organizations" (p. 38). It is not the number of jobs that matters to workers—it's the quality of jobs, both in their tangible rewards and in their opportunities for success, fulfillment, and challenging work. Unions need to speak out for good work in all its dimensions.

Thus we must ask, what is a "good teaching job" if it is not necessarily anchored in a single workplace? What would have to be the characteristics of teaching work that would attract talented people to teaching and evoke from them high levels of dedication, caring, and productivity? We believe the evidence favors a labor market that allows teachers to enter and leave as need be, one that allows teachers to recharge their intellects and their psyches, yet one that allows teachers a good measure of financial security through various transitions.

We believe that teachers would like to shape their jobs with individual preferences about the intensity and duration of their work. Teachers lead complex lives, and one of the attractions of teaching to both men and women is that the occupation allows a reasonably healthy balance between workplace, family, and community obligations. In the past, the relatively short on-campus duty day and the agricultural work year made teaching a welcoming occupation to mothers with child care responsibilities. Now, as school work has intensified and teacher's roles in site management and professional determination increase, school years and days become longer. Both male and female teachers find the need to somehow balance their lives. While other professions have approached the question of balance either with superhuman expectations or with separate "mommy or daddy" tracks of second-class workers, teaching could be constructed to allow workers to increase or decrease the intensity of their work.

We believe teachers would be attracted by the prospect of creating a professional practice, identifying themselves as teachers rather than as civil servants. Bureaucratic job definitions don't allow for a great deal of self-expression. Even the master and mentor teacher plans that have been developed over the last decade seem sterile alongside the kinds of interesting projects teachers develop for themselves.

It may well be that some teachers would choose a practice centered on creating curriculum or developing educational software. Any specific school might have need of such a person only for an intense period of development lasting a few months, so movement from place to place would be a normal part of such a person's practice. Other teachers would find high levels of identification with particular towns or communities, and thus would want to stay in the same physical location, but they might want to change areas of teaching or move from full-time teaching to counseling or developing a new program. Such teachers would need both the stability of a school and the freedom of change.

We believe that teachers want the ability to be proactive in the face of adversity. Currently, when bad things happen at school, teachers hunker down. They can engage in trench warfare with a bad principal and suffer through a place that they know has lost its spirit and academic integrity, but they rarely have an effective exit option. The system is set up to keep people in, and even golden handcuffs bind the wrists. Cobble's history of waitress unions showed an alternative system designed around a union's ability to assist employees in moving from unworkable situations to better ones. If a boss or headwaiter was abusive and dictatorial, the waitress sought work elsewhere, and eventually that establishment had difficulty in hiring qualified people. The idea of assigning people to work in places they didn't want to go disappeared, and many debilitating workplace grievances were relieved because the combatants were separated.

USING CHOICE

Teacher unions have edged toward embracing choice, and they now need to organize around it. The question is not whether the system will let people choose the schools they want to attend, but what structures will allow people to implement their choices. Will choice be effectively allowed only for people with money, or is it for everyone? Is it only for aggressive parents who find ways to beat the system by getting their children into elite schools, or is choice the system?

For the past half-century, the United States has been operating a massive choice-oriented educational program called *suburbanization*. In this system, the population stratified itself along economic class lines and to a significant extent divided itself racially. Even within schools,

students were tracked along academic lines that, again, strongly associated with race and class differences. While it is true that much of the
steam between choice systems comes from those who care little for social equity, it is also true that our current system of zoned schools
hasn't produced a great deal of equity despite very costly interventions
designed to make it do so. Carefully examining choice and putting it to
progressive use is a much wiser course than reflexive opposition. Well-
considered choice offers teachers and unions several advantages.

First, choice allows teachers to congregate in schools where they
favor the type and style of education being offered. A system of widespread choice, as opposed to a system with elite choice schools and
mass geographic bounded schools, allows what Hill (1990) calls
"schools of character" to develop around educational themes, central
visions, or guiding principles other than bureaucratic dictate and standardization. This type of choice legitimates individual preference for
styles of teaching and learning in the school organization just as modern psychology and pedagogy recognize individual differences in
learning styles. By allowing parents and children to choose schools,
teachers create a reciprocal right for themselves.

Second, choice is a necessary ingredient for decoupling bureaucracies, making schools more amenable to teacher voice, more flexible and, indeed, more fun. As Meier says of her work in East Harlem,
"It would have been impossible to create these successful experiments
without choice" (1995, p. 93). Choice allows school reformers a means
of rolling out change, of sidestepping resistance by building a parallel
system while the old one remains in place. No large social system can
overcome its own inertia all at once, and choice provides a viable alternative to the pilot project mode of educational reform, which often
fails to expand beyond initial trials.

Third, choice provides a system safety valve. There is much that is
uncertain about parenting and pedagogy, and different proponents
have strong attachments to their preferences. Rather than turn each
difference over religion, sex education, or the treatment of a child into
a matter for political debate or judicial due process, allowing parents
an exit option creates a system in which parents can match their expectations with a series of real schools.

The safety valve benefits teachers twice. It allows parents to shop
for alternatives when they or their children are not happy in school.
It also allows teachers to shop for schools where they want to work.
Teachers vary in organizational preferences just as students vary in

preferences for schools. The ability of a teacher to move easily from one school to another creates a useful alternative to debilitating and protracted disputes between principals and teachers. The ability to move easily may also moderate principal behavior, as principals react to the possibility of losing good staff.

Fourth, organizing around choice allows unions to avoid the trap of equating good with public and evil with private employment. The practical problem is that as we depart from civil service notions of public service, it is going to be increasingly difficult to draw a clear line between what is public employment and what is not. Which, for example, is the public employee—the teacher in a public early childhood center that charges tuition to defray part of its expenses, or the teacher in an independent school that accepts tax-supported students? Is the contract worker who performs duties in a building owned by the school district, and who may wear a uniform or insignia of the school, less a public worker than the teacher paid by the school district who works in a day care facility owned by a corporation? From hiring Berlitz to teach languages to creating professional contract relationships with school administrators, public education is headed toward substantial realignment in defining employment. By recognizing hybrid employment situations and organizing around them, unions gain rather than lose in a period of flexibility.

We should note that there are many things that choice does not do. Chief among them is the attribute conservatives most frequently ascribe to market competition: forcing bad schools to close. Bad schools don't close, because public agencies won't fund a surplus of schools to allow students from bad schools to flee to good ones. When Americans fled clanky Detroit autos in favor of the hum of Japanese engineering, it was because alternatives had entered the marketplace, not because their old choices were no longer available. Existing educational choice systems, in this country and Britain, do not have the ability to create viable alternatives in sufficient scale that bad schools close (Kerchner and Kerchner, 1994; Meier, 1995). Closing down bad schools is still an act of political will and courage, but a robust choice system makes the job easier.

THE ELECTRONIC HIRING HALL

Our hiring hall grows from the craft tradition of project-based employment, relatively frequent job changes, and peripatetic workers. In an era when the nature of work is rapidly changing, it is an idea whose time has come again.

Unlike the old craft union hall where men and women lined up for a call out or placed their union cards on a board to wait for an assignment in order of seniority, the modern hiring hall would function more as a sophisticated human resources organization offering placement and counseling services and access to training and development.

Thus the hiring hall carries with it both union security and a market facilitation function. It is, in the words of a half-century-old ruling, a means "to eliminate wasteful, time consuming, and repetitive scouting for jobs by individual workmen and haphazard uneconomical searches by employers" (*Mountain Pacific Chapter*, 119 NLRB 883 at 896, quoted in Morris, 1971). In this sense, the hiring hall serves the function of an employment agency, a registry, and a personnel office.

As employment becomes more fluid, the need for placement services increases, as witnessed by the growth of temporary employment agencies. The largest of these, Manpower, Inc., which used to provide only short-term clerical workers, now provides professional employees as well, and is the country's largest single employer (Rifkin, 1995).

If schools are to be much more autonomous in their operations, if a vision of a community of teachers is to have any practical means of coming about, then schools will need access to a registry of qualified potential workers. As was the case when unions represented waitresses and workers in other small service establishments, the hiring hall function serves an institutional purpose by assuring access to a well-trained and disciplined group of employees. It could take over much of the personnel function being performed in large school districts. The hiring hall would allow flexible employment without the problems that accrue to the current system of contracting out. Workers could essentially control the contracting-out process by creating norms of fairness and also norms of service and knowledge under it.

The legal tradition of the hiring hall was substantially changed after the 1947 Taft-Hartley Amendments that made illegal the requirement of union membership as a condition of employment. Unions that ran hiring halls were required to refer nonmembers as well as members, to specify that selection of applicants for referral was to be nondiscriminatory with regard to union membership, and to make it clear that the employer retained the right to refuse any applicant referred by the union and that announcements of job postings were to be open (Morris, 1971, pp. 712–713). There is a rich history of case law regulating the use of hiring halls for nondiscriminatory purposes.

In our concept, the hiring hall would have four functions:

1. *Registration.* Just as a personnel office now does, the hiring hall would receive and qualify applications. It would determine whether the person had the basic legal requirements for a job and whether the person met the requirements of an individual posting.

2. *Preparation and recommendation.* The hall would assist applicants in preparing employment portfolios, more compact versions of the presentations now being developed by the National Board for Professional Teacher Standards. Of course, for those teachers who were Board-certified, their certification would become part of their registration information. The hall might also provide screening, career counseling, and assistance in interview training.

A school could request the hiring hall to make an initial screening of applications. However, it would not be required to do so.

3. *Electronic database.* Registration information, including selections from a teacher's portfolio, would be made available to all schools in a hiring hall's service area and, given compatible data formats, could also be transferred between locations—thus creating a truly national labor market for teachers.

A school could screen applicants according to criteria it chose, with the knowledge that if it followed the proper screening techniques, the search would meet all antidiscriminatory and civil rights requirements. But all the information, including registrant preferences and work experience, would be available to a school.

4. *Employment broker.* Particularly for employees with highly specialized skills or a desire to work an unusual schedule, the hiring hall would serve an additional brokerage function. For example, it would be able to create full-time employment for a teacher of art or music, who might not be affordable at a single elementary school, but who might find a shared arrangement among several schools. This brokering function would allow the hiring hall to break down one of the most difficult and pernicious barriers in the existing employment market—the extreme economic difference between full-time and part-time workers, in which core workers have much higher salaries and benefits while those on the periphery work under harsher conditions.

A CAREER LADDER WITH TEACHING AT THE TOP

Most ideas for changing the teaching career begin with teaching at the bottom of a career ladder and build up from there. We believe this idea should be turned upside down, so that there are numerous jobs and occupations one could hold within education before one became a teacher; teaching would be the top of the career ladder rather than the first rung.

The need for differentiation described by Lortie (1975) a generation ago is still present. Teaching is an unstaged career. Unlike lawyering or professoring, public school teaching doesn't have much of an internal status hierarchy. Twenty years ago, the wages of a teacher at retirement were roughly twice those of a beginning teacher in real dollar terms. The roles and duties of a veteran were indistinguishable from those of a first-year teacher. To be sure, informal leadership and positions of respect and influence accrued with experience, along with a certain amount of job security based on the seniority clause in the union contract, but these arrangements fell far short of constituting the kind of career change that other occupations of highly trained individuals enjoy.

Teaching, it was said, offered little in the way of career motivation. A career ladder for teachers was thought to be the answer; a series of steps or stages above the role of beginning teacher would provide both extrinsic rewards for increasing capacity and intrinsic motivation for teacher growth and commitment. A career ladder, it was thought, would allow teachers to grow without going into school administration.

Since Lortie's time, we have witnessed substantial differentiation in teaching work. Both specialization and job enlargement have taken place. States such as California have instituted mentor teacher programs and simultaneously extended the variety of credentials for teachers going into special education, bilingual education, and teaching English as a second language. Many of the districts we studied adopted career ladder plans as a complement to their school reorganization plans. For example:

- In Pittsburgh, the union and district adopted the job title of Instructional Teacher Leader.
- In Rochester, a career system gave substantial responsibility to lead teachers and rewarded them with a $10,000 salary bonus.
- In Toledo and Poway, teachers were assigned as supervisors of novice teachers.

But most existing career ladder plans take entry-level teaching as their bottom rung. Even within their own scheme, classroom teachers, the ones who work with children every day, are at the bottom. Regardless of whether the title is an administrative one or a teaching career ladder one, the message is the same: those who work with children have the lowest status, and those who work with adults have the highest.

We suggest a different ladder, one that places classroom teaching at the top and creates an orderly career progression into teaching. The duties and responsibilities now ascribed to lead teachers would become a part of the normal responsibility of senior teachers, part of the world into which they become socialized. A career ladder with teaching at the top creates a natural situation in which teachers can train and socialize new entrants and ensure quality of entrants.

Putting teaching at the top of a career ladder allows those who are teachers to mentor, educate, and lead other adults. It allows real apprenticeships in the schools. It connects schools and communities, particularly in poor areas where senior teachers seldom live in neighborhoods surrounding schools. Para-educators can bring important qualities to schools. Particularly in rapidly changing communities, they are more likely to match the ethnicity, culture, and class backgrounds of the students than are the teaching corps. In Los Angeles in 1991, for example, about 60 percent of the students were Latino while 60 percent of the teachers were Anglo. But 48 percent of the para-educators were Latino (Hentschke, 1994, p. 5). Para-educators provide role models for students and often bring language facility that fully credentialed teachers lack.

The modern use of para-educators began with categorical programs initiated in the 1960s and designed to attract the poor into teaching. The logic was that of Pearl and Reisman's work *New Careers for the Poor* (1965), which rejected deficit theories of poverty and argued instead that poverty resulted from a lack of options. By 1970, there were about 57,000 para-educators employed in U.S. school districts, about one for every thirty-five teachers. By the early 1990s, the ratio had dropped to one para-educator for every six teachers, a total of more than 400,000 paraprofessionals (National Center for Education Statistics, 1993, p. 89).

However, for the most part, para-educator work is organizationally treated as casual labor, not particularly well integrated into the work of the school, and certainly not connected to a career ladder that leads to full-time work. Nevertheless, schools and unions have the ability to create career ladders. Somewhat fewer than one hundred of the twelve hundred teacher education programs in the country are designed to assist para-educators in navigating the training route toward becoming a teacher (Hentschke, 1994).

The career ladder plan at the San Francisco Unified School District approached this problem, though in a very limited way. The union and district crafted a plan that allowed aides to continue working while they finished an undergraduate degree and earned a teaching credential, and then the district guaranteed them a teaching job.

Creating a training program that begins with para-educator experience can pay substantive dividends for school quality. Conventional teacher education programs choose candidates on the basis of their scholastic record alone, assuming that good GPA, SAT, or GRE results will yield a good teacher. Para-educator programs have academic entrance requirements too, and the evidence suggests that they are comparable to those in other programs at the same schools, but they also pick candidates exclusively from para-educators who have had successful experiences with children in classrooms. These candidates have substantive experience before they begin teacher education.

Because para-educators are often funded through federal categorical programs, they tend to be found at the toughest schools, ones that frequently have high turnover and high vacancy rates among regular teachers. Where regular teachers frequently flee such schools after acquiring enough seniority under the contract to command a transfer, para-educators more frequently live in the neighborhood and are comfortable in the setting. It has been argued that financial support for paraprofessionals in college is highly rational because their attrition is so much less than for conventional teachers (Hentschke, 1994). On this basis, subsidy makes an economic as well as a social contribution to education.

Making workers other than teachers part of the educational process, part of the school decisional network, and part of the school also makes social sense. Education needs to be a way up for adults as well as for children. And jobs in education need to be decent jobs for those on the low end of the totem pole as well as those at the top. Connecting unions to the lowest-paid workers as well as the highest should be an important organizing strategy.

PORTABLE PENSIONS AND BENEFITS

Localized pensions and benefits create pronounced rigidity in the teacher labor market. Just as teacher job protection is tied to a particular employer, so too are benefits. Pensions are largely part of state plans in which employee contributions are only matched by the state at retirement. Moving employment out of state carries heavy penalties. Other fringe benefits, particularly health benefits, are usually school district specific. Within states, the patterning effect of collective bargaining has created similarity among districts, but movement is not seamless. These rigidities will not serve the fluid, school-based labor market we foresee. Career protection for teachers requires that they have the ability to move from place to place; their leverage in the market is their capacity to move, whether they exercise it or not. Moreover, to speak of careers means considering different intensities of work during a lifetime: highly intense activities during some years, less activity during periods of child rearing or other family responsibilities, work that may be split between schools for educators who practice a specialty or who work on special projects. Pensions need to travel and benefits need to continue through the ebb and flow of employment.

In health care and other benefits, where services must be locally delivered, the unions themselves should serve as the plan holder, contracting with HMOs and other care providers. Because the heath care industry is in such flux, including consideration of various national insurance plans, it is impossible to make specific recommendations about this point. The key is to move access to health care from the employer to the occupation so that benefits continue even when employment status changes or when one is not working for a time.

The Current System

Teachers' retirement plans are creatures of their individual state governments. Auriemma, Cooper, and Smith (1992), in their study of the fifty state teacher pension plans, found that these programs suffer from a least four deficiencies.

Perhaps first and foremost, they are not portable. A teacher who moves to a new teaching position in a different state must begin again in a different retirement plan. Most teacher retirement systems are structured as defined benefit plans in which benefit entitlement is determined by a formula that accounts for years of service and level of salary (Bodie, Shoven, and Wise, 1989). Moving to a new system results in lost vesting and a potential decline in lifetime retirement earnings.

In addition, teachers' retirement plans are not equitable. Different states offer different levels of benefit. Often it is difficult for a teacher who is considering a move to a different state to determine the precise nature of the retirement structure in force there.

Because teacher pension plans operate as state government services rather than as independent savings and capital accrual programs, investment in and withdrawal of dollars from the plans is highly restricted and restrictive. Teachers have little or no control over general pension policies and programs. Moreover, in recent years, teacher retirement plans have been subject to state political maneuvering; states have borrowed against the plans in times of fiscal crisis.

A Nationwide Pension System

We propose that a nationwide pension system be established for elementary and secondary teachers. The plan, which could be patterned on the model of TIAA-CREF, the organization that pioneered retirement plans for educators, would have several salutary effects.

A nationwide system would be portable. Teachers would be free to move to different states without jeopardizing accrued retirement benefits.

The system would be equitable. Interstate pension plan differences would disappear.

The program would be independent. Not administered by any state (or federal) agency, the new pension system would be established as a trust with responsibility for investment in the hands of a chief administrative officer (trustee) overseen by a pension committee.

The plan would be flexible. Designed as a defined contribution system, it would function for individual employees much like a tax-deferred savings account. The employer (and sometimes the employee) would contribute to the plan regularly and the dollars would be held in trust until the employee is ready to retire. Benefit levels would be determined by total contributions and investment earnings of dollars in the account, and employees would have some choice about where their money is invested.

We recognize that designing and implementing a nationwide pension system is a complex and difficult undertaking. Certainly no action should be taken that jeopardizes retirement earnings for the large numbers of teachers nearing the end of their careers. Thus a phased-in approach might be the best. For example, while the new plan is being fully developed, states could enact interim interstate pension portability agreements. In addition, for employees who are not within a few years of retirement, existing state plans might begin to serve as the base with multi-cross-state supplemental plans made available. Fully portable plans might be phased in for teachers hired as of a particular date.

REDEFINING TENURE

The assault on tenure now forming in state capitals is partly the result of the failure of school systems to create substantive evaluation systems and the failure of unions to develop peer review or other robust professional means of ensuring quality. It puts unions on the defensive, and that is unfortunate, because elements of tenure are undeniably necessary for a well-functioning education system.

Every teacher needs the basic free speech provisions that allow a teacher to choose books, make assignments, and initiate classroom discussion on controversial topics. No institution could long exist if its members were under constant doubt about what was approved speech and what was forbidden. It is in the interest of the state to retain these protections, and any union worth its salt will fight to the death for them.

The employment security aspects of tenure present another question. Ultimately, any organization must deal with the question of how much economic security is possible. In a setting where schools need the flexibility to combine the talents they need, and to recombine them frequently, seniority in assignment as a means of economic security makes little sense.

But seniority does make sense as an accrued property right. There are relatively high levels of societal agreement that over time people ought to gain the right to a continuing stream of economic payments—continued employment, severance pay, early retirement options. The violation of these norms over the last decade of corporate downsizing is just now beginning to prick the social conscience.

Under the hiring hall plan presented here, persons who were not employed at a school would become part of a pool of workers in transition between jobs. Members of the pool would be supported by a fund financed by all employees as a part of the districtwide bargaining agreements. The length of time an employee would be economically supported while in the pool would depend on the employee's seniority in the union.

Union members between jobs could be assigned temporary work for which they qualified. In this sense the pool would work just as the substitute pools in some city districts do now, and some temporary assignments could be performed in this manner. For example, districts or regions could maintain a small corps of teachers to fill in for school staffs engaged in professional development. The Pittsburgh, Pennsylvania, schools maintained such an arrangement during the 1980s, when high school teachers were absent from their schools for six-week periods while attending the district's Schenley Academy for professional development.

Meanwhile, the hiring hall would be performing its primary functions: trying to match members with positions and working with members on skill development to increase their attractiveness in the labor market. Because pensions and benefits rested outside the employing organization altogether, there would be much more fluidity among school districts, states, and regions of the country.

ENCOURAGING TEACHERS TO OWN THEIR PROFESSION

When the word *ownership* is applied to teachers, it is usually in the psychological sense: teachers feeling "bought in" or invested in program initiatives at their school. As crucial as this level of ownership is, we believe it is not sufficient. Teachers also need ownership of their craft or work, and they need ownership of the intellectual property involved. Unions can help in two ways.

The first is to allow teachers to create schools themselves—cooperative enterprises, professional service corporations, teacher-run schools. None of this denies the need for leadership; small schools need it even more than large ones. But it does deny the need for the brand of bureaucratic leadership that characterizes too many school principals today. To the extent to which schooling is marketized, unions will need to assist their members in full participation in those markets. Otherwise, the outside market forces will be pitted against the existing core of unionized teachers.

Second, unions ought to help teachers gain distinction as teachers. If the market for educators becomes more fluid, teachers will come to take on market value based on their reputation and skill. Those who are thought of highly will be sought after and—particularly in metropolitan areas—will have more opportunities to move from school to school.

Part of creating a quality labor market involves working with teachers to make them attractive to schools, and developing the capacity of teachers to gain notice and value in this fluid society. One of the reasons that teacher salaries remain undifferentiated compared with other occupations is the lack of ability on the part of any teacher to clearly demonstrate a disproportionate benefit to a school employer.

As schools are financed now, any teacher with thirty pupils creates the same flow of attendance-based funding as does any other teacher with thirty pupils. A good teacher, a bad teacher, a young and inexpensive teacher, an older and more expensive teacher, in revenue terms they are all the same. Under these conditions, it is not surprising that schools do not honor experience in teaching and that a senior teacher makes only about twice the wages of a beginner, this in marked contrast to most other occupations.

Changes in the way education is provided may alter the economic calculus of teachers in profound ways. Parental and student choice among schools creates strong pressures for differentiation among schools, an explicit mission or educational style, and a need to pick teachers with compatible style and talents. Choice inevitably challenges both district assignment plans and union seniority rules in job claiming.

Legal challenges to school financing practices also have the effect of making older, more experienced teachers more expensive to the individual school rather than the school district budget as a whole. Most districts allocate teaching positions to a school, not a specified number of dollars. Popular schools, usually those in more affluent neighborhoods, are often staffed by more experienced, expensive teachers. Lawsuits in Los Angeles and throughout the country have challenged this finance mechanism as a racial inequity. The Rodriguez decree in Los Angeles emerged from a 1986 complaint that alleged that "poor and minority children receive inferior educations" as a result of attending "aging, overcrowded schools where teachers are young and inexperienced." If schools are allocated dollars rather than positions, they will have to think and plan explicitly regarding what added talents and capacity senior teachers bring to a school. A market will begin to exist in individual talent and attractiveness that no seniority-and-education salary schedule can fully capture.

Individualizing the value of talent will then bring the question of productivity to local school consciousness. There will be strong incentive for schools to seek a differentiated mix of employees, to pay dearly for needed talent and to hire more readily available talent as inexpensively as possible. Education, like other avenues of work in the last generation, will become subject to strong rationalizing tendencies that favor contracting out and the substitution of technology for human labor.

Unions ought to make it possible for teachers and groups of teachers to create and own educational technology. The ability to produce portable educational products has the capacity to make not-so-minor media stars out of teachers who conceive of and develop products. Unions ought to fight for schemes where royalties from software used in schools reverts to public trusts to be reinvested in education.

And unions ought to fight the corporatization of technology. If one looks historically at the textbook field, teachers once played a much greater role in the development, authorship, and control of textbooks than they do now. To be a department chair in a lighthouse school district (a New Trier or a Gross Pointe) or to be a part of a large city school system with its own curriculum department, was to have a hand in the development of new material. Progressively over the last fifty years, product development has become the province of textbook publishers that produce anonymous, staff-written products.

The capacity of the knowledge society suggests that teachers again need to become the creators of the materials they work with. We are seeing a remarkable development among teachers associated with the professional societies in doing just this. The interesting work being done on standards and evaluation, as well as that taking place in developing teaching ideas, is largely coming from the disciplinary societies. Teacher unions ought to help this process by forming working alliances with the societies.

CONTRACTING OUT AND PROFESSIONAL PRACTICE

Contracting out seriously threatens existing union structures. The battle between the AFT and Educational Alternatives, Inc., in Baltimore and Hartford is emblematic of this problem. The Baltimore plan leaves the existing teachers in place but replaces the paraprofessionals with lower-wage college students and interns. Janitors and service personnel were replaced by workers from Johnson Controls. Work and workers once inside the union's bargaining unit are now in the hands of outsiders. The historic labor mission was to take wages out of competition. Contracting out explicitly puts wages back into competition.

In a highly bureaucratized system, the battle lines over contracting out—"taking work out of the bargaining unit"—are relatively clear, but in the evolving labor market both the merits of contracting out and the strategy for organizing around it become more difficult.

It is necessary to distinguish between contracting-out schemes that are driven by exploitation, a simple desire to sweat workers by paying them less for the same jobs, and contracting-out ideas that substantially increase productivity and aid organizational capacity. One of the advantages of contractors is that they can develop specialized service delivery knowledge. The reinventing government idea, in part, rests on freeing the capacity of specialized units, such as food services, to create better ways of working. "It makes sense," write Osborne and Gaebler, "to put the delivery of many public services in private hands (whether for-profit or nonprofit), if by doing so a government can get more effectiveness, efficiency, equity, or accountability" (1992, p. 47).

Some advantages accrue to workers in this. Organizations with specialized knowledge in delivering particular services create internal career ladders for employees, avenues that would be precluded in organizations where service workers were ancillary to the main work of the organization. A cook or a computer programmer will seldom rise in a school organization, but would have a chance of significant responsibility in an organization whose main concern is food service or computing services.

In education, contracting out has been done mostly in ancillary service areas: food service, maintenance, janitorial, legal services, transportation. But increasingly the use of contract workers is coming closer to the core functions of teaching and learning. As decentralization brings budgetary decisions to school sites, teachers themselves—as members of school site decision bodies—are likely to be involved in decisions about the division of labor. Thus it is highly important that the rules about contracting out be both transparently reasonable and enforceable. We suggest two rules.

First, no one should be forced to accept bad services. Janitorial and maintenance service in some school districts is a scandal, or should be. In others it is a model of efficiency, making much of limited resources. Food services show similar variation. No local school should be required to accept the services of either bad contractors or bad employees. Since the people who are most affected by bad services are those in schools, decisions about contracting out should be lodged in the schools themselves.

Second, all contracts should require basic worker protections. There is no question that wage rationalization pressures will be felt in education; one of the bitter ironies of the current workplace relationship is that work in the public sector, which used to be poorly regarded because of its economic sacrifices, is now sought after because of its relative rewards. Thus placing decency structures on contracts tends to level the field, allowing groups of workers internal to an organization to compete with outsiders for contract relationships.

CONCLUSION

Organizing teaching around career security rather than job security anticipates a decline in bureaucratic employment and a rise in more varied work arrangements in which job definitions change frequently and the freedom to move from one job or location to another is prized. It makes sense for unions to anticipate that public employment will evolve in directions unseen in the past. Likewise, it makes sense for unions to redefine the role of the union itself and to find ways to gain legitimacy with workers in a dynamic and knowledge-intensive society.

CHAPTER NINE

Creating New Representation Roles for Unions

U nder industrial unionism, a recognition agreement meant that a union became the exclusive bargaining agent for workers in specified job classifications. The powers granted the union were relatively narrow ones, circumscribed by the restrictions on the scope of bargaining, and the primary means of securing those powers was through collective bargaining. Labor statutes, case law, and practice all evolved around securing wages and working conditions for specified workers for particular employers.

As expectations for teacher unions change, focusing more on the artistic, craft, and professional aspects of teaching, the powers granted unions and the means of securing them need to change also. Craft unions succeed because they are able to extend themselves across an entire field, not just by organizing workers within a single firm. Unions of artists, such as the Screen Actors Guild, gain power over the flow of workers to particular projects, such as films. Professional organizations tend to organize strongly around licensure and certification of would-be practitioners and standards and reviews of practice for working professionals. This is far different from the powers granted in industrial union situations, where unions gain power by being the exclusive representative of all a company's employees in specified jobs.

To fill its representational roles in the evolving workplace for teachers, unions need to take on five roles and to be granted the powers to carry them out.

1. Exclusive representation, in which a school district, county, or regional authority agrees to recognize a union as the sole representative of its employees.

2. Hiring hall agreements, in which schools agree that the union will be the sole source of workers for the school for the jobs where the union represents workers. Teachers and others would not be required to be members of the union to secure their jobs through the hiring hall, but the hiring hall would be able to charge a fee for those services, just as would any personnel agency.

3. Professional services contracts, in which the union brokers an agreement whereby a group of teachers signs up to provide services for a school. In this case, the teachers would not be employees of the school but would be members of their own professional services corporation.

4. Technology agreements, in which the union represents teachers' intellectual property rights and influences the development and adoption of teaching technologies.

5. A strong stake in teacher licensing, education, and professional development, whereby unions support rigorous training and certification programs before the title *teacher* could be used, making unions full partners in initial teacher education and ongoing professional development.

EXCLUSIVE REPRESENTATION

An exclusive representation agreement for a school district or a local educational authority continues the American tradition of a single union for a given body of workers. Experiments in proportional representation, such as those that existed in California between 1965 and 1975 in which competing unions shared the same workplace, have largely proven to be unwieldy and a burden on management. If there are to be battles between unions, it is better that management not be caught in the middle.

Exclusive representation through a recognition agreement creates an obligation for education agencies to recognize unions who represent the majority of their employees. In fluid employment situations, where the question of who is or is not an employee comes into play, the matter becomes more complex, and we speak to this question in Chapter Eight, but the principle remains. For a labor relations system to be stable and fair, unions need the security of recognition and a master contract.

The history of labor relations teaches us that recognition agreements are essential. The legal tradition that prevailed before the Wagner Act (from which teacher labor relations statutes were drawn) allowed "yellow dog" contracts in which employers could demand agreements not to join unions as a condition of employment, allowed blacklisting of union sympathizers, and allowed the firing of union activists. Without protection from these measures, the idea of an independent worker voice, not controlled by management, is not viable.

Exclusive representation also places legal duties on the union to represent all the workers—not just the union members—covered by the agreement, and it requires that they be represented fairly and with a high degree of service. Individual workers are thus empowered to take legal action against their union.

HIRING HALL AGREEMENTS

The more employment relationships are settled at school sites, the more the craft-type hiring hall gains functional importance and needs to be considered as part of a union security arrangement.

The key consideration is whether the hiring hall should be granted the security of being the sole source of teachers (and other represented employee groups) for schools in areas with which the union has a representation agreement. We believe the hiring hall should be given a strong measure of organizational security, but not an absolute monopoly. Union membership as a condition of employment has been illegal under federal law for nearly half a century, and if this tradition were continued, anyone would be eligible to apply at the hiring hall just as they can now at a personnel office. Still, one faces the possibility of poorly run hiring halls that discourage or discriminate against applicants, just as there are poorly run school personnel offices.

For this reason, we advocate that hiring halls be the personnel office of first resort. Schools would be obliged to seek teachers through the hiring hall mechanism first, before turning to other sources. A persistent failure of a school or schools to use the hiring hall or the hiring hall to have qualified workers available would be grounds for an unfair labor practice complaint, just as failure to bargain in good faith is now.

The hiring hall mechanism also has another source of security, that generated by other workers themselves. Traditional craft unions and professional associations gained power through craft identity and solidarity, the association of workers with their occupation and their organization. A well-functioning hiring hall would find teachers in school sites—where employment decisions are being made—highly reluctant to choose people from outside their own association.

PROFESSIONAL SERVICE CONTRACTS

Although not yet common in education outside of top administrative posts, professional practice contracts are the means by which increasing numbers of high-paid workers link themselves to organizations. In some instances, such as the physicians at the huge Kaiser Permanente health maintenance organization, professional employees form their own corporation and contract with the HMO for professional services.

The ability of teacher unions to form this type of organization is an important ingredient in what is likely to be a long-lasting period of experimentation in how schools are to be organized. If charter schools become organizationally separated from parent school districts or if private corporations become empowered to compete with existing public schools for charters, then teachers will need a means of organization in these new arenas. Teacher unions should create machinery to allow members to form professional practice organizations and to support members in so doing. This approach will put the unions in a much stronger position than they will have if they persist in fighting a war of attrition against structural changes in the way education is delivered.

Our goal in these proposals is to link union security with an institutionally useful labor market, one that provides high-quality workers, adjusts for supply and demand, and offers career continuity for educators without hobbling school reform and change in the process.

Still, no area of labor law and practice is more controversial than that giving any exclusive powers to unions. Conservatives and libertarians consider these powers inappropriately coercive. Economic theorists answer that a measure of coercion is present in all large groupings, including industry and trade associations, as a means of solving the problem of some gaining a free ride at the expense of others.

Historically, labor practices and statutes have attempted to find a power balance between an institutional setting that keeps unions from a stranglehold on labor supply and one that makes unions powerless—for if the union is powerless, then other mechanisms for expression of worker interest and redress of grievances are required. It is beyond the scope of this book but nonetheless interesting to observe the enormous increase in employment litigation that has taken place precisely as union representation has dropped in the United States.

TECHNOLOGY AGREEMENTS

Unions need to be both knowledgeable and aggressive about educational technology. Clearly, the microcomputer revolution is unlike any previous ed-tech revolution, all oversold and many gone without a trace. Microcomputing is one of the legs of postmodern society and organization and is already much more invasive than most educators realize. Productivity increases in education will be tied to increased use of microcomputers and to the substitution of combinations of human and computer linkages for traditional teaching. The notion that computers can only supplement teaching will be swept aside as the cost of human services increases and the cost of computer intervention continues to plummet by as much as 25 percent a year. Increasingly, technology will allow students and parents to purchase instruction directly rather than going through teachers and school districts. Organizing around computing and its capabilities is as important for teachers today as organizing around the assembly line was for auto workers in the 1930s.

Intellectual Property

A lot of people stand to make a lot of money in the educational technology business. As currently organized, teachers will not be among them. While book publishers and multimedia companies reorganize around software design, teachers are relegated to occasionally testing new products or serving as consultants. This is the case even though thousands of teachers are well trained in educational software design and programming, and many more are proficient in applications usage.

While not all teachers want or need to become software and multimedia developers, many of them should, and their unions could help them. As we suggested in Chapter Eight, unions ought to make it possible for teachers and groups of teachers to create educational technology and have rights to the intellectual property they create. Some possibilities:

- *Negotiate royalty payments.* Unions operate as collective bargaining agents for large groups of teachers; they might also act as individual agents for software developers, just as actors or literary agents do now, bringing the work of new developers to the attention of publishers and distributors.

- *Provide venture capital.* Unions control or have influence over huge pension funds. Teachers' projects could be good investments, and a percentage of union funds ought to be invested in teacher-run enterprises for technology development.

- *Increase research and development.* A tiny surcharge on the price of software could finance a huge increase in educational research and development, the type of investment that will be necessary to move the United States forward in cognitive approaches to teaching. It could also finance, for the first time, real support for the continuing education of teachers and provide legitimacy to the position of teacher as researcher.

Direction of Smart Technologies

As the history of flexible manufacturing and numerically controlled machine tools shows us, technology is never worker neutral. Computer technologies can be arrayed in ways that make the underlying work inherently more complex and challenging or more routine and repetitive. Teachers know this is true of student work as well as their own, and the dumbing down of teaching has been a call to arms among activists for decades.

Control over computer technology is almost entirely a function of software design rather than of the design of computers and peripherals. Teacher unions are in a position to broker teacher participation in software development and design and to discuss its relationship to the way schools operate.

Unions can also act as a technology intermediary with teachers, parents, and children. Panels of teachers should review new software, and they should have students review the programs, too, for quite often students are the more adventuresome computer users.

TEACHER LICENSING, EDUCATION, AND PROFESSIONAL DEVELOPMENT

The old-line professions organized around educating and socializing new members, controlling access to the workplace, and establishing a lifelong economic and social relationship. In teaching, the relationship between unions and occupational development and access has been much more tangential. Unions clearly involve themselves in teacher development, but the function takes a backseat to collective bargaining. Considering unionism in an era of knowledge work invites rethinking labor's role in educating and developing teachers, particularly in teacher licensure, initial teacher training, and continuing professional development.

Credentials That Count

Without both specified training and a license, a lawyer, physician, or architect can't practice the profession. Licensure allows these occupations to control entry to their fields and to give great significance to the training programs leading up to acceptance into the occupation. For teaching, however, licensure is a muddle. Public policy and the market for teachers drives licensure in two directions simultaneously. Advocates of higher formal entry standards seek longer training programs and more rigorous examinations. Organizations such as the Holmes Group, to which both national unions belong, and the National Council for the Accreditation of Teacher Education (NCATE), strongly supported by the NEA, seek to raise the floor of standards under all teacher education. Meanwhile, the forces of supply and demand cause even existing licensure standards to be trivialized, and advocates of a more fluid and diverse supply of teachers seek alternative pathways that in some cases destroy the meaning of licensing altogether.

Of these two pressures, supply and demand is always the stronger. Providing education is a constitutional requirement in most states, and schooling is compulsory for students. Under these conditions, states and school districts do what they must to fill classrooms. For most of the century, there has been a serious undersupply of teachers, and even during times when job seekers outnumbered classroom positions, there were still large areas of chronic undersupply, including bilingual teachers, special educators, and teachers for central cities and isolated rural areas. As a result, states and school districts routinely provided waivers. In 1982, emergency credentials represented between 10 percent and 20 percent of all those issued in California, Colorado, Florida, New Jersey, Ohio, and Pennsylvania. It is estimated that as many as 200,000 teachers hold emergency credentials (National Center on Education and the Economy, 1990). The pressures that produced these credentials are not likely to abate.

Even though teacher unions have taken strongly worded positions against compromised licensure, it has been mostly a war of words. In 1990, the NEA Representative Assembly resolved that "Emergency, irregular, or substandard licenses, together with misassignments out of field, must be eliminated in all forms" (National Education Association, 1990). Still, the numbers of cases in which teachers have taken direct action, refusing to teach alongside an improperly credentialed coworker, are extremely rare. These kinds of actions, universal understanding, and workplace enforcement of the credential system would be routine in a craft- or profession-based job market.

Yet, even in those occupations that have traditionally maintained high occupational specificity and strong boundaries in the right to practice, we are seeing substantial changes. Work formerly done by physicians is now routinely done by physician's assistants or registered nurses, and bedside nursing is frequently undertaken by workers with lower levels of certification than registered nurses. "Across the country, many nurses have been shifted to outpatient centers where the daily action is swifter and continuous and their responsibilities are very specific to their education. There is very little 'care' delivered in terms of patient comforts and housekeeping" (Herrmann, 1995, p. 26). The change in health care delivery has caused great stress for the American Nurses Association, whose members face layoffs as the health care system attempts cost containment. Some 25 percent of hospitals planned staff reductions in 1995 (Herrmann, 1995). At the same time, nurse unions face the problem of job role reidentification, with representatives of Registered Nurses seeking the ability to do higher-skilled work while holding on to jurisdiction over nonmedical patient care.

Education has only begun to feel the pressures for rationalization noted in the health care industry. As forms of instructional technology increase, and as certification of student competence is achieved by tests created outside the schools, consideration of instructional alternatives is likely to follow. Software and telecommunications have the ability to transform the class size discussion into a discussion about the meaning of a class itself.

A workable certification system responds both to the need for high standards and to the need for labor market flexibility. The career-ladder-with-teaching-at-the-top proposal designs a flexible teaching labor market that can bring in novices or people with skills needed in a given setting without violating standards. By accommodating various descriptions of paraprofessionals, paying them fairly, and making them part of a community of educators, the title *teacher* and the status that accrues to that title could be protected.

At the same time, drawing a line in the sand over the teacher assignment is likely to be unsuccessful, either because teachers are not willing to enforce the distinction, as in the case of colleagues teaching outside their area of proper certification, or because the work of teachers will change markedly, making it difficult to associate a single teacher with a group of students. In a situation in which students learn a lesson or topic—or a whole course—from interactive software in a room overseen by a para-educator applied to a project directed by a certified teacher, and are examined by a portfolio viewed by a panel of educators and noneducators, who is the teacher in charge?

As autonomous organizations, schools will gain some control over the mixture of personnel they want to use. School committees, as they negotiate their enterprise compacts (see Chapter Seven), can decide the mixture of teachers and other personnel they want to use. A school with a large immigrant population might decide to use multilingual paraprofessionals to conduct certain classes and talk to the parents in their own language. The school would be allowed to tap into this pool of talent, but *it would be forbidden to use the word* teacher *to describe such uncertified paraprofessionals.* Over time, being able to attract certified teachers would be one of the marks of a good school, just as being able to attract faculty with earned doctorates became a hallmark of high-quality colleges and universities. Partly because the quality of the doctorate remained high, and in many disciplines increased in rigor, it continued to be desirable, and the supply of doctoral candidates rose to meet the demand. There is nothing inherently keeping elementary and secondary teaching from the same market dynamic. High standards may actually increase the numbers of applicants.

The Education of Teachers

How teachers are certified reflects how they are trained. The traditional model of train-test-teach shows signs of cracking. Increasingly, the distinction between learning how to teach and teaching itself is being questioned, and the notion that a novice can be fully or even adequately trained as a teacher is being challenged by a more apt model of long-term growth and development. Since the late 1980s, more than two hundred new institutional arrangements called professional development schools have come into being, many of them connected to major school reform networks, such as the Comer School Development Program and the Coalition of Essential Schools. These models have gained favorable notice from the Holmes Group, the Carnegie Forum on Education and the Economy, and the National Board for Professional Teaching Standards (Darling-Hammond and McLaughlin, 1995).

The excitement about substantive changes in teacher education and professional development challenges unions to rethink their relationship to professional development. Historically, unions have sought to influence teacher education by gaining control of teacher licensure boards. Their own union-run teacher development activities have been a markedly ancillary part of teacher training and development. As a part of the 1980s reforms, both unions evidenced renewed interest in actively participating in professional development as opposed to governing it. In the process, the idea that continuous learning should be embedded in teaching began to come to the fore. The AFT founded its QuEST conferences, whose attendance now rivals that at its biannual convention, and the NEA set up the National Center for Innovation. In Miami, Cincinnati, Rochester, Louisville, New York, and several other cities, teacher unions created specific programs for teacher development tied to the reforms being undertaken there. Some consider this a failed experiment. As the economy worsened, many of those programs were abandoned or curtailed. Programs founded by foundation grants and volunteerism were largely unsustainable in the face of budget cuts and the departure of key personnel.

However, it is possible to build on these experiences. While unions are not likely to be successful in going it alone to create a new genre of teacher professional development, they can be powerful collaborators. The professional development school model offers an institutional structure for unions to help teachers embed learning in their own work. The model has the potential to overturn the traditional view of staff development in which virtually any workshop or conference conducted outside a school counts as legitimate staff development, while "authentic opportunities to learn for colleagues *inside* the school do not" and the understanding of people outside the field is regarded as more important than that of teachers (Lieberman, 1995, p. 591).

Unions are potentially powerful collaborators because they negotiate the allocation of time in school and define a teacher's official duty day and psychological work role relationships. "You just don't have time available to you to think of new ideas, to reflect. So time is number one," one teacher said (Wilson, 1993, p. 92).The pacing of the school day and the allocation of time within it are so intense that there remains little reflective time available. Finding time to go to the bathroom, get a glass of water, or make a phone call is difficult enough; reflection is impossible. It does not have to be this way. Teachers in other countries, notably Japan, spend much of their working time outside of direct instruction, and the experiments of past decade suggest that teachers in the United States could do the same. We know that there are a number of ways of integrating learning into the act and practice of teaching. (For additional discussion of this point, see Lieberman, 1995.) Here are some examples:

• *By building new roles such as teacher leader, peer reviewer, and teacher researcher.*

The staffing pattern of U. S. public schools is in stark contrast to that in other countries. In the United States, leadership is equated with administration—in 1986, for instance, our schools employed approximately one administrative staff member for each 2.5 teachers; about 38 percent of the budget went for teacher salaries and less than 1 percent for staff development. This differs substantially from the pattern in other countries (Darling-Hammond and McLaughlin, 1995).

Expanding teacher roles helps get the work done without feeding the hierarchy. But it is not simply a question of adding duties. New teacher roles have to fit into the life of the school.

• *By creating new structures, such as those that evolve in site-based management.*

For openers, school schedules that allow teams of teachers to work together and create common preparation periods both break down the isolation and begin to instill a culture of "we" rather than "I." The notion that "all of us are smarter than any of us" was explicitly part of work life reforms in Jefferson County, Kentucky, for example.

Learning to work in teams taxes teachers accustomed to solitary practice. Just as practices from successful schools do not easily flow to other schools, practices from successful teams do not necessarily infuse whole schools. Jealousy and competitiveness may result rather than collegiality and mutual assistance.

There is a decent history of union experience about teaming. The NEA's Mastery in Learning Project, which ran for a decade before coming to a conclusion in 1995, did a highly credible job of tracking its own progress, and other experiments have been subject to documentation—not all of it glowing—about the success of teamwork (McClure, 1995). What is lacking is recognition that changing structures are likely to be a relatively permanent force within education, something that unions need to organize around for the long run, not for a quick turnaround.

Although it may be true that without other reforms, school-based management does not lead anywhere, it is equally true that without changes in teacher work roles, the changes in curriculum and pedagogy required to move toward teaching for understanding are highly unlikely. There is no way for unions to duck the manifest conflicts between the existing work role system and the needs of new schools.

•   *By working on new tasks, such as proposal writing, creating standards and assessments, and documenting practices that work.*

Teachers can influence changes in their work by developing the voice to effectively describe what they do. When part of teaching work becomes the documenting of effective practices, then a sequestered voice is brought into discussions about what teaching should be like.

This can take place in straightforward ways such as teachers documenting their own best practices. The teacher-run staff development program developed in the Petaluma (California) school system allowed teachers for the first time to think of themselves as experts with something to say to other teachers.

Although a sea change in teaching is vital if schools are to cope with the demands they face, it is unlikely that such a change will occur on its own. Teachers will need extended opportunities to "practice" in different ways, to seek their own grants and create their own programs, to explore learning outside the usual one-day in-service programs, and to become articulate about their own standards and practice. Teacher voice can only become strong and articulate through use.

• *By creating a culture of inquiry in the school and also in the union.*

It's hard to be a learner and a teacher at the same time. But it is necessary. The idea of a school as a center for inquiry has roots as deep as Dewey, and running back to some of the heroic teachers in Chicago who were instrumental in founding the teacher union movement. Becoming a learner in one's own classroom runs counter to most of the structures schools have in place. There is very little time available in the current school day for teachers to review their work, comment on one another's success or moments of frustration, or examine the lessons inherent in an interaction between teacher and student.

Unions can be much more influential in creating a culture of inquiry than they commonly believe. Under existing collective bargaining arrangements, and even more so under the ideas we are presenting in this book, unions are the initiating party with ideas about changing teaching work. If unionists believe that new ideas in schooling must flow from teachers rather than from school administrators, then they must first organize around this proposition. They must treat alternative ways of designing school days and years seriously, so that it is physically possible for teachers to learn in their workplaces. Union leaders, as some now do, need to make this issue their own. The notion of "time to teach" needs to be expanded into "time to learn."

One of the best ways to model inquiry in the schools is to model it within the union. Both unions, but the NEA in particular, develop conversational orthodoxies in which some subjects are virtually undiscussable. A serious outbreak of free speech would be of great benefit.

Outside Schools

There are also things unions can do outside of schools to influence teacher professional development. Clearly, unions have a representational role in the organizations that devise curriculum, set teacher education standards, and devise enforcement. However, unions are not important solely as a means for teachers to gain parity or control over these agencies. Rather, the important question is the nature of policies decided upon and how they bring what we are calling knowledge creation into the classrooms. Unions are important, not so much because they represent teachers' prejudices about training and development as because their leaders or representatives understand the practice and psychology of teaching and how to move and shape teaching as an occupation using policy interventions.

Unions should bring craft knowledge of teaching to policy construction, thus allowing, as Cohen and Barnes (1993) suggest, educational reform to be built into the everyday activities of teaching. Some examples: Curriculum and curriculum frameworks could be much more educative than they are. States such as California and Vermont, which have adopted curriculum frameworks, pride themselves in having done so with teacher "input," but this means that they have involved at the most a few dozen teachers. The process of diffusing the frameworks has largely been modeled on old, behavioristic pedagogy, not teaching for understanding and knowledge. Teachers still go to short-term in-service workshops, get notebooks, and are handed the rules relating to the new curricula. They adopt a new curriculum rather than coming to understand it, and in particular without understanding their own teaching in relation to it.

Several years ago, Philadelphia teachers participated in creating a splendid ninth-grade world history program. Groups of teachers, supported by Rockefeller Foundation grants, collaborated with faculty members from Temple and Penn in rethinking the standard Eurocentric approaches to a course that was thought to be important but not highly popular with students. They came to understand history and culture as scholars. They devised stunning alternatives, with projects, artifacts, and action-related projects. The process changed the teaching of the participants. But once adopted, the program was installed in binders and "taught" to successive groups of teachers, who, it was reported, grew progressively more resistive and less enthusiastic. Their experience was one of received wisdom rather than learning through experience.

One approach for unions would be to make the policy construction process educative for teachers and their representatives. Unions have not been particularly good at modeling good pedagogy in this regard. While they generate lots of policy—much of it clearly stating what they are against—they seldom link policy construction to deepening the collective wisdom about the object of policy. It is one thing to stand against standardized testing, for example, and quite another to understand the ways testing has evolved in our national educational culture, the role that it plays in sorting students, and what alternatives might be. It is one thing to rest on a policy line that holds that technology can only supplement and never supplant the classroom teacher. It is another to explore the pedagogical implications of technology, how its introduction can profoundly affect learning and authority relationships in classrooms.

Learning about pedagogy can be built into even very ordinary activities. For example, most school districts have textbook selection committees that periodically review basic or supplementary materials for adoption. The usual conversation about these offerings concerns the apparent ease of use, the package of goodies being offered by the publisher or vendor as an inducement, and the quality of the instructor's manual. Why could not unions, in cooperation with organizations such as the National Conference of Teachers of English and their counterparts in other subject areas, create programs that allow teachers who are evaluating textbooks to understand the frontiers of each discipline, the economics of textbook purchasing, and alternatives available to teachers who want to deviate from publisher-paced curriculum. Much could be gained from rethinking what is in the daily work lives of teachers and how these activities could be made more educative.

CONCLUSION

Organizing teaching for the knowledge society logically entails expanding and reshaping the roles played by teacher unions. Unions do not relinquish concern for teachers' economic welfare or the fairness of the workplace, but these traditional matters are regarded from a new context in which teachers claim rights to both intellectual definition and intellectual property. Expanding the roles played by teacher unions would be greatly aided by revising the statutes under which teachers organize, a topic considered in the next chapter.

CHAPTER TEN

Reforming the Labor Law

~~~

Teacher unions, like other labor organizations, started as social movements, but they gained status and influence because they gained a statutory anchor. Labor law legitimates, protects, and spreads the work of organizers. As Bell (1973) notes, union growth in the United States has always been dependent on government support. Although it is clear that the upsurge of unionism in the 1930s was indigenous, its *institutionalization* was possible only under the National Labor Relations Board.

In teacher labor relations, it was only after states began to adopt "little NLRA" statutes that collective bargaining expanded rapidly across the country. Statutes could be copied from one state to another, and the introduction of a statute provided an orderly way to make the transition into collective bargaining. It is not accidental, for example, that the educational labor relations statute in California bears a strong resemblance to that in Indiana. Statutory borrowing from one state to another generated a common ethos and indeed a common handbook of law and practice, Wollett and Chanin's *The Law and Practice of Teacher Negotiations* (1974), which served as the touchstone for the institutional patterning of the NEA. Collective bargaining was able to spread from place to place relatively easily because each school district and each union did not have to invent it anew. While they had to go through a psychological and political revolution that we have called generational change (Kerchner and Mitchell, 1988), the behaviors and structures of collective bargaining could be copied from other districts (DiMaggio and Powell, 1983). Without a similar patterning effect, unionism for the knowledge society is not likely to spread very far very fast.

Much of the current discussion about labor relations has been focused on repairing perceived flaws in the structure and application of the National Labor Relations Act construct, and it is necessary for the framers of worker protection laws to grapple with the special problems of knowledge workers as well as power inequities in organization that make it easy for determined employers to defeat unions. However, drafting within the current framework is not sufficient to reflect the enormous change taking place in the nature of work.

The framework of the Wagner Act (1935) was a triumph when both work processes and employment were stable. The law itself came into being when industrial work was relatively mature; it was only five years later that the census revealed that the rapidly growing service sector of the economy employed more people than did manufacturing. Thus a statute intended by its framer to create a new dialogue between labor and capital (Barenbaum, 1993) became more narrowly construed as a law of employees and managers.

Today, the stable corporation is losing ground to short-term ventures, network forms of multinational organizations. Work is changing, too, as the boundaries of traditional jobs are shattered by technology and reengineering. Homework, labor brokering, contracting out, the use of contingent workers, and independent contracting have made the old employee-based systems of worker protections both ineffectual and increasingly irrelevant. Quoting Pleasure and Greenfield (1995, p. 181), the problem we face is, "How do we facilitate worker representation in an economy in which work is unstable and the marketplace increasingly resembles a bazaar?" The answer involves both rethinking conventional labor relations law governing public workers within the framework established by the National Labor Relations Act and the similar state statutes, and attending to the broader law of work affecting everyone.

LAW OF WORK

Particularly since the Civil Rights Act of 1964, employee rights have been more widely advanced by statute than through collective bargaining. Giving women and persons of color recourse to the courts has caused a revolution in personnel law and has created worker protections frequently more potent than those provided by bargained contracts. The advancement and enforcement of rights for women, African Americans, Latinos, students, and persons with disabilities has created an interest group democracy that we recognize as both advancing rights and leading to an enormous rise in workplace litigation (Heckscher, 1988).

The existing law of work creates simultaneous insecurity for employees and danger to employers, who face unsure waters and the possibility of large jury awards regarding employment discrimination, wrongful dismissal, and occupational health and safety violations. It is still, as Fox (1974) observed, a mistrustful, legalistic work society that reflects a declining spiral of faith and commitment at a time when expanding knowledge work seeks to create the opposite.

Historically, the law of work was determined by the needs of the surrounding society. For example, the English common law concept of master-and-servant derived from a set of social and economic relationships embedded in agricultural and artisanal society. Each successive mode of production created its own law of work—including industrial society, which edged toward making unions a partner in the enterprise but which never involved the structural forms of involvement, such as works councils, found in European social democracies.

For the first time in many decades, serious attention has been given to reshaping work relationships. Both the report of the Commission on the Future of Worker-Management Relations (1995) and the critical commentary following release of the report suggest that observers of all political stripes believe a new legal environment is needed (Troy, 1995). A knowledge-era law of work needs to solve specific problems of the emerging labor market. First, it needs to *encourage knowledge work* rather than routine production or service work. Our national policy about work ought to encourage employers to form jobs requiring the creation, exploitation, and application of knowledge: smart jobs rather than dumb ones. Second, it ought to *exploit flexibility without exploiting workers* and make a virtue of the relative openness in the U. S. labor market and labor force. This requires a set of general protections and guarantees that apply to all workers, whether employed at the moment or not. Third, *the capacity for dispute resolution should be increased and the legalisms attached to the law of work should be decreased.*

These changes in work statutes are all extremely important for teachers. Each of these areas represents a sizable undertaking, and to explore them fully would detract from our more specific and immediate task of considering a new labor law for teachers. Still, it is important to understand the extent to which the law of teaching work rests within the context of law for workers in general. Teachers are not likely to gain fair treatment and progressive policies for their work if the people who vote in school board elections and send their children to school do not have those conditions in their own lives.

A NEW LABOR RELATIONS STATUTE FOR EDUCATORS

It is both good news and bad news that the educational reforms of the past decade have been accomplished without major changes in labor relations statutes. It is true, as traditionalists argue, that the current law is intended to be organic and flexible. That the experiments of the last decade or so were possible is evidence that changes in law are not necessary to permit experiments with changing labor relations. However, a closer look reveals a legal structure designed to preserve industrial-style labor relations rather than allow them to change easily. First, current statutes are subject to interpretation that would chill any substantive workplace reforms of the sorts we have described and reduce educational reform to narrow managerialism resulting in employee participation within an entirely management-controlled environment. Second, the current statutes have no incentives for schools and districts to change. Labor law as we know it is built around large hierarchies and centralized control. If we want schools to change, we need to alter the institutional incentives for change, and the labor code is one of these incentives.

We see eight substantive mismatches between the existing laws and educational reform:

- *Coverage:* Which workers are eligible for protection under labor statutes?

- *The bargaining unit:* Which employees should be grouped together to be represented by unions?

- *Cooperation:* Under what legal aegis can unions and employers develop joint working arrangements?

- *The scope of bargaining:* What issues are employees and unions supposed to discuss?

- *Peer review:* How can employees take on the professional responsibility of judging the quality of work performed by their colleagues?

- *The hiring hall:* How can educational workers' jobs be organized around schools rather than school districts?

- *Dispute resolution:* How can workers and managers learn to solve workplace problems peacefully, and what recourse will the system offer when they fail?

- *Statute administration:* What role do state labor boards (or other jurisdictional bodies) play in making the new statute run smoothly?

Which Workers Are Covered?

Both employed professionals and independent contractors have precarious status under existing labor law.

Professionals and others whose work definition includes making organizational decisions run afoul of the legal tradition that excludes managers from protection under labor law. The NLRA posits a fundamental dividing line between labor and management. Legislative history and court decisions interpreting the law assert that collective bargaining by people on the management side of that line would create intolerable divided loyalties. Employees affiliated with management would be torn between their responsibilities to their employers and their solidarity with other employees in the union movement. These conflicts could impair job performance and threaten the organization (Rabban, 1989, p. 1778).

The tradition of denying bargaining rights to supervisors causes potential problems when the work of teachers takes on decisions that traditionally were the province of managers. The 1980 U.S. Supreme Court decision in *National Labor Relations Board* v. *Yeshiva University* reinforced the separation of workers and managers in higher education, as did a recent case involving nurses (*National Labor Relations Board* v. *Health Care and Retirement Corporation of America,* 1994). The 1947 Taft-Hartley amendments to the NLRA specifically excluded supervisors from coverage under the law, specifying in section 2(11) that supervisors are those who have the authority to hire, transfer, suspend, lay off, recall, promote, discharge, assign, reward, or discipline other employees. Faculty members at Yeshiva were denied collective bargaining rights because their faculty senate and its committees made substantive decisions at their university. Thus they were considered "supervisors" under the law and ineligible for bargaining rights. Although this federal legal doctrine has never been applied to a state case governing public school teachers, it stands as a symbolic barrier, a monument that the law did not intend workers and management to share decisional power (Schlossberg and Fetter, 1986). "In the end the *Yeshiva* case is troubling because it is at war with the idea of consensus between professional employees and their administrators" (p. 15). This legal status is troubling not only to teachers but also to other professional employees.

A second legal issue arises among independent contractors, persons who may work at an organization but are not considered employed by it. With the increasing use of contracting-out mechanisms and part-time contingent labor, and even of professional service contracts, it is becoming a matter of the utmost importance to include independent contractors within the protection of labor laws.

When it passed the Wagner Act in 1935, Congress had in mind protecting workers who moved from workplace to workplace. The scope of protection was not to be limited to single enterprises. The Supreme Court even extended the law's protection to newspaper boys, coverage that outraged publishers, and that was removed by the 1947 amendments. Over time, however, coverage under the labor law has come to be associated with current employment (Pleasure and Greenfield, 1985, p. 184). If education is to be formed around individual schools, and if the relationship of teachers and other employees to those schools is to be flexible and fluid, the rights to representation and coverage need to apply when persons are between jobs. These rights also need to apply whether people are employed directly by the school or serve as independent contractors working within a professional corporation, as many physicians currently do.

The Bargaining Unit

Bargaining unit provisions determine how workers are grouped together for the purposes of negotiation and representation. The goal is to form what the law calls a community of interest among workers, and thus groups are formed according to the type of work they do. Almost always, teachers and professionals wind up in separate units. Classroom aides, janitors, cooks, secretaries, and school security workers nearly always have their own bargaining units. In larger districts they tend to be separated one from another; in smaller ones they are often combined. Sometimes credentialed or licensed workers other than teachers are placed in separate units, too. Thus nurses, counselors, and librarians bargain separately from teachers.

This arrangement undermines two of our reform ideas: the idea embodied in the educational compact—that every adult in the school should be an educator—and the idea of a career ladder with teaching at the top. If everyone who works for money in schools, and students and parents (who work but don't draw salaries), are to be included as part of an enterprise compact, we clearly change the community of interest. It is necessary to do this in order to create learning organizations. There are a number of different ways to think about this problem.

One option would be to create omnibus bargaining units, so-called wall-to-wall arrangements covering all workers in a school. Another is to allow separation by employee group, as is now done, but create through statute parallel responsibilities toward the educational compact arrangements. This parallel arrangement would work well for those workers whose careers are not directly connected to the teacher job ladder, but the para-educators who are in the teacher career ladder need to be in the same bargaining unit as the teachers—mostly because their relationship with the teachers is a very delicate one. At the job site, teachers are colleagues and mentors, but within the occupation teachers are superiors. Teachers will determine who is hired and who is not and the career steps of para-educators. Thus para-educators need to have provisions for equity and fair treatment within the bargaining unit.

Cooperation and Joint Enterprises

Cooperation between labor and management is still legally suspect. Although Senator Robert Wagner espoused cooperation among workers, the law for which he is remembered, and the state statutes derived from it, nearly universally place barriers in the way of a close working relationship between unions and managements. The framers of the law were concerned about so-called company unions, organizations that looked like unions but were dominated by management and formed to forestall worker organization by independent unions.

Section 8(a)(2) of the NLRA provides that it shall be an unfair labor practice for an employer to: "Dominate or interfere with the formation or administration of any labor organization or contribute financial or other support to it: Provided, that . . . an employer shall not be prohibited from permitting employees to confer with him during working hours without loss of pay." Employee organizations—defined in Section 2(5)—included virtually any kind of employee representation committee or organization that deals with wages or working conditions.

Now, however, there is a felt need to form substantive joint enterprises such as professional practice committees and professional development schools without violating the employer assistance or domination prohibition. While recent lower court decisions have seemed to recognize that changing conditions strengthen the case for cooperative employer-employee relations, the Supreme Court has yet to clarify the situation.

We believe that development of a legal structure more conducive to the implementation of professional values requires changes in the concept of company domination. Collegial committees or actual joint operations *need* support from employers. Teachers should be able to form committees that advise and actually make policy, and school authorities should be able to assist those committees with staff support and budgets without violating the labor statute.

We agree with Rabban (1990), who suggested that the definition of company domination should be limited to actual interference with the independent decision making of employee committees. Employees and companies should be able to work together to promote professional values, as long as the employer stops short of attempting to control decisions that have been entrusted to employees. Whether or not an employer's intervention stems from anti-union animus, it can render committees of professional employees useless, so legal limits are still needed. However, the law should stop short of preventing the attempt to work together.

The Scope of Bargaining

As we have in previous work, we advocate an increase in the scope of the relationship between teachers and educational managers. Industrial-style bargaining evokes a legal fiction: that wages and the work rules of teachers can be separated from educational policy. While many critics of collective bargaining have taken pains to show that unions have encroached on the educational policy arena, they miss the point. Even the narrowest constriction of the scope of bargaining— wages, classification of workers, benefits, and hours of work—effectively encumbers virtually all the operating budget of a labor-intensive organization such as a school system. Moreover, the scope of bargaining has a tendency to expand over time as the parties to labor agreements use that vehicle to solve personnel problems and settle disputes. This is most often done without reference to the educational consequences of the agreement, thus creating what we have called *accidental* policymaking. It is the worst of all worlds, preserving the legal position that educational policy remains in the hands of legislatures and school boards while operating in an environment where professional-level employees effectively control the budgetary expenditures and time allocation.

Before the widespread adoption of collective bargaining, public schools attempted to answer the problem of scope through "meet-and-confer" practices that allowed wide-ranging discussions, but left the obligation to act in the hands of management. In some states, such as California, meet-and-confer became a statutory practice of labor relations; in many others it was an informal practice. It was almost universally unpopular. In some locales, meet-and-confer gave rise to very elaborate labor agreements that were indistinguishable from collective bargaining agreements, thus causing outcries from the public and board members who charged that management "had given away the store." In other cases, the process was so inconclusive that teachers dubbed it "meet-and-defer." Thus broad-scope interaction gave way to narrow-scope collective bargaining.

Narrow-scope bargaining, as embodied in the NLRA framework, makes it impossible to solve the problem of professional judgment and public accountability. The Taft-Hartley Amendments of 1947 introduced a phrase that has been adopted in most state teacher bargaining laws. It specified a duty to "confer in good faith with respect to wages, hours, and other terms and conditions of employment" [29 U.S.C. Sec. 158(d) (1982)]. Eleven years later, the U.S. Supreme Court ruled that the requirement to bargain extended only to those subjects mandated by the law, and the law thus created a second category of "permissive" items over which employers could bargain if they wished. During bargaining, employers were restricted from taking unilateral action on mandatory subjects. Thus, for example, an employer could not raise or cut wages. Much of the legal dispute between employers and professional employees, including teachers, surrounds the boundary line between mandatory and permissive issues (Rabban, 1990).

Where some commentators have argued that the solution is simply to broaden the scope of bargaining by eliminating the permissive section and requiring virtually any subject to be bargained to impasse, we feel another route is desirable. Our notion requires a very narrow contract at the school district, regional, or state level, depending on the structure of public schooling. As we suggested in Chapter Six, these contracts would cover only a recognition agreement, salary minimums, the school calendar, basic safety conditions, and the charters of any jointly operated programs such as professional practice schools.

Substantive policy bargaining would be included in the school enterprise compact, and these agreements would be without any restriction whatever. As discussed in Chapter Seven, the rights of the public would be represented in these agreements through the parent representatives. The rights of school district managers to oversee operations and demand quality would be protected by their right to accept or reject completed enterprise compacts. The rights of individual students and parents to choose a good school, and one that responded to their educational concerns, would be protected by the right of choice among different schools.

The rights of the profession to gain flexibility and control over its actions would be represented by the teachers and para-educators, who could create highly restrictive situations or highly dynamic relationships if they so chose. What makes open scope possible in an educational compact where it was impossible under meet-and-confer is the coupling of rights and responsibilities at the school site level. Teachers and local schools could create any sort of work rules they wished, so long as they remained responsible for the budget and the outcomes.

Peer Review

Peer review challenges both the ideology and the practice of current labor relations in rather obvious ways. It also is legally suspect. The courts have held that by achieving the status of exclusive representative for a group of employees, a union also takes on a duty to "exercise fairly the power conferred upon it in behalf of all those for whom it acts, without hostile discrimination among them" (*Steele* v. *Louisville and N.R.R.*, 323 US 192, pp. 202–203).

This duty is felt in several circumstances, but the one most associated with peer review is the representation requirement when employees are disciplined or discharged. The courts have held that a union has discretion in deciding how far to press a grievance brought by a member in these cases, so long as it does not discriminate against or among groups of members (Morris, 1971). Thus not every grievance needs to be carried to arbitration or into the courts. But in peer review cases, the union approves of and participates in a process in which members judge other members, and unions have generally agreed that they will not challenge the substance of peer review rulings. While the existing peer review experiments have produced no legal challenges from teachers who were judged to be incompetent, the status of unions remains unclear, and a statute that anticipates workers serving in a professional peer review situation should be adopted.

Peer review also challenges sections of education statutes that reserve the managers' right to evaluate employees. Principals in Rochester, New York, unsuccessfully challenged the teacher union's introduction of peer review on this ground. In California districts that adopted peer review, administrators still sign the final recommendations—thus complying with the letter of the law.

The Hiring Hall

Craft unions flourished in the nineteenth century because labor organizations were able to control entire fields of work through a combination of solidarity, coercion, and licensure. Indeed, the modern professions followed in the footsteps of the guilds by regulating entry to work through education and apprenticeship and setting the standards of practice. Membership in medical or bar associations became a matter of social expectation and functionally often a requirement for forming a successful practice.

Thus the practicality of the form of unionism we envision, extending beyond one employer, depends on the legitimated right of unions to undertake activities that create representation throughout a field of employment. Current law discourages such activity.

Creating a hiring hall itself would be permissible under existing law, and could be part of the recognition agreement between school employers and unions. But if the intent of the statute was to encourage movement from industrial-style collective bargaining to knowledge-era representation, then recognizing the hiring hall function in statute would have the desired patterning effect.

For a hiring hall to work, unions would have to have statutory rights to compel membership or charge a service fee for representation, just as employment agencies or headhunting firms now do. Currently, unions in some states have the right to form what is called an *agency shop* by vote of its members after the union has been recognized. The extent of agency shop representation varies widely. Agency shop operates much like the more traditional union shop, in which an employee must become a member of the union within a certain period after employment, usually a month or so. The agency shop allows those who are opposed to unionism on political grounds or forbidden to join a labor organization by their religious beliefs to pay the union a fee for representing them rather than actually joining the union.

The existing form of agency shop is restricted to a single employer and is instituted by the vote of employees. Obviously, for a hiring hall concept to work, the hall would have to serve whole regions, and a network of these arrangements would have to cover the country. Otherwise, the system would lack the fluidity we have described and teachers and others would not gain the ability to move easily from school to school. In a regional setting, the right to charge an agency fee would have to be provided by statute, rather than by membership vote.

Because the hiring hall, in effect, replaces the personnel service function of school employers, the union would need to be subject to civil rights requirements for job posting, advertisement, and procedural due process. Some of the counseling and other functions of the hiring hall may be extensive, larger than a teacher applicant can reasonably be expected to afford, and thus it may be in the interest of states or school employers to subsidize hiring hall operations. To do this, the ability of schools to support cooperative and joint enterprises, noted earlier, needs to be clarified.

To enforce the hiring hall's status as the exclusive provider of employees—and to preserve equality—employees in individual schools need the right to refuse to work with someone hired into a school without having gone through the hiring hall. However, this right would not need to restrict a school's ability to contract out work to external firms: to hire a janitorial service, to contract with Berlitz to teach French, or to use a multimedia firm for educational resources. These decisions would be carried out within the purview of educational compact decisions.

Dispute Resolution

While we hope that the system we have devised will be cooperative in the sense that it forms a community of professionals and a broader community of support and nurture around schools and schoolchildren, any system of employment relations that does not anticipate disputes is doomed from the outset. For labor relations, the question is always how to accommodate workers' rights to voice their interests in ways that do not lead to unreasonable disturbances in the work or to overly costly, protracted, and cumbersome dispute resolution techniques. Under school-centered organizations, and using enterprise compacts, we anticipate that the range and nature of conflict will be different, not that the level of conflict will necessarily be higher or lower.

Conventional labor law differentiates disputes over *rights* from those over *interests*. Rights disputes usually take the form of grievances, typically an employee's charge that management failed to do what was required under the contract. Most often, grievances arise when the contract is unclear, for example about which employees are to have preference in transfers to a different school or whether a principal's called staff meeting was allowable under the contract. Rights disputes are subject to a contractually required step-by-step dispute resolution process familiar to most educators. The endpoint in this process is frequently binding arbitration. In contrast, interest disputes arise during collective bargaining or union organizing when agreements can't be reached over the terms of a contract or whether a union will be recognized. These disputes are the most difficult and frequently explosive, leading to overt conflict and direct action through strikes and other means.

In the system we have designed, the line between rights and interests is less clear than in conventional systems. Teachers and administrators will carry with them the rights to set work parameters and also the responsibility to make the school function smoothly. The ability to engage in conflict as if it is someone else's responsibility to run the school will vanish, and neither labor nor management will be able to leave disputes unsettled without consequences.

Because setting an educational compact establishes a different kind of workplace democracy than we currently have, the nature of dispute resolution is different. Existing forms of representation are built on an interest group depiction of democracy. As a result, existing law needs to define the rights to form interest groups and the rules of engagement for combat with other groups. The educational compact proceeds from the idea of unitary democracy (Mansbridge, 1990), in which all members of workplace organization have a primary responsibility for making it successful. There is a realization that common interest binds the parties as much as differences divide them and that the organizations will fail unless people organize around them.

The primary need of the new system is for high levels of dispute resolution training and skills. Where the primary skill of labor activists in the industrial setting is to rally workers around clearly (if sometimes artificially) articulated divisions with management, the dominant skill in the knowledge era is to form communities of interest. If the experience of labor relations reform efforts over the last decade are any guide, a great deal of training, expertise, and support will be necessary in process, problem-solving, and dispute resolution skills. Teachers and administrators in Glenview, Illinois, for example, invested heavily in meeting process skills, and those in Pittsburgh, Pennsylvania, in consensus decision making (Kerchner, 1991; Smylie, 1991; Smylie, Brownlee-Conyers, and Crowson, 1992). Interestingly, the origins of emphasizing dispute resolution had less to do with labor-management relationships and much more to do with controlling the conflict among students that was preventing school reform programs from going forward. Teachers then found that they needed the medicine they were giving the children.

Second, the new system must to come to grips with the right to strike. Striking remains controversial in the public sector: a blasphemy to detractors and ideological bedrock for unionists. Increasingly, however, strikes are seen as of dubious utility, a right that is essential but rarely useful.

Under a school-based enterprise compact system, we do not believe the right to strike should be extended to individual schools except under two specific cases: when employees are brought into the school improperly, that is, without going through the hiring hall mechanism, and when work is contracted out in contravention of the educational compact processes.

Failure to reach a compact, or protracted and inconclusive deliberations over one, indicate a serious problem at the school, but not necessarily one for which a strike is the best remedy. Because the educational compact is also the school's operating plan and the basis for an ongoing school–central authority charter, persistent inability to forge an educational compact would trigger the central authority's responsibility to intervene.

The central authority would be required to dissolve the school as an organization and reform it. Instead of the doctrine of no contract, no work, the operating model would be no compact, no school. This is harsh medicine indeed, and it signals to the school community that compact making is a serious responsibility requiring high levels of professional engagement.

Teachers should retain the right to strike against the central authority. Since the contract with the central authority is relatively slim, and since wage setting becomes partly the function of individual schools and partly the function of the professional practices board, we would expect that the occasion for economic strikes would arise less often than currently. Yet there would certainly be economic disputes with school authorities, and in states with centralized funding, with state governments. Both need to be permitted, or statutes need to provide for mandatory third-party settlements—which are often more costly to the public purse.

If the experiences of the last decade are any guide, the most contentious aspect of labor negotiations may well be the boundaries of joint operations—professional practice schools and similar combined activities that impinge on what managers traditionally think of as their prerogatives. Negotiating a hiring hall agreement, thus transferring much of the personnel function outside the school authority, may prove highly charged. Setting agreements about what percentage of a district's budget will be delivered to the schools is a point of constant conflict in existing school reform settings.

The labor statutes form both an instrumental and a symbolic connection between union organizing and labor as an institution. Both organizing and labor law connect labor and the hopes Americans have for themselves and their children, a subject to which we turn next.

CHAPTER ELEVEN

Organizing for the Knowledge Era

I nstitutions matter deeply to society, and teacher union activity over the next decade will affect the future of both the institution of public education and the institution of organized labor. Teacher unions are vital to education's primary function of delivering new forms and standards of learning and literacy, bringing truth to the phrase "all children can learn." Teacher unions can also serve as a prototype for organized labor to use in organizing other knowledge workers. If teacher unions have the will, they can play an important part in both institutional changes.

Thus this final chapter addresses two kinds of organizing: organizing education and labor organizing. It first addresses the concrete steps teacher unions can take within education. Then it considers the ways in which organizing in education also serves as a key to organizing knowledge workers. The chapter ends with a return to the theme of historical change, reconnecting labor to the dreams of Americans and the American dream.

ORGANIZING EDUCATION IN THE KNOWLEDGE SOCIETY

Organizing "the other half" of teaching—teachers' craft, art, and profession—is both daunting and doable. It is daunting because, as we suggest in Chapter Three, much of the way teachers work and the way they think of themselves as workers will change over the next twenty years or so. The task is doable because, given a general vision of where the institution is headed, it is possible to develop a strategic plan for institutional change and construct the new system in a series of incremental steps, some taken in schools and classrooms and others in legislatures and public forums.

Talking with Teachers

The first task of union leadership is to prepare their members for change. This is a difficult task because members, whom union leaders depend on for political support and whom leaders are pledged to represent, live in the old institution. Their attachment to the old is not simply a question of employment security. Workers' sense of craft and vocation are tied to jobs they know and know how to do. Axial changes in teaching work are very threatening to a union membership, and they are quickly associated with underlying principles of what is right and proper. Opposition to institutional change is not simple stubbornness; it's rooted in deeply held ideology.

Bridging the chasm between what is and what may be requires clear understanding that change is not optional. The institution of public education will be swept along with the changes brought about by the new economy and changes in the instructional core of education. Bridging the chasm between the old institution and the coming one obliges union leadership to visualize institutional change, find the alternatives for worker organization, and identify viable and attractive paths for teachers.

Driving home the change message requires both information and action. Teachers need to know what the knowledge-era society looks like and they need to know what they can do about it. Union leaders have read and discussed books and reports that look over the information-age crest, but to most teachers books such as Marshall and Tucker's *Thinking for a Living* (1992) or reports such as *America's Choice: High Skills or Low Wages* (National Center on Education and the Economy, 1990) remain remote abstractions unconnected to their professional lives.

But while labor force economics remains an abstraction to most teachers, the conditions under which their children live and learn are concrete. Why not connect the global message of change to practical steps that teachers could take to understand the economic and social changes being faced by the children in their schools and their families? Why not use the same sorts of inquiry-driven pedagogies used in model classrooms to drive staff development? Action research would help teachers to understand the economic struggles faced by many children and their families. Teachers could then cross the divide between decrying lack of parental support and understanding the daily challenges of a two-earner family in which half the parents' combined income goes to pay the rent. Interviews with parents and community members would help surface both the aspirations and frustrations teachers have for their children. Ultimately, teacher action and inquiry will lead to a specific, concrete teacher knowledge about where their own system of education doesn't work, thus connecting the message of change to things that teachers do every day and to the children with whom they work (Poplin and Weeres, 1992).

Professional Development and Peer Review

Once teachers are convinced that change is not optional, it becomes possible to build powerful professional development and peer review programs. Using professional development and peer review, teacher unions can seize and pull the levers of educational quality.

Peer review is a natural outgrowth of professional development, a claim about expertise. No one else does teacher evaluation very well—not the state accrediting agencies, not the universities, and certainly not the school districts. If teacher unions demonstrate their capacity to enhance educational quality through peer review, little can stand in their way, and the governance and school operations issues with which reformers concerned themselves during the 1980s will become tractable.

As we argued earlier, we believe peer review provides great leverage in getting teachers to articulate, define, and improve professional practice. The most important aspect of peer review is not that it moves teacher evaluation from administrators to teachers; it is that it allows teachers to gain knowledge of their work and gives them the opportunity to tell other teachers about it. Thus if peer review is linked to an ongoing system of professional development, teachers gain a real purchase on defining their own occupation. If these two developments take place, we may in reality see a "second academic revolution"—to quote again the happy phrase Grant and Murray (1996) coined to discuss a process like the one college professors underwent in the 1950s and 1960s.

The organizational beauty of staff development and peer review is that unions can both advocate and act on an educational quality issue that the public deeply cares about. Unions not only have the ability to bargain forms of peer review, as was done in Toledo, Poway, Rochester, and other places, but they also have the capacity to initiate programs on their own. Union-run staff development programs are commonplace already. Increasing their intensity and rigor is within the capacity of both national and state union organizations.

Peer review becomes a powerful union policy campaign issue. Even if management balked, unions could assist members to prepare for National Board for Professional Teaching Standards certification. They could adopt some of the National Board's techniques in creating their own observation and evaluation mechanisms. Unions could ally themselves with disciplinary associations—English, math, history—that are developing domain-specific pedagogy. Contemporary standards and pedagogy could be offered on a voluntary basis for the formative assistance of new teachers and as a benefit of union membership.

Peer review allows unions to take the initiative rather than react. Teachers in general and unions in particular often present an extraordinarily whiny face. They contrive victimization. "If only class size were smaller, if only the kids came to school well fed, if only we could get the parents to help us, if only Congress cared." Cincinnati Federation of Teachers president Tom Mooney has a sign in his office with an apt response: "Don't whine; organize." Organized teachers would gain unbeatable influence by saying:

- We will take joint custody of reform.

- We will evaluate ourselves and hold ourselves to high, and public, professional standards.

- We will come to understand our students' lives and advocate for them before we advocate for ourselves.

By pointedly taking risks and by investing their brains and their bodies, teachers will gain for themselves both status and influence.

Making Schools Smarter

Once teachers start to organize around their own practice, they gain a vision of how schools need to be reorganized. Thus school reorganization becomes an exercise in building what is called a learning community rather than simply dividing up managerial responsibility.

The reforms of the 1980s clearly indicate that the process is much more difficult than we thought it was and that school districts and unions have invested far too little in it. School-level organization has always been unionism's weak link. Union structures are basically hierarchical, just like management structures, and prestige, influence, and attention flow upward. The building representative or steward is largely an afterthought, as is the functioning of the union at an individual school.

But current structural reforms, such as school site management or charter schools, much less the large-scale changes we anticipate, alter the location of knowledge within the hierarchy. "Teachers at the local level know more about school reform than the union staff," said the late John Kotsakis, assistant to the Chicago Teachers' Union president on education issues, "and more about its operational requirements, such as how to create a budget" (Kerchner and Koppich, 1993, p. 192). Kotsakis indicated that teachers are learning from each other at the building level, inventing practical responses to concrete problems, and soliciting training not from the school board or the union, but from outside community advocacy groups.

The position of union stewards or building representatives also takes on new importance. During the 1980s experiments with site-based management in the Dade County Public Schools, one union steward noted, "In the past before we went to SB [site-based management] I was the person that stood in between the bricks that were flying. But now it is just the opposite. The union is behind SB and they work right along with all the decisions that are being made." Asked whether it didn't feel as though someone had taken away the job, the steward replied, "No, I feel great! Before I felt like I was the bad boy of the school. If somebody had a grievance I had to go to the principal, but now it is nothing like that."

The stewards' role changes, but their historic complaint-handling function does not disappear. Someone is still needed to make sure that all staff have a voice in the decision-making process. The steward or building representative serves as a security blanket for teachers, making sure that change efforts fall within the spirit of the compact and joint reform initiatives. Finally, teachers need someone they can grumble to—someone who is not an administrator—though they may have no intention of filing a grievance.

The paid staff of unions take on a new role as the unions commit themselves to the organizational change of school districts. Full-time union executive directors often play an important role in school reform, particularly in teacher locals affiliated with the NEA. Field representatives find themselves doing a lot of counseling in support of reforms. As a field staffer for the Jefferson County (Kentucky) Teachers Association said, "You have to understand . . . sometimes [teachers] will not feel comfortable making decisions. And the administration has been under a certain mindset, and they are not going to change simply because there is PM [participatory management]. We come often to buoy the faculty . . . give them some assertiveness training, or a good talk so they don't have PM in name only."

Once adopted, new roles and expectations for teachers and union staff tend to persist even through changes in administrative personnel and sometimes through the demise of particular programs. Changes in union staff function create new organizational cultures: a sea change in the ways in which unionists think about their work roles. Kerchner and Mitchell (1988) described the change from one union ideology to another as a *generational change,* one often marked by overt conflict and replacement of union or management leadership. What we have termed professional unionism is profoundly different from industrial unionism, and the break between the two constitutes intensely fought terrain within both unions and management (Kerchner and Koppich, 1993). Unions, in particular, face an ongoing struggle both with management and with their own traditionalist wings.

Organizing Parents

Organizing schools requires organizing parents, historically regarded as the "enemy within" by teachers. Not insignificantly, organizing parents allows unions to define membership on a basis other than employment. Parents can be powerful allies, and unions have substantive services to offer them, both advocacy and support in raising their families. But neither national teacher union has done a very good job of courting parents. Part of the reason lies in outmoded ideas about profession.

Much of the existing institution of education is designed to create a system of professional superiority over educational decisions and to diminish the voice and influence of parents. However, parents are increasingly seeing themselves both as customers of education, desiring to choose appropriate schooling for their children, and as public critics of the system. In addition, educators have come to realize that family resources of time, discipline, and support are necessary for children to succeed in school.

There are two paths for gaining parental and public support for the broadly inclusive type of educational labor market we envision. First, parents need to believe that teachers and teacher unions are on their side, that they support things that parents want done, and that they can communicate directly with parents. This means teachers will have to master the art of translating ideas out of educational jargon. It also means that a great many of our teachers need to speak a second language in addition to English.

When teachers establish good communication, parents and families are much more likely to believe that unions are engaged in creating fairness rather than featherbedding. It is fairly easy for parents and other citizens to gain the impression that unions seek jobs for teachers and disregard education for children. However, changing this impression is not impossible. When teacher unions gained initial bargaining contracts, particularly in states where recognition agreements were not required by state labor statute, they had to appeal to parents and the public. Teachers won these battles by seeming more reasonable and educationally relevant than did administrators, who easily could be cast as protecting their own domains.

If teachers are again to create a base of support among parents, they will have to be able to construct a vision of workplace justice and gain its acceptance by parents and the community. Not only will teacher unions have to be in an organizing mode regarding other workers, they will need to become civic missionaries. Convincing parents of the justice of teachers' and para-educators' occupational needs becomes easier when unions also demonstrate that they are on the parents' side in the raising of their children and improving the quality of schools that their children or grandchildren attend. Ironically,

this is exactly the role played by school administrators at the beginning of the century when the last great institutional change occurred
in education.

Teacher contact with parents needs to be viewed as both instrumental and strategic, as much a part of a strategy for school renewal
as is contact with school board members. Part of teaching work thus
has to be defined as regular and consistent contact with parents. Making a shift in teacher work roles of this magnitude is no small matter
and lends credence to the educational compact idea. At the outset,
teachers will have to buy this time with sweat equity; few school
boards are likely to provide teachers with extended-day payments for
the purpose of forming coalitions with parents that can pressure or
potentially embarrass school administrations or boards. But this is
part of the political and social movement work of unionism.

The second path for gaining parent support is more instrumental:
create a classification of membership for parents or form partnerships
with parent-based organizations. Teacher unions can help parents in
the tough job of child rearing. Heckscher's idea of *associational unionism* (1988) applies to creating a linkage between educational unions
and parents. Union development of educational aids, union assistance
in helping parents help their children with homework and with emotional problems—all this is within the capacity of unions to create and
to circulate using computer technology. If educational software can
be sold at 1–800-ABCDEFG, unions can operate their own 1–800-
HELP-KID. (Indeed, unions in several cities operate homework hot
lines already.)

Sustained and helpful contact between teacher unions and parents,
between individual teachers who perceive themselves as unionists and
individual parents, is the first stage in creating an attentive public that
will support both teachers and the idea of unionism. If educational
unions want to build support for public education or a larger social
agenda, they need to renew their ties to the grass roots.

ORGANIZING UNIONISM IN
THE KNOWLEDGE SOCIETY

Just as teachers are part of the institution of public education, they are
also part of organized labor. In many ways, teachers and their unions
are superbly positioned occupationally to become a productive model
of worker organization in the United States. Unionized teachers are

the "United Mind Workers" for whom success depends on ability to work through highly abstract, ill-defined situational problems typical of knowledge-based production. Teachers work in the service sector where jobs are growing, not the manufacturing sector where they are declining. Teachers have historically worked in large, bureaucratic organizations. They understand the tension between individual discretion and organizational control in the workplace. Finally, most teachers are female, and relative to other highly educated work-forces, teaching includes a high proportion of persons of color. Indeed, teaching has always served as a route for upward occupational mobility. Thus the occupation brings a voice and perspective to the workplace that is largely missing among the traditional professions and among most other unions.

The challenge of knowledge workers comes at a propitious time for organized labor, which has been in decline for the last forty years. It makes too little of the matter to say that the house of labor has not faired well in the last generation (Hoerr, 1991; Geoghegan, 1991). Only about 11 percent of the private-sector workforce now belongs to a union, down from 35 percent in the mid-1950s. The lack of union density sends ripple effects through the society. When unions were strong, nonunion companies would pay similar wages—sometimes even a premium—to forestall unionization. When unions are weak, the momentum goes the other way, with unionized companies facing pressures to keep wages down. When unionism is so rare, union wages and benefits are seen as "bastions of social privilege" that unfairly aid the few.

More damning, however, is the damage done to the institution of organized labor: "A generation ago, leaders of the AFL-CIO could think of themselves, with only slight exaggeration, as full partners in the power elite that governed America. Now, they have lost their membership, or rather they were kicked out of the club. Unions are mostly reduced to rear-guard battles fighting cheap-labor imports or defending the pensions of retired workers or competing expensively with each other for membership jurisdiction" (Greider, 1992, p. 192).

Recently, the *Los Angeles Times* (Bearak, 1995) reported a confidential AFL-CIO commissioned survey of worker attitudes toward labor. For most of those interviewed, unions were "not an important part of how they see the world" and although workers had plenty of complaints "it literally did not occur to them to look to unions as a solution." In ways reminiscent of the 1920s, writers have begun to speculate about employee relations without unions (Garbarino, 1984).

Fortunately, organized labor shows signs of seizing the initiative. Organizing is on the union agenda again after fifteen years in which the AFT, the Service Employees International Union, and the American Federation of State, County and Municipal Employees accounted for virtually all the new members gained within the AFL-CIO (Bearak, 1995).The AFL-CIO's Organizing Institute captured the energy of young activists and Generation Xers long thought lost to the union movement. Campaigns such as Justice for Janitors tap wellsprings of support among immigrant communities, particularly among Latinos. The Union Summer of 1996 took several hundred college students and activists into the field, spreading an interest in unionism among those who had never encountered it before. If nothing else, the campaign brushed up unionism's dowdy image, maybe even made it hip (Levinson, 1996). Labor organizing's revival comes at a time when a large segment of the white-collar workforce finds itself threatened as firms and government agencies move into the information age.

White-Collar Blues

For the better part of this century, white-collar workers, particularly managers, were protected by corporate paternalism. "They were treated as permanent members of permanent enterprises. They were well paid and could confidently expect careers of steadily increasing responsibility and rewards. Their jobs, unlike those at the highest levels, were not very stressful: they generally worked 9 to 5 and within clearly delimited boundaries" (Heckscher, 1995, p. 4). Corporations implicitly pledged—and public employers followed suit—that they would take care of their employees if the employees would subordinate their needs to those of the company.

That pattern has been shattered. There is now more white-collar unemployment than blue-collar, and although higher education is still the key to upward mobility, a college degree no longer guarantees employment. Among middle-class Americans, the worry is over unemployment, not the national deficit (Beatty, 1994). Corporate executives may bemoan the loss of employee loyalty, but they shouldn't be surprised by it.

Just-in-Time Workers

One of the characteristics of Japanese manufacturing is a production process so well timed and connected to its resources that it needs very little inventory. Parts arrive from suppliers just in time for assembly into increasingly sophisticated products. Information technology allows suppliers to know what is required and when. This precision in scheduling and integrating work by capturing the power of technology has been subsequently applied to thousands of processes. Supermarket scanners capture customer purchase information and create precise replacement orders. A teenager buys a sweatshirt in Los Angeles, and a subcontractor in a small town in northern Italy gets an order to dye up another batch of hunter green.

A parallel change has been occurring among workers. The expectation of long-term employment is gone as employers shrink and expand their workforce. Although the tendency is worldwide, the United States in particular is notable for having created a highly flexible workforce, as the *Wall Street Journal* (Aug. 7, 1995, p. 1) commented in an article on increasing foreign investment in U.S. companies: "There's also a more subtle reason why non-U.S. corporations are looking so favorably on expansion here. Compared to operating within most European or Asian societies, laying off workers is easier in America. If demand falls, the American system is more flexible. Just as Japan perfected the just-in-time inventory system, America is well on its way to perfecting the just-in-time workforce, notwithstanding the grim toll it takes on labor. The harsh truth is that it is a major productivity plus."

Particularly for younger Americans, work has become much more fluid, and full-time jobs that include health and other benefits more difficult to find. Part-time work is on the increase in the United States and now accounts for at least one-fifth of all workers, and almost a quarter of these—some 4.7 million workers—are *involuntary* part-timers who would prefer full-time employment (Tilly, 1992). Part-time employees have lower wages than full-time workers—in 1987, part-timers earned an average of $4.42 per hour or about 60 percent of the median $7.43. By comparison, education part-timers are relatively well paid even though the contrast between classroom aides and certificated teachers is still striking. Part-time workers for the most part lack fringe benefits, with only 22 percent covered by health care. They also keep their jobs for much shorter periods, and the jobs are nearly always without advancement possibility.

The fluid labor market is not confined to part-time workers. Large numbers of workers, professional and technical workers in particular, toil as temporary or outsourced workers—those working for a contractor. Although the image of the temporary worker is the Kelly

Services receptionist or secretary, professional employment is also becoming explicitly temporary, more than 125,000 professionals working as temps every day (Rifkin, 1995, p. 192). Federal agencies, school districts, and particularly colleges and universities make extensive use of part-time, temporary, and outsourced workers, often paying them badly and treating them worse.

Indeed, fluidity in the workforce could be an important organizing principle for the economy, and it could be an important organizing principle for workers, too. Depending on how the labor market is organized, it could mean greater opportunity and greater individual control over time and labor: more choices, better ability to increase and decrease work intensity at different times during a career, or more freedom to seek interesting work assignments.

The urge toward fluidity can support innovative forms of work design, including flextime, job sharing, and telecommuting. But if fluid work is also poorly paid work, without benefits, then these workers are simply expendable: throw-away people. Organizing around fluid employment, by means of such devices as the union hiring hall and professional service contracts, is a way to preserve some of the flexibility that is attractive to employers—and to some workers, too—without creating a two-tier labor market.

Work Scarcity

One of the reasons that the just-in-time workforce exists is the perception of work scarcity. In Henry Ford's economy, high-wage workers were a necessity, for without them there was no one to purchase the burgeoning output of America's industries. The globalization of work, however, has made it possible for owners and investors, including worker pension funds (which send a huge chunk of capital flowing into the system), to prosper without creating jobs at home. This decade has been termed one of "prosperity without jobs." Between 1987 and 1991, the real wages of college-educated workers fell 3.1 percent (Rifkin, 1995, p. 172). Up to 35 percent of recent college graduates have been forced to take jobs that don't require a college degree, and the job market for college graduates has been called the worst since World War II. Throughout the industrialized world, unemployment has been at levels not seen since the Great Depression, with official unemployment in some European countries running to 13 percent.

Writers from highly diverse perspectives contemplate a world without enough jobs to go around (Rifkin, 1995, p. 7). Drucker foresees a world in which both labor and capital, in the traditional sense, are displaced by knowledge work. He notes that "disappearance of labor as a factor in production" will emerge as the critical unfinished politics in capitalist society (1993, p. 68). British business consultant and commentator Charles Handy advocated constructing a society around useful forms of work outside the market economy (1984). Radical theologian Matthew Fox similarly calls for finding vocations outside employment (1994).

This is, of course, not the first time that society has contemplated an absolute shortage of work. Marx's "surplus value" theory of labor derived from the decline of agricultural work in the nineteenth century. Immigration to and migration within the United States at the turn of the century resulted from agricultural mechanization and falling farm prices. As recently at the early 1960s, it was widely believed that automation would permanently dampen employment. (In the latter case, the onset of the Vietnam War and increases in military production chased manpower concerns from the public agenda and diverted public attention from employment issues until the oil shortages of the 1970s.)

In each period, general employment shortages proved transitory. New economies proved so robust that both employment and wage levels generally increased, and analysts are divided over whether we are likely to face a period of employment nirvana or a period in which for most people, work is not central to their identity and being. It is not necessary to decide between the two alternatives.

Rather, it is important to recognize the turmoil that exists now and that colors the lives of the great majority of American workers and their families. This condition of instability and insecurity is important to teachers both because it affects the communities in which they live and the lives of the children they teach and because it holds the keys to worker organization within education.

Pressure to Produce

The rationalizing pressures that hammered manufacturing are being duplicated in white-collar jobs, and there is every reason to believe teaching will feel them too. The pressure to drive down the cost of services is virtually universal. The NEA, for example, considers the cost of health care a major problem for teacher collective bargaining, and it devotes a high-level staff member to considering policies to stem runaway health costs. Every state finance department in the country has a staff member similarly working on ways to decrease the cost of education.

Simply put, the service sector has grown so large—and the manufacturing sector so vulnerable—that the economy suffers when productivity fails to increase. As Drucker notes, "Unless we can learn how to increase the productivity of knowledge workers and service workers, and increase it fast, the developed countries will face economic stagnation and severe social tension. People can only get paid in accordance with their productivity. Their productivity creates the pool of wealth from which wages and salaries are then paid. If productivity does not go up, let alone if it declines, higher real incomes cannot be paid" (1993, p. 84).

The computer holds the keys to changing productivity for service and knowledge workers. Computer usage used to be subject to what is called the productivity paradox: despite heavy investments in information technology, only very small gains in efficiency could be seen. No more. The application of aptly named *smart technology* to managerial and service tasks is revolutionizing the service sector. Smart technology is not simply automation, the replacement of a human function with a mechanical one; it is the introduction and application of knowledge and judgment without direct human intervention.

Automated teller machines generally provide more information than human tellers did. Sophisticated machines allow users to inquire into their account balances, see which checks have cleared, and transfer funds between accounts. Meanwhile, they suggest—in any of several languages—that users think about refinancing their houses. A human teller can handle a maximum of two hundred transactions a day and works thirty hours a week. An ATM can handle two thousand transactions a day and works 168 hours a week, if asked. Between 1983 and 1993, banks eliminated about 179,000 human tellers, or 37 percent of their workforce (Rifkin, 1995, p. 144).

The effects of smart technology are by no means restricted to routine or low-skilled jobs. Computer-aided design is now a standard part of architectural work, and even medicine is experimenting with Robodoc, a 250-pound machine with a scanner that can develop three-dimensional pictures and a robotic arm that can drill holes with high speed and great precision (Rifkin, 1995).

In education, computer applications are rapidly moving beyond "drill and kill" rote applications to incorporate analytical capacity and knowledge creation. Grammar and spelling checkers are routine parts of word processing software. Mathematics programs can contain powerful error analysis algorithms that guide students to an understanding of their mistakes. An electronic humanoid known as A.D.A.M. teaches physiology with accuracy and graphic quality. Looking at off-the-shelf software alone, there can be little doubt that human teachers have lost the monopoly on direct instruction. Indeed, the increasing use of technology for distance learning may render the definition of a "school" as a building in which a group of students receives instruction from an on-site teacher a twentieth-century anachronism. The questions that remain relate to the role that technology will play in changing schools as organizations and the role teacher unions will play in reengineering education.

Corporate reengineering typically involves losing about 40 percent of jobs and sometimes as much as 80 percent of those in middle management (Rifkin, 1995, p. 7). Hammer and Champy, who coined the term reengineering, use the example of reengineering IBM's credit processing system. In that situation, sophisticated microprocessing allowed a case manager to process an entire credit application in four hours, a reduction from the seven days it previously took. The change eliminated five departments (Rifkin, 1995, p. 101).

Reinventing government is scheduled to take 252,000 workers from the federal service, some 12 percent of the workforce (Rifkin, 1995). But rationalization of federal government work is a minor adjustment compared with that facing state and local governments. Contrary to the popular belief, the federal government has grown only modestly in recent years; it has been the states, counties, and cities where public employment has increased most rapidly. It is those same governments that are feeling enormous fiscal pressure. Federal revenue sharing, which used to supply as much as 25 percent of city budgets, is gone, and Congressional efforts to cut social spending will put great stress on local governments to both constrict programs and reinvent how they are delivered.

Largely because of union protections, teaching—despite some cutbacks—remains one of the few large occupations where workplace protections and stability have not been stripped away. Despite teachers' threadbare self-image, they are among the more privileged of American workers—they enjoy decent pay, generally good benefits, and high job security. Teaching has not yet been connected to reengineering. It will be.

The New Knowledge Class

It is increasingly obvious that the labor market has bifurcated, creating what is seen as the crisis of the middle class. Instead of a large—virtually ubiquitous—middle range, we are producing very good jobs at the top and very bad ones at the bottom. When Bluestone and Harrison first published their "shrinking middle class" research in 1987, it ran into a firestorm of criticism. It is still contested, but something approaching consensus has emerged over the position that there is a growing polarization in wages. (For a review of this research see Harrison, 1994, pp. 190ff.)

The occupational structure in the United States, which used to be hinged around the great middle class, now hinges around the top 20 percent. Below the one-half of 1 percent of Americans who own 37 percent of corporate stock and bonds and 55 percent of all private assets is a growing and privileged knowledge class comprising about 20 percent of the workforce. Here, incomes continue to increase. This top fifth, including the super rich, controls more of the economy than the bottom four-fifths (Rifkin, 1995, 174).

Reich (1991) divides the labor market into divisions that are particularly meaningful to educators. Jobs fall into three broad classifications. *Routine production services* involve repetitive tasks and routine supervision. They are typically thought of as blue-collar, but routine work is found in the most glittery of high-tech firms and the most prestigious professions, for example, the routine creation of computer codes. Computerization, restructuring, and globalization all take a bite out of these jobs, and they are increasingly vulnerable.

In-person services may be just as routine, but they are delivered face-to-face and are less subject to global competition. This category includes retail sales workers, hotel workers, cleaners, health aides, and security guards. This category of work is expanding, but the work is often poorly paid.

It is Reich's third category, the *symbolic analysts*, that encompass the top 20 percent of wage earners and may well form a new class of American workers. Their work is problem identification, problem solving, and brokering of services. The symbolic analyst classification includes some of the traditional professionals, but it is distinguished by a set of emerging occupations—biotechnology engineers, multimedia designers, investment bankers—all of whom solve problems by manipulating symbols. They live in a world of cognitive construction, and their work presents the proof of relevance of changes in psychology and learning theory.

The good news is that symbolic analysis work is increasing and that we expect to add more well-paid thinking jobs. As Berryman and Bailey (Berryman, 1993; Berryman and Bailey, 1992) show, occupations involving professional skill, technology, management, and sales are increasing much more rapidly than production and traditional services. The trend is projected to continue, and not unexpectedly one of the distinguishing features of growing occupations is continued education.

This new occupational structure exposes enormous weaknesses in American society and poses equally enormous challenges to education. The all-too-apparent danger is the recreation of a class structure in America. As Drucker notes, "There is a danger that the post-capitalist society will become a class society unless service workers attain both income and dignity" (1993, p. 16). The existence of income differentials, of course, does not constitute social class separation, but persistent differential and a tendency toward greater inequity have reinvoked the concept of an underclass and sparked renewed discussion of an overclass that some call the cognitive elite. Like underclass, *overclass* refers to a group with a common culture and interest, "with the obvious difference from the underclass that nobody is trying to get *out* of the overclass" (Adler, 1995, p. 33).

The American conventional wisdom of a middle-class society requires a belief that almost everyone can get in (Ehrenreich, 1990). The poor are an exception, and thus unionism is seen as a struggle for *rights* rather than as a class struggle, as it is in the European tradition. For manufacturing workers, access to decent pay and safe working conditions was "simple justice" (Aronowitz and DiFazio, 1994, p. 211). We do not yet have a definition of simple justice for the 1990s. We face a society with large amounts of unfocused anger; discontent wrapped in nostalgia for a time that never was and aimed at virtually all institutions, including families and children. Dissatisfaction is the stuff of political organization.

RECONNECTING LABOR TO THE AMERICAN DREAM

While this is primarily a book about schools and the people who work in them, the implications of reorganizing education and reorganizing unionism within education reach beyond schooling to the institution of education and beyond education to the organization of American society. Some time ago, labor lost its connection to the American dream. Most workers, and most Americans, don't include unions in their list of the institutions that made America great, and precious few see worker organization as a way through the transition from an industrial society to the identification of postindustrialism. Teacher unions have unique characteristics that place them in a good position to change the popular view of labor and to reconnect unionism to achievement of the American dream.

Teacher unions are huge, well organized, uncorrupted, and competently run. Unlike the case with school board members, we can cite no examples of union leaders convicted of official corruption; unlike the case of school districts, we can cite no instances of union locals declaring bankruptcy. Teacher unionists are well educated, predominantly female, and increasingly racially and ethnically diverse. They represent the occupationally mobile edge of the knowledge society. Their work involves knowledge creation, the stuff of social organization and wealth creation for this age. Simultaneously, teachers and para-educators face all the problems encountered in the transition from industrial assumptions about organizing to knowledge-era organizations.

The problems teachers face are the problems American workers face. The solutions teachers find may be solutions others can use.

Teachers will have to tend to the dying elements of their own institution. The rebirth of an institution requires a death first, and with it the questions of pain and loss. As a people, Americans see work as very much a part of national identity, and when the character and nature of work changes—as is the case currently with physicians—it is an occasion for mourning and loss. The pain of change inclines workers and their leaders toward conservatism, and even an odd form of romanticism that lauds the very bureaucracies that teachers organized against.

If teachers can master the task of allowing parts of an old institution to die with dignity, and convey dignity and respect to those who have spent their lives working in it, they will be in a position of leadership and also connection. No group of workers will discard itself, but unions have been capable of making transitions to new technologies, and we believe that unions are more likely to do this in ways that create dignity and protection than are managers.

In *The Second Industrial Divide* (1984), Piore and Sabel describe the passage from one production era to another as a period of conscious choice. It is a time in which the society, through a series of decisions, determines how work will be done and what will be the relationship of workers to the work. In the transformation to industrial work, the Western world opted for a construction of work that traded high wages for low control over the work content. That may not have been the only choice available.

Teachers face the problem of how to construct work, whether to dumb down work with computer-driven routines, or whether to use the same technology to make both work and workers—both teachers and students—smarter. The history of digitally controlled machine tools, and even the saga of astronaut training, shows that the design of all real jobs faces these choices. Unions can help keep teaching smart.

If unions can master the transition to jobs built around knowledge work and to teaching that educates the worker while it educates the student, then this mode of unionism and work organization may well become attractive to people in other sectors of knowledge work—in medicine, banking, and arts-related industries—who will make up an increasing percentage of the workforce.

Teachers face the problem of inclusion, bringing nontraditional entrants into knowledge-based occupations. Creating a career ladder into teaching may allow the first traditional "women's occupation" to transform itself into an explicitly knowledge-generating career. Teaching may also be the first large occupation in which the balance among work, family, civic, and religious life roles is purposefully examined for the benefit of workers, whether female or male. If unions can solve these structural problems, then they can continue to work as agents of social mobility while creating jobs that allow their occupants to be both productive and fully human.

Finally, teachers face the largest problem of inclusion of all: who is to be included in the American dream. It is one thing to teach the poor and quite another to teach in a culture of poverty. Teachers are in a position to advocate for children and to assist parents and families in building safe, decent communities. Teachers, in greater numbers to a greater extent than any other adults, spend time with the nation's children. They are in a position to help bridge the now widening gap between *I* and *we* in America. We pay a huge price in this country for our failure to create community—in our cities, among our workers, and in our classrooms. This lack is palpable in the statements of those who seek a solution to the daily violence that has become endemic in American life and the loneliness and isolation that captures our families.

If unions can effectively advocate for children and can succeed in telling their stories, they can lead in recreating a politics of justice, tolerance, and kindness. It is work worth doing.

~~~ References

Adler, J. "The Rise of the Overclass." *Newsweek,* July 31, 1995, pp. 33–46.

Aronowitz, S., and DiFazio, W. *The Jobless Future.* Minneapolis: University of Minnesota Press, 1994.

Auriemma, F. V., Cooper, B. S., and Smith, S. C. *Graying Teachers: A Report on State Pension Systems and School Districts' Early Retirement Incentives.* Eugene, Ore.: ERIC Clearinghouse on Educational Management, 1992.

Ball, D. L., and Cohen, D. *Developing Practice, Developing Practitioners: Toward a Practice-Based Theory of Professional Education.* New York: National Commission on Teaching and America's Future, 1996.

Barenbaum, M. "The Political Economy of the Wagner Act." *Harvard Law Review,* 1993, *106,* 1381–1496.

Bascia, N. *Unions in Teachers' Professional Lives: Social, Intellectual, and Practical Concerns.* New York: Teachers College Press, 1994.

Bearak, B. "Staggered by Hits, Unions Need Ways to Regain Punch." *Los Angeles Times,* May 18, 1995, pp. 1, 13.

Beatty, J. "Who Speaks for the Middle Class?" *Atlantic,* 1994, *271*(5), 63–87.

Bell, D. *The Coming of Post-Industrial Society.* New York: Basic Books, 1973.

Berliner, D., and Biddle, B. *The Manufactured Crisis: Myth, Fraud, and the Attack on the American Public Schools.* Reading, Mass.: Addison-Wesley, 1995.

Berryman, S. E. "Learning for the Workplace." In L. Darling-Hammond (ed.), *Review of Research in Education.* (Vol. 19). Washington, D.C.: American Educational Research Association, 1993.

Berryman, S. E., and Bailey, T. R. *The Double Helix of Education and the Economy.* New York: Institute on Education and the Economy, Teachers College, Columbia University, 1992.

Block, F. *Postindustrial Possibilities: A Critique of Economic Discourse.* Berkeley: University of California Press, 1990.

Bluestone, B., and Bluestone, I. *Negotiating the Future: A Labor Perspective on American Business.* New York: Basic Books, 1992.

Bodie, Z., Shoven, J. B., and Wise, D. A. (eds.). *Pensions in the U.S. Economy.* Chicago: University of Chicago Press, 1989.

Brimelow, P., and Spencer, L. "Comeuppance." *Forbes,* Feb. 13, 1995, pp. 121–127.

Brody, D. *Workers in Industrial America: Essays on the Twentieth Century Struggle.* (2nd ed.). New York: Oxford University Press, 1993.

Brookover, W., and others. *Creating Effective Schools.* Holmes Beach, Fla.: Learning Publications, 1982.

Bruer, J. T. *Schools for Thought: A Science of Learning in the Classroom.* Cambridge, Mass.: MIT Press, 1993.

Bryk, A. S., and Hermanson, K. L. "Educational Indicator Systems: Observations on Their Structure, Interpretation and Use." In L. Darling-Hammond (ed.), *Review of Research in Education.* (Vol. 19). Washington, D.C.: American Educational Research Association, 1993.

Carnegie Forum on Education and the Economy. *A Nation Prepared: Teachers for the 21st Century: An Overview.* Washington, D.C.: Carnegie Forum on Education and the Economy, 1986.

Chubb, J. E., and Moe, T. M. *Politics, Markets and America's Schools.* Washington, D.C.: Brookings Institution, 1990.

Cibulka, J. G., Reed, R. J., and Wong, K. K. (eds.). *The Politics of Urban Education in the United States: The 1991 Yearbook of the Politics of Education Association.* Washington, D.C.: Falmer Press, 1992.

Clegg, S. R. *Modern Organizations: Organization Studies in the Postmodern World.* Thousand Oaks, Calif.: Sage, 1990.

Cobble, D. S. "Organizing the Postindustrial Work Force: Lessons from the History of Waitress Unionism." *Industrial and Labor Relations Review,* 1991, *44*(3), 419–436.

Cobble, D. S. "Labor Law Reform and Postindustrial Unionism." *Dissent,* Fall 1994, pp. 474–480.

Cohen, D. K., and Barnes, C. "Pedagogy and Policy." In D. K. Cohen, M. W. McLaughlin, and J. E. Talbert (eds.), *Teaching for Understanding: Challenges for Policy and Practice.* San Francisco: Jossey-Bass, 1993.

Coleman, J. S. *Parents, Teachers, and Children.* San Francisco: Institute for Contemporary Studies, 1977.

Collective Bargaining Agreement for Teachers and Other Professional Employees Between the Pittsburgh Board of Public Education and the Pittsburgh Federation of Teachers. (Sept. 5, 1988–Sept. 6, 1992).

Collective Negotiations Contract Between the Board of Education-San Diego Unified School District and the San Diego Teachers Association. (July 1, 1992–June 30, 1995).

Commission on the Future of Worker-Management Relations. *Final Report*. Ithaca, N.Y.: School of Industrial and Labor Relations, Cornell University, 1995.

Conley, S., and Odden, A. R. "Linking Teacher Compensation to Teacher Career Development." *Educational Evaluation and Policy Analysis*, 1995, *17*, 219–237.

Contractual Agreement Between the City School District of Rochester, New York, and the Rochester Teachers Association. (July 1, 1987–June 30, 1990).

Costa, A., Garmston, R., and Lambert, L. "Evaluation of Teaching: The Cognitive Development View." In S. Stanley and W. J. Popham (eds.), *Teacher Evaluation: Six Prescriptions for Success*. Alexandria, Va.: Association for Supervision and Curriculum Development, 1988.

Cremin, L. A. *The Transformation of the School: Progressivism in American Education, 1876–1957*. New York: Knopf, 1962.

Cubberly, E. P. *Public School Administration: A Statement of the Fundamental Principles Underlying the Organization and Administration of Public Education*. Boston: Houghton Mifflin, 1916.

Cushman, K. "Less Is More: The Secret of Being Essential." *Horace*, 1994, *11*(2), 1–10.

Darling-Hammond, L. "Reframing the School Reform Agenda: Developing Capacity for School Transformation." *Phi Delta Kappan*, 1993, *73*(10), 752–761.

Darling-Hammond, L., and McLaughlin, M. "Policies That Support Professional Development in an Era of Reform." *Phi Delta Kappan*, 1995, *76*(8), 597–604.

DiMaggio, P. J., and Powell, W. W. "The Iron Cage Revisted: Institutional Isomorphism and Collective Rationality in Organizational Fields." *American Sociological Review*, 1983, *48*, 147–160.

DiMaggio, P. J., and Powell, W. W. "Introduction." In W. W. Powell and P. J. DiMaggio, eds., *The New Institutionalism in Organizational Analysis*. Chicago: University of Chicago Press, 1991.

Doeringer, P. B., and Piore, M. J. *Internal Labor Markets and Manpower Analysis*. San Francisco: New Lexington Press, 1971.

Doyle, D. M. "Choice, Politics, and Public Schools: A Case Study of the California Proposition 174 Voucher Campaigns." Unpublished doctoral dissertation, Claremont Graduate School, 1994.

Drucker, P. F. *Post-Capitalist Society*. New York: HarperCollins, 1993.

Drucker, P. F. "The Age of Social Transformation." *Atlantic*, Nov. 1994, pp. 53–80.

Dunlop, J. T. *Industrial Relations Systems*. (Rev. ed.). Boston: Harvard Business School Press, 1993. (Originally published 1958.)

Edmonds, R. R. "Making Public Schools Effective." *Social Policy,* 1981, *12*(2), 56–60.

Ehrenreich, B. *Fear of Falling: The Inner Life of the Middle Class*. New York: HarperCollins, 1990.

Farham-Diggory, S. *Schooling*. Cambridge, Mass.: Harvard University Press, 1990.

Finn, C. E. *We Must Take Charge: Our Schools and Our Future*. New York: Free Press, 1991.

Fisher, R., and Ury, W. *Getting to Yes*. London: Simon & Schuster, 1987.

Flower, L., and Hays, J. R. "The Dynamics of Composing: Making Plans and Juggling Constraints." In L. W. Gregg and E. R. Steinberg (eds.), *Cognitive Processes in Writing*. Hillsdale, N.J.: Erlbaum, 1980.

Fowler, F. C. "The Politics of School Reform in Tennessee: A View from the Classroom." In W. L. Boyd and C. T. Kerchner (eds.), *The Politics of Excellence and Choice in Education*. Bristol, Pa.: Falmer Press, 1988.

Fox, A. *Beyond Contract: Work, Power, and Trust Relations*. Winchester, Mass.: Faber & Faber, 1974.

Fox, M. *The Reinvention of Work: A New Vision of Livelihood for Our Time*. San Francisco: Harper San Francisco, 1994.

Fullan, M. G., and Stiegelbauer, S. *The New Meaning of Educational Change*. New York: Teachers College Press, 1991.

Garbarino, J. W. "Unionism Without Unions: The New Industrial Relations." *Industrial Relations,* 1984, *23*(1), 40–51.

Gardner, H. *The Mind's New Science: A History of the Cognitive Revolution*. New York: Basic Books, 1985.

Geoghegan, T. *Which Side Are You On? Trying to Be for Labor When It's Flat on Its Back*. New York: Farrar, Strauss & Giroux, 1991.

Glenview Public Schools Constitution: An Agreement Between the Glenview Education Association and the Board of Education of the Glenview Public Schools. (1989–1992).

Good, T. L., and Brophy, J. E. "School Effects." In M. C. Wittrock (ed.), *Handbook of Research on Teaching*. (3rd ed.). Old Tappan, N.J.: Macmillan, 1986.

Grant, G., and Murray, C. "The Second Academic Revolution." In R. L. Crowson, W. L. Boyd, and H. B. Mawhinney (eds.), *The Politics of Education and the New Institutionalism: Reinventing the American School*. Bristol, Pa.: Falmer Press, 1996.

Greider, W. *Who Will Tell the People? The Betrayal of American Democracy.* New York: Simon & Schuster, 1992.

Hage, J., Powers, C. H., and Henry, J. *Post-Industrial Lives: Roles and Relationships in the 21st Century.* Thousand Oaks, Calif.: Sage, 1992.

Halberstam, D. *The Reckoning.* New York: Morrow, 1986.

Handy, C. B. *The Future of Work: A Guide to a Changing Society.* Oxford, England: Blackwell, 1984.

Hanushek, E. A. "The Economics of Schooling: Production and Efficiency in Public Schools." *Journal of Economic Literature,* 1986, *24*(3), 1141–1171.

Harrison, B. *Lean and Mean: The Changing Landscape of Corporate Power in the Age of Flexibility.* New York: Basic Books, 1994.

Harrison, B., and Bluestone, B. *The Great U-Turn: Corporate Restructuring and the Polarizing of America.* New York: HarperCollins, 1990.

Heckscher, C. C. *The New Unionism: Employee Involvement in the Changing Corporation.* New York: Basic Books, 1988.

Heckscher, C. C. *White-Collar Blues: Management Loyalties in an Age of Corporate Restructuring.* New York: Basic Books, 1995.

Hentschke, G. "Paraeducators: New Plumbing in the Teacher Education Pipeline." Unpublished manuscript, 1994.

Herrmann, J. "Restructuring the Health Care Delivery System." *Health Systems Review,* 1995, *28*(2), 18–29.

Hill, P., Foster, G., and Gendler, T. *High Schools with Character.* Santa Monica, Calif.: Rand, 1990.

Hoerr, J. "What Should Unions Do?" *Harvard Business Review,* 1991, *69*(3), 30–45.

Hunter, M. "What's Wrong with Madeline Hunter?" *Educational Leadership,* Feb. 1985, pp. 57–60.

Iannoccone, L., and Lutz, F. W. *Politics, Power and Policy: The Governing of Local School Districts.* Columbus, Ohio: Merrill, 1970.

James, W. *Talks to Teachers on Psychology.* New York: Holt, 1909. (Originally published 1900.)

Jencks, C. *Inequality: A Reassement of the Effect of Family and Schooling in America.* New York: Basic Books, 1972.

Jennings, J. F. "School Reform Based on What Is Taught and Learned." *Phi Delta Kappan,* 1995, *76*(10), 765–769.

Johnson, S. M. *Teachers at Work: Achieving Success in Our Schools.* New York: Basic Books, 1990.

Johnston, G. "The Educational Implications of Occupational Change."

Unpublished master's thesis, Department of Education, University of Chicago, 1939.

Kelley, C. "Teacher Compensation and Organization." Paper presented at the Consortium for Policy Research in Education (CPRE) Conference on Teacher Compensation. Madison, Wis., 1995.

Kelley, C., and Odden, A. *Reinventing Teacher Compensation Systems.* New Brunswick, N.J.: Center for Policy Research in Education, 1995.

Kerchner, C. T. "Union-Made Teaching: The Effects of Labor Relations on Teaching Work." In E. Rothkopf (ed.), *Review of Research in Education.* Washington, D.C.: American Educational Research Association, 1986.

Kerchner, C. T. *Pittsburgh: Reform in a Well-Managed Public Bureaucracy.* Project Report. Claremont, Calif.: Claremont Project VISION, Claremont Graduate School, 1991.

Kerchner, C. T. "Rethinking City Schools." Working paper, California Education Policy Seminar of the Claremont Graduate School, 1995.

Kerchner, C. T., and Kerchner, L. B. "Radical Toryism: Lessons from England About Changing Schools." Unpublished manuscript, 1994.

Kerchner, C. T., and Koppich, J. E. *A Union of Professionals: Unions and Management in Turbulent Times.* New York: Teachers College Press, 1993.

Kerchner, C. T., and Mitchell, D. E. *The Changing Idea of a Teachers' Union.* Bristol, Pa.: Falmer Press, 1988.

Kidder, T. *Among Schoolchildren.* Boston: Houghton Mifflin, 1989.

Kochan, T., and Osterman, P. *The Mutual Gains Enterprise.* Boston: Harvard Business School Press, 1994.

Kochan, T., McKersie, R., and Capelli, P. "Strategic Choice and Industrial Relations Theory." *Industrial Relations,* 1984, *23,* 16–39.

Kuhn, T. S. *The Structure of Scientific Revolutions.* Chicago: University of Chicago Press, 1970.

Landers, A. "Discouraged in Mass." *Los Angeles Times,* July 23, 1995, p. E2.

Lawrence, D. "The Toledo Plan for Peer Evaluation and Assistance." *Education and Urban Society,* 1985, *17*(3), 347–354.

LeMahieu, P. G. "Up Against the Wall: Psychometrics Meets Praxis." *Educational Measurement: Issues and Practice,* 1986, *5*(1), 12–16.

Levin, H. M. "Cost-Effectiveness and Educational Policy." *Educational Evaluation and Policy Analysis,* 1988, *10*(1), 51–69.

Levin, H. M. *Cost-Effectiveness: A Primer.* Thousand Oaks, Calif.: Sage, 1983.

Levinson, M. "It's Hip to Be Union." *Newsweek,* July 8, 1996, pp. 44–45.

Lieberman, A. "Practices That Support Teacher Development: Transforming Conceptions of Professional Learning." *Phi Delta Kappan,* 1995, *76*(8), 591–596.

Lieberman, M. *Public Education: An Autopsy.* Cambridge, Mass.: Harvard University Press, 1993.

Lightfoot, S. L. *The Good High School: Portraits of Character and Culture.* New York: Basic Books, 1983.

Linn, R. L., and Dunbar, S. B. "The Nation's Report Card Goes Home: Good News and Bad About Trends in Achievement." *Phi Delta Kappan,* 1990, *72,* 127–133.

Little, J. W. "Teachers' Professional Development in a Climate of Educational Reform." *Educational Evaluation and Policy Analysis,* 1993, *15*(2), 129–151.

Locke, R., Kochan, T., and Piore, M. J. (eds.). *Employment Relations in a Changing World Economy.* Cambridge, Mass.: MIT Press, 1995.

Lortie, D. C. *Schoolteacher: A Sociological Study.* Chicago: University of Chicago Press, 1975.

Maeroff, G. I. *The Empowerment of Teachers.* New York: Teachers College Press, 1988.

Malen, B. *Bellevue: Renewal and School Decision Making.* Claremont, Calif.: Claremont Project VISION, Claremont Graduate School, 1992.

Mansbridge, J. J. (ed.). *Beyond Self-Interest.* Chicago: University of Chicago Press, 1990.

March, J. G., and Olsen, J. P. *Rediscovering Institutions: The Organizational Basis of Politics.* New York: Free Press, 1989.

Marshall, R., and Tucker, M. *Thinking for a Living: Education and the Wealth of Nations.* New York: Basic Books, 1992.

Master Contract Between the Hammond Teachers' Federation and the Board of Trustees of the School, City of Hammond, Indiana. (Jan. 1, 1990–Dec. 31, 2001.)

McClure, R. "Sharing a Decade's Lessons." *Doubts and Certainties,* 1995, *9*(5), 1–5.

McGreal, T. *Successful Teacher Evaluation.* Alexandria, Va.: Association for Supervision and Curriculum Development, 1983.

McNeil, L. M. "The Politics of Texas School Reform." In W. L. Boyd and C. T. Kerchner (eds.), *The Politics of Excellence and Choice in Education.* Bristol, Pa.: Falmer Press, 1988.

Meier, D. *The Power of Their Ideas: Lessons for America from a Small School in Harlem.* Boston: Beacon Press, 1995.

Meyer, J. W., and Rowan, B. "The Structure of Educational Organizations."

In J. W. Meyer (ed.), *Environments and Organizations.* San Francisco: Jossey-Bass, 1978.

Miller, G. A. "Human Memory and the Storage of Information." *IRE Transactions of Information Theory,* 1956, *2–3,* 129–137.

Mincer, J. "On the Job Training: Costs, Returns, and Some Implications." *Journal of Political Economy,* 1962, *70*(5, part 2), 50–79.

Mitchell, D. E., Ortiz, F. I., and Mitchell, T. K. *Work Orientation and Job Performance: The Cultural Basis of Teaching Rewards and Incentives.* Albany: State University of New York, 1987.

Morgan, G. *Images of Organization.* Thousand Oaks, Calif.: Sage, 1986.

Morris, C. J. (ed.). *The Developing Labor Law.* Washington, D.C.: Bureau of National Affairs, 1971.

Murnane, R. J., and Cohen, D. K. "Merit Pay and the Evaluation Problem: Why Most Merit Pay Plans Fail and a Few Survive." *Harvard Educational Review,* 1986, *56*(1), 1–17.

Murphy, M. *Blackboard Unions: The AFT and the NEA, 1900–1980.* Ithaca, N.Y.: Cornell University Press, 1990.

Myers, M. *Changing Our Minds: Negotiating English and Literacy.* Champaign-Urbana, Ill.: National Council of Teachers of English, 1996.

National Center for Education Statistics. *Digest of Education Statistics.* Washington, D.C.: U.S. Department of Education, 1993.

National Center on Education and the Economy. *America's Choice: High Skills or Low Wages.* Rochester, N.Y.: National Center on Education and the Economy, 1990.

National Commission on Excellence in Education. *A Nation at Risk: The Imperative for Educational Reform: A Report to the Secretary of Education.* Washington, D.C.: U.S. Department of Education, 1983.

National Commission on Teaching and America's Future. *What Matters Most: Teaching for America's Future.* New York: Author, 1996.

National Education Association. *Ensuring High Standards in Nontraditional Routes to Licensure.* Washington, D.C.: National Education Association, 1990.

National Education Commission on Time and Learning. *Prisoners of Time.* Washington, D.C.: Government Printing Office, 1994.

Osborne, D., and Gaebler, T. *Reinventing Government: How the Entrepreneurial Spirit Is Transforming the Public Sector from Schoolhouse to Statehouse, City Hall to the Pentagon.* Reading, Mass.: Addison-Wesley, 1992.

Pearl, A., and Reisman, F. *New Careers for the Poor: The Nonprofessional in Human Services.* New York: Free Press, 1965.

Perelman, L. J. *School's Out: Hyperlearning, the New Technology, and the End of Education.* New York: Morrow, 1992.

Peters, T. J., and Waterman, R. H., Jr. *In Search of Excellence: Lessons from America's Best-Run Companies.* New York: HarperCollins, 1982.

Peterson, P. G. *Facing Up: Paying Our Nation's Debt and Saving Our Children's Future.* New York: Simon & Schuster, 1994.

Piore, C. F., and Sabel, M. J. *The Second Industrial Divide: Possibilities for Prosperity.* New York: Basic Books, 1984.

Pleasure, R. J., and Greenfield, P. A. "From Servants to Workers: A Modern Law of Work in the United States." In P. Voos (ed.), *Proceedings of the Forty-Seventh Annual Meeting, Industrial Relations Research Association Series.* Madison, Wis.: Industrial Relations Research Association, 1995.

Poplin, M., and Weeres, J. *Voices from the Inside.* Claremont, Calif.: The Institute for Education in Transformation, Claremont Graduate School, 1992.

Porter, A. C., Archbald, D. A., and Tyree, A.K.J. "Reforming the Curriculum: Will Empowerment Policies Replace Control?" In S. H. Fuhrman and B. Malen (eds.), *The Politics of Curriculum and Testing: The 1990 Yearbook of the Politics of Education Association.* Bristol, Pa.: Falmer Press, 1990.

Poway Unified School District and Poway Federation of Teachers. *Trust Agreement, Alternative Evaluation Program.* Poway, Calif.: Poway Unified School District and Poway Federation of Teachers, 1990.

Poway Unified School District. *Alternative Evaluation Program.* Poway, Calif.: Poway Unified School District, 1991.

Pring, R. "Is Teaching a Profession?" Unpublished paper, Department of Educational Studies, University of Oxford, 1993.

Rabban, D. M. "Can American Labor Law Accommodate Collective Bargaining by Professional Employees?" *Yale Law Journal,* 1990, *99*(4), 689–758.

Rabban, D. M. "Distinguishing Excluded Managers from Covered Professionals Under the NLRA." *Columbia Law Review,* 1989, *89*(8), 1775–1860.

Ravitch, D. *The Troubled Crusade: American Education, 1945–1980.* New York: Basic Books, 1983.

Reich, R. B. *The Work of Nations: Preparing Ourselves for 21st Century Capitalism.* New York: Knopf, 1991.

Rifkin, J. *The End of Work: The Decline of the Global Labor Force and the Dawn of the Post-Market Era.* New York: Putnam, 1995.

Rowan, B. "Domain II: Teaching and Learning Processes: Taxonomy and

Overview." In University Council for Educational Administration (ed.), *Educational Administration*. New York: McGraw-Hill, 1994.

Rutter, M. *Fifteen Thousand Hours*. Cambridge, Mass.: Harvard University Press, 1979.

Rutter, M. "School Effects on Pupil Progress: Research Findings and Policy Impressions." In L. Schulman and G. Sykes (eds.), *Handbook of Teaching and Policy*. New York: Longman, 1983.

Schlossberg, S. I., and Fetter, S. M. *U.S. Labor Law and the Future of Labor-Management Cooperation*. (No. BLMR 104). Washington, D.C.: Government Printing Office, 1986.

Schön, D. A. *The Reflective Practitioner*. New York: Basic Books, 1983.

Schultz, T. *Investing in People*. Berkeley: University of California Press, 1981.

Schumpeter, J. A. *Capitalism, Socialism and Democracy*. New York: Harper-Collins, 1942.

Senge, P. M. *The Fifth Discipline: The Art and Practice of the Learning Organization*. New York: Doubleday, 1990.

Shanker, A. *Linking School and Work*. New York: American Federation of Teachers, 1995.

Shedd, J. B., and Bacharach, S. B. *Tangled Hierarchies: Teachers as Professionals and the Management of Schools*. San Francisco: Jossey-Bass, 1991.

Sizer, T. R. *Horace's Compromise: The Dilemma of the American High School*. Boston: Houghton Mifflin, 1984.

Sizer, T. R. *Horace's School: Redesigning the American High School*. Boston: Houghton Mifflin, 1992.

Smylie, M. *Glenview, Illinois: From Contract to Constitution*. Project Report. Claremont, Calif.: Claremont Project VISION, Claremont Graduate School, 1991.

Smylie, M. A., Brownlee-Conyers, J., and Crowson, R. L. "Teachers' Responses to Participatory Decision Making: The Nexus Between Work Redesign and the Classroom." Paper presented at the American Educational Research Association Annual Meeting, San Francisco, 1992.

Special Study Panel on Educational Indicators. *Education Counts: An Indicator System to Monitor the Nation's Educational Health*. Washington, D.C.: National Center for Education Statistics, 1991.

Stroud, J. *Detroit Free Press*, Sept. 6, 1992, p. 2F.

Tilly, C. "Short Hours, Short Shrift: The Causes and Consequences of Part-Time Employment." In V. L. du Rivage (ed.), *New Policies for the Part-Time Contingent Workforce*. Armonk, N.Y.: Sharpe, 1992.

Toch, T. *In the Name of Excellence.* New York: Oxford University Press, 1991.

Toffler, A. *Power Shift.* New York: Bantam Books, 1990.

Toledo Public Schools and Toledo Federation of Teachers. *The Toledo Plan: Intern Intervention, Evaluation.* Toledo, Ohio: Toledo Public Schools, Toledo Federation of Teachers, 1991.

Troy, L. "Sacred Cows and Trojan Horses." [http://www.cato.org/pubs/regulation/reg18nlb.html]. 1995.

Tyack, D., and Hansot, E. *Managers of Virtue: Public School Leadership in America, 1820–1980.* New York: Basic Books, 1982.

Tyack, D., Kirst, M., and Hansot, E. "Educational Reform: Retrospect and Prospect." *Teachers College Record,* 1980, *81*(3), 253–269.

Tyack, D., Lowe, R., and Hansot, E. *Public Schools in Hard Times.* Cambridge, Mass.: Harvard University Press, 1984.

U.S. Bureau of the Census. *Statistical Abstract of the United States.* Washington, D.C.: Government Printing Office, 1962.

U.S. Buearu of the Census. *Historical Statistics of the United States: Colonial Times to 1970.* Washington, D.C.: Government Printing Office, 1972.

U.S. Bureau of the Census. *Statistical Abstract of the United States.* Washington, D.C.: Government Printing Office, 1992.

U.S. Bureau of the Census. *Study of Wages and Education.* Washington, D.C.: Government Printing Office, 1994.

Walsh, M. "Baltimore to Terminate EAI Schools Contract." *Education Week,* Nov. 29, 1995, p. 1.

Walton, M. *The Deming Management Method.* New York: Dodd, Mead, 1986.

Walton, R. E., and McKersie, R. B. *A Behavioral Theory of Labor Negotiations.* New York: McGraw-Hill, 1965.

Weiss, C. H. "Research for Policy's Sake: The Enlightenment Function of Social Research." *Policy Analysis,* 1977, *3,* 531–545.

Wilson, S. M. "Deeply Rooted Change: A Tale of Learning to Teach Adventurously." In D. K. Cohen, M. W. McLaughlin, and J. E. Talbert (eds.), *Teaching for Understanding: Challenges for Policy and Practice.* San Francisco: Jossey-Bass, 1993.

Wise, A., Darling-Hammond, L., McLaughlin, M. W., and Bernstein, H. *Teacher Evaluation: A Study of Effective Practices.* Santa Monica, Calif.: Rand, 1984.

Wollett, D. H., and Chanin, R. H. *The Law and Practice of Teacher Negotiations.* Washington, D.C.: Bureau of National Affairs, 1974.

━ᴥ━ Index